The
Long-Distance
Runner

ALSO BY MICHAEL HARRINGTON

The Other America

The Retail Clerks

The Accidental Century

Toward a Democratic Left

Socialism

Fragments of the Century

Twilight of Capitalism

The Vast Majority

Decade of Decision

The Next America

*The Politics at God's Funeral:
The Spiritual Crisis of
Western Civilization*

The New American Poverty

*Taking Sides: The Education of
a Militant Mind*

*The Next Left: The History
of a Future*

The Long-Distance Runner

AN AUTOBIOGRAPHY

Michael Harrington

Henry Holt and Company

New York

Published by Henry Holt and Company, Inc., 115 West 18th Street,
New York, New York 10011.
Published in Canada by Fitzhenry & Whiteside Limited,
195 Allstate Parkway, Markham, Ontario L3R 4T8.

LIBRARY OF CONGRESS CATALOGING-IN-PUBLICATION DATA
Harrington, Michael, 1928–
The long-distance runner : an autobiography / Michael Harrington.
—1st ed.
    p. cm.
Bibliography: p.
Includes index.
ISBN 0-8050-0790-3
1. Harrington, Michael, 1928–   . 2. Social scientists—United
States—Biography.   3. Political scientists—United States—
Biography.   I. Title.
H59.H36A3 1988
300'.92'4—dc19   88-10334
[B]   CIP

First Edition

Designed by Beth Tondreau Design / Carol Barr
Printed in the United States of America

10 9 8 7 6 5 4 3 2 1

ISBN 0-8050-0790-3

To the movement, of course, and above all to those, too numerous to be named, whose sacrifice and devotion enriched my life.

Contents

The Long-Distance Runner

The Long-Distance Runner

I am a long-distance runner.

On a rainy day in 1949 in St. Louis, I went into a decayed, beautiful house, near the Mississippi River, which stank of stopped-up toilets, dead rats, and human misery. It was a terrible shock to my privileged, middle-class nostrils. I had come there as a temporary and opportunistic social worker trying to save up enough money to go to New York and be a poet and a Bohemian. An hour or so later, riding the Grand Avenue streetcar, it dawned on me that I should spend the rest of my life putting an end to that house and all that it symbolized.

I have been running toward that goal now for almost forty years, and I am not tired, even though the finish line keeps receding.

That decision on the Grand Avenue streetcar was the most Protestant thing I ever did. Protestants, it seems to me, tend to have dramatic conversions. They are "born again" and do not look back. Catholics—and though I have been an atheist for years, I am culturally and psychologically a Catholic—are forever backsliding, deconverting, returning to their previously sinful life. That is one of the reasons why confession is such a central institution in the Church.

That experience in St. Louis was, for me, a Protestant deviation. I was Saul on the road to Damascus that day. Or, to return to the thematic image of this entire book, that was when I decided to be a long-distance runner.

Why should anyone care? Because that career has taken me into some of the most significant social movements and political struggles of our time. In *Fragments of the Century*, I described what that meant in terms of pre–Vatican II Catholicism, Bohemia, the socialist and civil rights movements, and the New Left. That book, like this one, was a social autobiography in which I talked of my life only insofar as it was evidence of the times in which I live. To be sure, I told of a nervous breakdown, but I depicted it as a historical, rather than an intimate, experience. Not, of course, that my life has been merely public; it has not. It is just that what I want to write about—what I think interesting to other people— is the social dimension of my autobiography.

This book, then, will deal primarily with the meaning of my encounters with the political and social movements of the Left during the seventies and eighties, nationally and internationally. I will, however, try to convey the experiences of my public self's daily life: teaching at Queens College in the City University of New York; moving to the suburbs after thirty years in the Bohemian heartland of Greenwich Village; and what it is like to be a writer. And there is one experience I will describe that simply refuses to be reduced to its sociological dimensions: facing up to premature death through cancer.

And yet I cannot resist, in this opening chapter, probing my own psychology and confessing that there are aspects of it that strike me as inexplicably, even mysteriously, individualistic and unhistorical, a consequence of my inner self rather than of the times in which I live. Since I have been a democratic Marxist for about thirty years, that requires some explanation.

When I became a father, I was astounded that my sons seemed to emerge from the womb with personalities. To be sure, I was never a vulgar Marxist, explaining all things through social structure, ignoring the genetic and the personal. I had always known that a human being, like a poem, is infinitely more than the "re-flection" of the class struggle, even though no one can be really understood apart from his or her historical time and place. But with fatherhood, that simple truth became overwhelming as I got to know my sons as unique individuals before society even had the chance to act upon them.

Now, looking back, I have to compound that mystery by sug-gesting that, in my case at least, the self I did not choose, the self I was before I knew it, has shaped much of my life, even its accidents. Three Germans—two of them poets, the other a mis-understood philosopher who has generally been seen as impossibly abstract—illuminate my point.

Rainer Maria Rilke wrote in "The Seventh Elegy" of his *Duino Elegies*:

> *Don't think Destiny's more than what's packed into childhood.*

Our personal fate, he was saying, is to a considerable degree de-termined in the early years of our lives. (Freud would agree.) And in his *Letters to a Young Poet* he commented, "Only because so many people, all the time their destinies were living inside them, did not absorb them and transform them into themselves, have they failed to recognize what came out of them." We obviously do not create the accidents that happen to us, and yet something inside of us often shapes the meanings that those accidents will have for us.

For Hegel, all life and all history are a process whereby indi-viduals and societies become fully what they are in the first place. (I disagree with Hegel's historical fatalism in this regard, but that is not relevant here.) In the same vein, Goethe wrote in *Faust*, "You must struggle for what you inherit from your father in order to possess it." I should immediately add that these perceptions of Rilke, Hegel, and Goethe—as well as my own life—define a middle-class truth: most people since the dawn of human time have been simply programmed by their birth to a short and brutish life that is not shaped by them or anyone else. But to the degree that social struggle raises women and men above mere survival, it allows us to find at least a good part of our destinies inside ourselves.

My personal gloss on these insights is that I did not *become* a long-distance runner. I seem to have been born one.

As far back as I can remember, when I was a four-year-old in kindergarten at St. Rose's School, I used to give my lunch money to the missions so I could help save a baby in China for Christ. Taking religion very seriously while I was growing up was a critical part of the destiny my childhood packed into me. It meant, above all, that I accepted the idea that life was a trust to be used for a good purpose and accounted for when it was over. I have been an atheist for about thirty years, yet in this fundamental conception of the meaning of existence I am as Catholic as the day on which I made my first communion. Without knowing it, I was destined, at the age of four, to be a long-distance runner.

Perhaps that is why the movie *Lost Horizon* made such an impression on me when I was about ten. James Hilton's story about Robert Conway, the philosophical man of action who was mysteriously spirited away to the lamasery in which the spiritual richness of civilization was being protected from the violent political ravages of the twentieth century, so gripped my youthful imagination that I cannot remember how many times I saw it. Not too long ago I went to a revival of the film, which even added some lost footage and dialogue. Seeing the movie was an embarrassing experience—it seemed dated, stilted, obvious. And my Marxist, analytic self categorized it in a millisecond: an escapist product of the thirties, a typical intellectual's utopia in which humanity is saved, not by its own action, but by an elite acting out of noblesse oblige.

All that is true, and yet for a youth in St. Louis, it still gave a social, and even political, dimension to the religious impulse. At the end of the movie, when Robert Conway is overcoming impossible odds to return to Shangri-La, a group of hearty colonialists in a London club drink to his passion. The man who had tried to bring Conway back to England says that he hopes every one of us will find our Shangri-La. Sophisticated as I was when I saw the revival, my eyes teared up.

But there is a problem in that little incident. I tend to cry indiscriminately, for reasons good and bad, in response to both the profound and the trivial. While listening to Bach's Goldberg Variations there are moments when I temporarily believe in God again and weep for joy; but certain popular songs, and even artful commercials on television, can have the same apparent effect on me. When Jo, the street boy, dies in *Bleak House*, Dickens writes, "Dead, your Majesty. Dead, my lords and gentlemen. Dead, Right Reverends and Wrong Reverends of every order. Dead, men and women, born with Heavenly compassion in your hearts. And dying thus around us every day."

Those words are wrenching every time I read them. Even as I write, I find it emotionally difficult to copy them here. Fine, for they are Dickens at his angry, decent best and they are about my own deepest sense of what should be. I am hardly ashamed at being moved by such a scene. But what about the tears shed while watching the hokum of the one-hundredth anniversary of the Statue of Liberty? More seriously, my vision sometimes takes me by surprise. In Paris in 1983, I was writing the first draft of the opening chapter of *The New American Poverty*, explaining why I thought of history as a pilgrimage toward the City of Humanity. And suddenly I found myself sobbing at my own thought.

Yet if I am somewhat ashamed of my own sentimentality and the way it apes my deepest emotions, most people who cry in movies do not usually live their entire lives in response to the experience, nor do they reflect analytically upon their tears. I have.

My romantic identification as a ten-year-old with Robert Conway led to one of my first literary essays, a study of André Malraux published in *Partisan Review* when I was twenty-three. Malraux was, of course, a Robert Conway much larger than fiction. An archaeologist in Indochina, a revolutionary in China, the author of one of the great books of the age, *Man's Fate*, a commander of the Loyalist air force in Spain during the Civil War, a colonel in the Maquis in France during World War II, a Gaullist leader, and an art critic, he was the quintessential philosopher-artist-militant. And at the same time I was fascinated by and writing about Malraux, I discovered Albert Camus. Reading *L'Homme révolté* (*The Rebel*) before it was translated into English, excited in me the same mix of thought and action.

I never thought of myself as a Trotskyist, even though the movement that most influenced me when I became a socialist had emerged out of a factional fight with Trotsky. And yet there is no doubt that I responded positively to him—even though he unwittingly helped create the Stalin who murdered him—because he, like Malraux and Camus, combined thought with action. In Mexico City I once went to his house in Coyoacán and was deeply moved, looking at the gun slits that failed to keep the assassin from insinuating himself into the house. I imagined the revolutionary intellectual, sitting at his desk and trying to work even as the Soviet secret police surrounded him because Stalin feared his mind and his principles as much as an armored division.

In part this was sheer youthful romanticism, a Byronic conception of the hero. And, no mistake about it, even though these heroes were militant men of action, there was an irresponsible aestheticism at work in my admiration for them, as well as an incipient social conscience. When I was a teenager, I sometimes took my dates to Lambert Field in St. Louis to watch the planes take off. (This was not quite as bizarre a date as it might seem now because in the forties the airplane was still a novelty.) And when, at the age of twenty-one, I read Baudelaire's line

Happy are those who leave in order to be leaving

its truth struck me as self-evident.

And yet, as my choice of heroes proved, very early on I rejected mere aestheticism. There is an image in Thomas Mann's *Doctor Faustus*—I first encountered it in my twenties—that has long seemed to me a marvelous statement of what I felt about a life dedicated only to beauty or "experience." Adrian Leverkühn, the Faustian character, who is an inspired modernist composer, has gone mad as a result of both the horrors of World War II and the degeneration brought on by a venereal disease. In an unforgettable scene, he proposes to "take back" Beethoven's Ninth Symphony on the grounds that no one has the right to imagine such beauty in a world of such violent ugliness. The Ninth Symphony, Leverkühn says, is a lie.

Yes and no. If we knew nothing about Beethoven's life, the music of that symphony—particularly its last movement—would tell us of a vision of harmony and reconciliation. But we do know Beethoven's life and Schiller's words, which are the text of the choral section. The symphony was written after deep disappointment with the hopes of the Enlightenment—and particularly the disillusionment with Napoleon. It is an affirmation whose scope lies in the future, not in the present; it expresses an ideal. And Schiller's words are even more explicit: all men *shall be* brothers. Leverkühn was right in that World War II was the utter breakdown of all the best hopes of the finest minds and spirits of more than a century of German culture, of a dream that could be symbolized by the choral movement of the Ninth Symphony. But World War II was not, in fact, the end of that ideal.

For me that scene in *Doctor Faustus* meant one could never content one's self *simply* with the contemplation of beauty in the midst of an intolerable world. Just as the poet I wanted to be as a young man did not disappear, but became a part of the activist militant and the theoretical analyst, so did Beethoven's Ninth Symphony and art in general become a part of my social vision, not a contradiction of it. To me justice was, and is, beautiful, not stern. That is one of the reasons why I have not tired during all of these years.

I theorize too much. Ultimately, the most important thing I want to say about being a long-distance runner is that, prior to all the books and music and movies, there was in me a hunger and thirst for justice. For me this was a second nature, a drive more powerful and lasting than romantic love or sexual desire. And in a profound sense I feel that I showed no morality, no will, in acting upon that instinct, because I could not have done otherwise.

Chariots of Fire is a movie that dramatizes what I am trying to say. Superficially it is about running. But its profundity lies in its trying to understand *why* the heroes run, why they punish and discipline themselves. For Harold Abrahams, one of the two main characters, running means forcing Cambridge University, and polite English society in general, to accept his Jewishness. He is going to "run them off their feet," and the movie ends with the affirmation that he did precisely that.

The other main character, Eric Liddell, is a deeply committed Christian, a Scot, who would eventually die as a missionary in China at the end of World War II. He is in conflict because the trial heats for his race at the 1924 Olympics in Paris are scheduled for a Sunday, but he is committed to strict observance of the Sabbath. He cannot violate that principle, the movie rightly portrays, because his speed is a way of giving glory to his God. As he himself puts it in a sermon after a race that takes place long before the Olympics: "Where does the power come from to see the race to the end? From within."

Later, just before he is to run in the Olympics—not in his specialty, the sprint, which he refuses because of the Sunday trial, but in a distance race that is much more difficult for him—he preaches another sermon in a Paris church. He quotes Isaiah 40:31: "But they that wait upon the Lord shall renew their strength / they shall mount up with wings as eagles / they shall run, and not be weary / and they shall walk, and not faint." My face was bathed with tears when I watched that scene because I felt what was being said was a personal revelation.

Yet obviously I do not believe that it is God who has permitted me to "run and not be weary." Still, as I wrote in *The Politics at God's Funeral*, it is possible to have a religious nature without being religious. That does not for a minute mean that I think my socialism is a substitute for religion. I have always thought such a notion to be dangerous, for it implies that a finite human movement can satisfactorily answer questions about the infinite. Socialism could make life better and even beautiful, but it can never conquer death or evil itself. And whenever political movements go in search of a messianic perfection, they end either in triviality or totalitarianism.

My political vision is not the equivalent of a supernatural response to the limits of mortal life. Indeed, it is a vision I share with religious people who do affirm that supernatural response, but it is hardly a substitute for it. I am convinced, as I will explain in Chapter 10 in a very nonacademic setting, that when I die I will be dead, that there is only one life, and that it will come to a definitive end. I am not, like Eric Liddell, running toward the Kingdom of God and therefore unwearied. I am running toward the kingdom of humanity, and I know perfectly well that I will never see it. Perhaps no one will.

And yet the reasons I run are similar to Liddell's; they come from within and seem to have been a part of me from a time so early I can barely remember being without them.

I do not picture myself in this way in order to claim precocious— or mature—sanctity. For there is another side to this drive: it is not at all nice, and I can hardly look back upon it with pride. My ideals have indeed been a passion. And the intellectual life that went along with them can only be described as libidinous, as being swept by joy and exaltation and exhaustion, as insistent as desire for a woman, often as frustrating, and just as renewable. To shift the metaphor from eros to agape, when at times I am engulfed by music or possessed suddenly by the utter clarity of an idea I had been struggling to comprehend, a prayer from my youth—the Magnificat—suddenly wells up in my atheistic consciousness, and I overhear myself rejoicing in the words of Mary when she is told that she is to be the mother of Christ: My soul doth magnify the glory of my lord.

That makes for a long-distance runner—and a defective human being. For if one is intoxicated and seduced by ideas and ideals, then there is not too much energy left over for the intimacy and personal love that is supposed to be the essence of my imagined future. Brecht, in what was objectively an apology for Stalinism— as well as a great poem!—wrote in "To Posterity,"

We who wanted kindness itself could not ourselves be kind.

I will not attempt to rephrase the line but simply to say prosaically that I, who want a world built on love, did not love too well and for that very reason.

I say this because the present book will not recount my intimate failures, only my public defeats; ironically, that makes me look much more noble than I have been. And since I will make no further confessions that are not social in nature, the reader is duly warned of this distortion. The impulse for social involvement that was in me from the beginning would be much more complex, and even ambivalent, were I to write a different kind of book.

Circumstances, of course, had much to do with what actually happened to that impulse—or did they? There was that rainy day in St. Louis in 1949 when I accidentally happened to be a social worker and blundered into an encounter with an outrageous, unnecessary misery. The point is, I was waiting for that accident to happen; I all but summoned it. That was the moment when my life changed, when I was born again; but in a secular sense—I was hardly transformed on the spot. I went to New York and caroused and wrote my poems, not very successfully. Still, I was a haunted man.

Then came a day in the spring of 1950. I was a writer-trainee at *Life* magazine, twenty-two years old, drunk with youth and Manhattan. I was living on the Lower East Side, at Fifth Street between avenues C and D in the midst of a Jewish ghetto. On this day I was taking a bus to Union Square and talking to a lovely young woman by the name of Peggy Brennan. We got into one of those conversations that went with our age and class: what would you do if you had a million dollars? And I heard myself saying, "I would give it away." The next day, I wrote to the American Friends Service Committee and volunteered to work full-time without pay. As it turned out, they didn't even have the money to cover my expenses.

Two or three months later, the Korean War broke out and I,

with fear and trembling, declared myself a conscientious objector. About eight months after that casual conversation, as the bus circled Tompkins Square on a spring afternoon, I showed up at the Catholic Worker and stayed, living in voluntary poverty, for two years. Having been born to be a long-distance runner, I started the race. What follows are some of the things I saw during the last fifteen or so years of running.

CHAPTER TWO

The Seventies:
From the Left

The seventies were the decade that wasn't.

Historical-political decades do not, of course, necessarily follow the calendar. If the thirties clearly belonged to Franklin Roosevelt, they lasted through the campaign of 1948 when Harry Truman mobilized the classic New Deal coalition with the rhetoric of the Depression. There were no forties. The Eisenhower fifties were clear enough and so were the left-wing sixties. Indeed, the sixties broke down into two distinct periods. There was an "era of good feeling," from the black student sit-ins of February 1960 to the Selma-Montgomery march of 1965. Then came the years of increasing anger, from the escalation of the Vietnam War in the spring of 1965 to the McGovern primary campaign and convention victory of 1972, when the sixties ended.

If history were orderly, Richard Nixon would have stamped the seventies with his personal seal during his second administration. There was Watergate instead, and that pushed the elections of 1974 well to the Left of where they otherwise might have been. Gerald Ford was hardly the charismatic leader who models a period in his own image. In any case, his presidency lasted only a little more than two years. And Jimmy Carter, moving from a timid liberalism to a timid conservatism, may have reflected the times, but he certainly did not dominate them.

So it was that the genuine figure of the seventies, Ronald Reagan, did not come to power until 1981. I thus characterize Reagan as a man of the seventies, since I do not believe that he created any kind of a "revolution." That is, he carried out the reactionary response to the crisis of welfare-state liberalism that took place during the seventies and belongs to the political calendar of that decade. He created no new institutions—for instance, nothing as solidly enduring as Social Security or Medicare, and his monuments are therefore two tax laws that can be easily reversed, unlike the structures of the New Deal and the Great Society.

For all his ebullient optimism, Reagan will eventually be seen as a man—a remarkable, incredibly lucky man, a political magician ("now you see it, now you don't"), a sincere ideologue, and conceptual incompetent—who tried to take revenge on the past rather than creating the future he so often proclaimed.

I also assume as I write—in the late 1980s—that the seventies will come to an end in the not too distant future and that the nineties will begin. It is too late for there to be any eighties. I write from the perspective of a Left activist, a leader in two radical organizations, the Democratic Socialist Organizing Committee (DSOC) and the Democratic Socialists of America (DSA), which resulted from the merger of DSOC and a group primarily composed of New Left alumni and alumnae, the New American Movement (NAM). What value, you may ask, is there in an assessment of mainstream politics written from the viewpoint of a tiny, a politically marginal group?

The answer is easy enough. The outsider often has insights that elude people immersed in the exercise of power or counterpower. So it was, as Karl Marx observed, that the conservative Balzac wrote the most profound account of the social consequences of the French Revolution in his incomparable *Comédie humaine*.

Perhaps, one might reply, that justifies looking at the seventies from the vantage point of the mainstream Left. But what value is there in comments from the Left wing of the Left wing about a period that was moving from the center to the right? Strangely enough, the *Wall Street Journal* provided an excellent answer to that question. When the tiny Socialist party split in 1972 through 1973 into three even tinier groups, a *Journal* article said that this seeming tempest in a radical teapot refracted some of the conflicts within the larger, and quite important, liberal and labor movements.

I think that the *Journal* was right. Our caucus in the Socialist party was the defeated remnant of an already defeated remnant, and DSOC and DSA were indeed sometimes shunted to the sectarian margins of American society. But they were, more often than not, resolutely antisectarian and interacted with some of the most important movements of the mainstream Left—with feminists, minorities, trade unionists, and peace activists—sometimes even playing a catalytic role within them. Our microcosm was, then, a significant part of the larger world, and this memoir of our experience is a part of the social history of our times. It shows, I think, that we played a role quite out of proportion to our very modest numbers.

The *Wall Street Journal* was also right about our main opponents in that socialist faction fight, who became involved with the emergent neo-conservatism of the seventies. They became Social Democrats, USA. Their members helped create the Coalition for a Democratic Majority, the Scoop Jackson caucus of the Democratic party; played a significant role around Lane Kirkland in the AFL-CIO (one of them, Tom Kahn, is the international affairs director of the Federation); organized the Institute for Religion and Democracy to fight the "Left" in the churches; held important leadership posts in the American Federation of Teachers; ran the A. Philip Randolph Institute, the major labor-funded group dealing with civil rights; and so on.

Carl Gershman, the present director of the National Endowment for Democracy (NED), was the executive director of the SDs in the seventies. Once, at a meeting of the Socialist International in Lisbon, he actually abstained on an otherwise unanimous motion of condolence for an African liberation leader in protest against the dead man's politics. In 1981 that kind of hard-line activism brought him appointment to a high position in the United States mission to the United Nations under Jeane Kirkpatrick. From there he went on to the directorship of the NED. I found it strange that socialists had finally made their way into the corridors of American power under a right-wing Republican administration.

Slightly more bizarre, but less important, was the history of Linda Chavez, originally a member of the *Left* faction in the Socialist party who moved to the SDs, the Teacher's Union, the Reagan White House, and finally in 1986 became Maryland's Republican candidate for the U.S. Senate.

There are some who have even argued that my personal commitment to DSOC and DSA has been primarily motivated by hostility to the SDs. That is not true. And yet, I was hurt when I discovered that the comrades of my youth—who, like me, had been harassed by the FBI—had turned sharply to the Right (although I did not know that this move would carry some of them all the way to Ronald Reagan). Moreover, I realized that I had trusted them longer than I should have, that I kept giving noble socialist speeches to the public while they were plotting and conniving behind my back. And that did have a real impact on my life: it convinced me that, in both DSOC and DSA, I had to be an organizational leader, not just a spokesperson.

In any case, I do not want to rehearse this history once again, but I cite the mainstream work of these antagonistic heirs of that Socialist split as a way of saying that my remembrance has to do with something more significant than a handful of sectarian individuals.

DSOC, NAM, and DSA were the focus of all of my public, and much of my private, life from 1972 to the present. I cannot write this social autobiography without placing them at its center.

I

The Democratic Socialist Organizing Committee (DSOC) was formally organized in 1973. Its strategy was to make an impact upon both the mass and the ideological Left. In our analysis of the Nixon landslide of 1972 (and, for that matter, of Humphrey's defeat in 1968), we stressed the fragmentation of what was potentially a progressive majority coalition. I used to say that we had to unite the constituencies of the "three Georges": the largely middle-class, antiwar forces of George McGovern; the blue-collar partisans of AFL-CIO President George Meany, a dedicated hawk; and the largely working-class and "redneck" followers of George Wallace, people who were responding not simply to a very real racism, but to a phony populism as well.

How were these contraries to be yoked? On the basis of economic interest, we replied. Without backing off from the struggle with the Meanyites on the war question, we had to reach out to them on issues such as national health and full employment that were, even if most of them didn't know it yet, as important to antiwarriors, feminists, and environmentalists as to trade unionists. And while attacking Wallace's racism head on, we proposed to emphasize the antielitism of the real Left, which meant a rejection of the bureaucratic social engineering of the right-wing liberals. Under the changed economic circumstances of the seventies, we argued, full employment, which was the moderate demand of the sixties, had turned into a radical issue. So if the constituencies of the three Georges were to come together around that demand, it would mean pushing American politics well to the Left.

This theory defined a unique function for DSOC. We were going to be the link between the warring factions of the potential majority. Our labor credentials were good, and we counted a significant number of antiwar trade unionists among our members and friends. And all of us had been active in the broad antiwar movement, even though we were often attacked from the Left because we rejected a shrill, anti-American and utterly counterproductive tactic in that struggle. We had some access, then, to the followers of two of the three Georges. And, we thought, if we could bring them together, we would create a populist, but antiracist, pole of attraction for the Wallacites. After all, we knew from the survey data that there had been a significant number of people who had voted for Robert Kennedy in the 1968 primaries and for George Wallace in the general election.

All of these things could only be accomplished within the Democratic party. In our faction fight within the Socialist party, our prowar adversaries agreed with us on this point even as we battled one another over Vietnam. And indeed, most of our first recruits were people who had long since been carrying on their socialist work within the Democratic electoral framework. That was obviously true of our trade unionists, but it also held for those who had come from the Kennedy and McCarthy campaigns of 1968 and the McGovern effort in 1972. But if we tended to agree among ourselves—and at the outset, "ourselves" meant between two hundred and fifty and five hundred people in the United States—we were opposed by most of the anticapitalist Left.

For them, the Democratic party was purely and simply the party of Lyndon Johnson and the Vietnam War, of Southern racists and oil magnates, of sexists and union busters. We conceded every one of the specific indictments, since they were essentially true. But we then added that this same Democratic party was, for historical reasons beyond our control, also the rallying point of the antiwarriors, minorities, feminists, and trade unionists. Under the special—and often frustrating—conditions of American life, this contradictory, unprincipled swamp of an institution was the Archimedian lever for social change.

There were about five hundred people at our founding convention in the fall of 1973. Our *Newsletter of the Democratic Left* reported six months earlier that there were some 1,200 participants at a Maoist meeting in New York exploring the possibilities of a "new Communist movement" in America. At the outset, then, DSOC was very much in sync with the liberal-labor forces on our right flank and was considered to be selling out by many of the profoundly alienated heirs of sixties radicalism to our Left.

And yet, at our founding convention I made a speech in which I defined our task as putting an end to the fights and recriminations of the sixties. That speech itself was not merely a personal statement. It had been drafted and redrafted in consultation with all of the leaders of our tiny remnant from the Socialist party wars. We wanted, it said, to become the multi-tendency rallying point of the entire anticapitalist Left. No one, it continued, should define present political and organizational positions on the basis of historic differences. Those could be amicably debated over drinks *after* the demonstration or campaign based on agreements about our immediate and future tasks.

And finally, our strategy was based upon what turned out to be a most productive error. We were coming together in the wake of the McGovern debacle, and we did not anticipate what Watergate would mean. So we set our sights too low. We said that all we wanted to do was to survive, to preserve those cadres which, once there was a basic change in the American political atmosphere, would help create the future Left. Usually socialist grouplets announced that history would soon rescue them from their temporary isolation. We, on the contrary, hunkered down for a long, miserable stay in the trenches.

Thus our quite modest success came as a marvelous surprise.

I I

DSOC was carefully created as a noncadre organization by a determined cadre.

Cadre. To the distinct minority of Americans who have even heard of the word, it has a Leninist, or even Stalinist, ring to it. And indeed, Lenin had, under the conditions of underground struggle against czarism, built a centralized and disciplined party of professional revolutionaries—a "cadre" party. Given the circumstances, that was hardly unreasonable; Lenin himself looked to the German Social Democracy, the very model of a mass party with practically no membership requirements, as *the* incarnation of Marxism (he changed his mind in 1914 when the German Socialists supported the war). And, as Stephen Cohen has shown, the Bolsheviks themselves were far from internally cohesive. On the eve of the October Revolution, two of their leaders who were opposed to an insurrection went public with the party's plans to make one—and remained leaders.

Stalin falsified this reality, created the myth of a totally disciplined and infallible party, and used it to legitimate his own totalitarian purposes.

All of us who founded DSOC were, of course, opposed to that idea of the cadre. But some of us had come from two genuinely democratic sects, the Independent Socialist League and the Young Socialist League, with cadre standards of membership. (During the Joe McCarthy years, when I joined, such standards were not a choice but a necessity, since no one who was not deeply committed could be recruited in the first place.) Yet those of us from that past were the most vociferous in fighting any attempt to reduplicate our own experiences, however enriching they were in many ways. We were determined to break out into the mainstream of American life and wanted a multi-tendency, obstreperous, and irreverent organization. There were to be no more long, theoretical resolutions, passionately debated and carefully refined, which established every historical and political nuance of a "line." We would, we said, encourage every member to arrive at our common conclusions in their own way, via religious socialism or humanism or Labor Zionism or the dozen varieties of Marxism. Our "positions" would refer to action in the present and future. Period.

That was, of course, an obvious corollary of our decision to try and become the broad and inclusive movement of the democratic socialist Left in the United States. There was just one problem: it takes a cadre to build a noncadre organization.

Any group that lasts—a local church, a Little League, a political campaign—has to have an inner core of responsible people who are willing to sweep the floor, stamp the envelopes, and articulate a vision. That is a cadre. So when I say that we began DSOC with about two hundred and fifty people, that is an individualistic understatement of our strength. We were two hundred and fifty women and men with a shared, collective experience, not simply in socialist organizations, but in social movements, the unions, civil rights, and antiwar struggles above all. We also participated in a political culture where everyone had a working knowledge of the theory and history of the Left. A reference to a dispute between the Bolsheviks and Mensheviks in 1903, whose very terms would be incomprehensible to most of our fellow citizens, was the commonplace of our casual discussions.

Let me name just a few individuals, not to make a historic record (for the list is utterly incomplete), but to evoke the kinds of lives that were our only resource. We were antiwar trade unionists and prolabor peace activists, a tiny band of long-distance runners. Over the years, some from that original core would drift away from the organization, but none were to defect from the struggle.

There were veterans of the Socialist party mainstream such as Harry Fleishman, who managed Norman Thomas's last campaign in 1948; UAW activists from Detroit such as Oscar Pascal, who had gone from college to the shop floor in order to be part of the workers' movement and became so effective as a trade unionist that he went on the staff; intellectuals, including a majority of the editorial board of *Dissent* magazine, the most important publication of the American democratic Left; activists from the youth section of the presplit Socialist party, among them a dedicated cadre of women from Chicago; David Bensman, another youth leader, who was to become a very serious labor historian; and many others.

At our founding convention we also reached out beyond the Socialist party remnant. I had asked Victor Reuther, the last of the legendary Reuther brothers, who had played such a critical role in the UAW, to come to the founding convention and speak. To my surprise, he accepted. He stayed for the entire three days, sitting as a member of the rank and file, which delighted me even more. So I asked him to be a vice-chair of the organization, and he accepted on the spot. My old friend Ralph Helstein, formerly the president of the CIO Packinghouse Workers union, signed on and became a vice-chair. A young woman who had once worked as my assistant at the League for Industrial Democracy heard about the convention on a car radio and, with her husband, literally turned around and drove from Washington, D.C., to New York to attend it.

Peter Steinfels, a leading Catholic intellectual and harbinger of our involvement with the religious Left, was there. So were some veterans of the New Left, deeply suspicious of reformists such as myself who had championed "moderate" tactics in the antiwar movement. We also attracted young people without a political past. Steve Davis, from Texas, had found out about us by reading *Dissent* and recruited himself.

But there was one glaring absence: there were practically no blacks or Hispanics present. That was a problem at the very outset of our work; it was to be a critical failure in our modest success.

We also began with what might be called the cadre's cadre, the organizers of the organizers. Jack Clark was a young Irishman from Boston who had been the protégé of another one of our key founders, Julius Bernstein, the director of the Jewish Labor Committee and a vital force in every progressive cause in Massachusetts. Jack was a thoughtful labor and political intellectual, at twenty-three a veteran of the antiwar and student movements. The simplest measure of the man was that when I phoned him in 1972 and offered him the job of organizing a losing caucus in the defeated Socialist party at fifty dollars a week along with a spare bed in Debbie Meier's house, he accepted immediately. For the next eight years he was indispensable in everything we did. It was simply natural that, in 1985, I turned to him when someone had to be given the difficult task of telling the movement that I had cancer.

Jack was a youth leader. But four other members of the cadre's cadre had been the friends and comrades of my own youth.

Debbie Meier was a second-generation socialist. Her father was a fund-raiser for Jewish causes and her mother a tremendously energetic Social Democrat in the Norman Thomas tradition. When I met her in 1953, she and her then husband, Fred Meier, had an apartment on the South Side of Chicago. A civil rights activist who lived in interracial neighborhoods and always sent her children to the local public school, she became an impassioned and very effective teacher and is now the principal of an integrated school on the border between Harlem and the West Side of Manhattan. In the seventies, her house on Seventy-seventh Street was our effective national center, and we called it Smolny (which was the name of the Bolshevik headquarters in Petrograd on the eve of the revolution).

Carl Shier, named for Karl Marx, was a Chicagoan and second-generation activist. A long-time militant in the trade union movement, he had become a leader in Local Six of the United Auto Workers in Chicago, was a key figure in the left-socialist caucus that gave critical—often very critical—support to Walter Reuther in the internal battles in the union, and ended up as one of the most respected staffers in the UAW. He is the kind of a man who, when a French Socialist intellectual visited Chicago doing research on the labor movement, took him down on the line to talk to the workers for himself. He was our trade union conscience.

Bogdan Denitch was born in Yugoslavia, the son of a pro-Tito mother and a diplomat father who was a bourgeois republican. I met him in 1951 when I was at the Catholic Worker, and we joined forces in an anti-Franco demonstration. It was, in fact, Bogdan who got me to sign up in the Socialist party in 1952. A City College dropout who had majored in student politics rather than get a degree, he became a shop floor activist in the union movement in New York and California, eventually qualifying at the highest skill level as a tool and die maker. Then he went to Columbia University, acquired a Ph.D. in sociology, and wound up in a nine-year stint as head of the graduate sociology program at the City University of New York.

Irving Howe was in some ways the most surprising member of our nucleus. Arguing that socialist education and thought were more important than maintaining make-believe sects, he had re-signed from the Independent Socialist League in 1952 just as I was coming into its orbit. I first encountered him when he was creating *Dissent*, and at its conferences in the mid-fifties would accuse him, in a friendly way, of having "turned his back on the working class," i.e., of not belonging to our sect. Over the years our lives and opinions increasingly converged, but Irving remained "unorganized" on principle. So when he signed up and committed his considerable reputation and unquestionable integrity to our enterprise, it was a significant morale lift for all of us.

The featured speaker at the opening meeting of the founding convention was David Lewis, the leader of the New Democratic party of Canada, and we have retained that connection with a Left so much more successful than ours to this very moment. Things were slightly chaotic—a delegate from Pittsburgh spoke in favor of a united front with the Communist party and then realized he had come to the wrong place—but a declaration of principles, which I had drafted, entitled "We Are Socialists of the Democratic Left," was adopted. The Lyndon LaRouche sect, then in transition from the New Left to a kind of fascism, distributed a leaflet saying that our extremely modest little beginning was nothing less than the creation of a "Brandt-Brezhnev axis," of the rapprochement of socialism and Communism on a world scale. That exercise in paranoid fantasy particularly delighted one of our members from a Communist past. He thought we were a bunch of Red-baiters, he told us with a grin; he didn't know we were as good as the LaRouche people claimed.

After the convention, we moved our office out of Debbie's house into a tiny basement, which stank of the neighboring sewer just down the street. Indeed, we had to shift our meager office furniture every time the superintendent had to fix the sewer. Jack was joined by Gretchen Donart, who did an excellent job of organizing our founding convention. And Frank Llewellyn, a youth activist of enormous devotion—which he liked to conceal behind a cynical air—with a shrewd sense of practical politics, volunteered his way into being a full-time and key member of the staff. Then, in the winter of 1974, we hired Selma Lenihan as a part-timer assigned, among other things, to coordinate my personal schedule.

Selma was a magnificent woman—and in a sense a victim of the times. She had been around the Communist party and its fronts for years, but was never a member. Still, when we talked to her about the job, we had a long and embarrassed discussion about whether the difference in our histories would make joint work impossible. What if, I asked, she had to help organize a picket line in front of the Soviet United Nations delegation in protest against some Communist outrage? She felt that she could handle the situation. In the years that followed we were to laugh about that strained interview, since there was never the slightest problem in that area. But the way we gingerly approached the topic showed how nervous we were when exploring a territory largely unknown to the American Left: unifying rather than splitting.

Selma was an incredibly talented woman and a free spirit. Yet she had spent years performing routine clerical tasks with exemplary efficiency even though she had the capacity to be a leader in her own right. As our own feminist consciousness increased, we realized that she had belonged to a generation of the radical movement in which women were exploited and discriminated against in the fight against exploitation and discrimination. And, worst of all, a generation in which the victims did not know that they were victims. So Selma began to take on more and more important duties and by 1981 had become a major leader of the organization.

Then, when she was just about to come into her own, she discovered she had cancer. Two years later, after an operation, the miseries of chemotherapy, and a brave, relentless struggle for survival, there was no hope and she decided to end all treatment and die. I was in Paris at the time and phoned her for what she and I knew was going to be our last conversation. I did not have the courage to give her courage and broke down along with her. But perhaps that was a message in its own way.

In 1974, all we knew was that we had recruited a warm woman who was more efficient than any three of us. We were doing all the standard things: the dinner where you honor some important labor or liberal leader and thereby blackmail all of her/his friends to buy a ticket (Carl Shier in Chicago turned that perfunctory rite into a marvelous family reunion of the Left); the petition (Nine Nobel Laureates Greet 1975 Convention; Trade Unionists and Liberals Rally to Support of Portuguese Democracy; and so on);

the Labor Day issue of the *Newsletter* in which friendly unions took out ads to hail us; fund-raising from the handful of wealthy people who were sympathetic (the job I hated the most); organizing a tax-exempt educational organization, the Institute for Democratic Socialism; and on and on according to the hallowed traditions of the antitraditionalists.

But something unexpected and shocking began to happen. There were trade unionists who joined, often because we were the opposite of the prowar Social Democrats. We organized a broad liberal labor coalition within the Democratic party around programmatic issues and eventually were taken seriously by *Business Week*. We became an affiliate of the Socialist International, which, as later chapters relate, had considerable ramifications within this country as well as abroad. And our notion of a broad coalition strategy within the Democratic party ceased to be a lonely heresy on the American Left and turned into a model for a whole series of ventures (the Citizen Labor Energy Coalition and, indeed, the entire citizens' action movement; Big Business Day in 1980).

We became, in short, a modest success for about eight years and then survived a series of crises, some of our own making, some created by the atmosphere of Ronald Reagan's America. The accomplishments—and the problems—came from our ability to bring together the most extraordinarily disparate forces. And that story is bound up with the social history of the seventies.

I I I

There was a profoundly symbolic moment at DSOC's founding convention in 1973. The critical second day of that event had gone better than we expected, and I went with my wife to Debbie Meier's house for a party where I could relax with the delegates. When I walked in the door, I was hustled into a bedroom where about ten people were already deeply involved in an intense, even tearful, acrimonious discussion of our insensitivity to women. I emerged five hours later; the party was, of course, over.

In the preconvention planning period, Ronnie Steinberg (then Ronnie Steinberg Ratner), a young graduate student at NYU, tried to educate us on the importance of the nascent feminist movement. She raised the issue at all of our committee meetings and lectured on it at a discussion group in New York. The problem was that many of us did not really hear her, or rather, we heard her, but only politically, abstractly, in terms of public policy and not at all in terms of our own lives. What follows is a man's history of how a group of men were educated by feminists. But this is not simply an American or sectarian history: at the 1986 congress of the Socialist International, as the principal author of a draft of a new declaration of principles by the seventy-five parties of the International, I included in a preliminary document that was unanimously adopted by delegates from all over the world much of what I had learned about feminism.

The familiar, Hegel said, is often not known. It is the taken-for-granted, the unthought, the obvious that is not really true. And that is why that tense exchange took place at Debbie Meier's.

We socialist men, after all, knew ourselves to be among the enlightened. When we were putting together the slate for the national committee that would be elected at the convention, we included a good number of women: Debbie Meier, of course; Ruth Jordan, a trade union activist and journalist who was one of the most important leaders in the new organization; Liz McPike, another trade unionist who would play a very important role at the founding convention of the Coalition of Labor Union Women (CLUW).

How, then, were we ignoring the question of women in America? Because at that time, none of those magnificent women was primarily identified with the feminist movement as such. They had forged their political identities prior to the re-emergence of that movement in the late sixties, and even if they shared and worked for feminist goals, those goals were not then the source of their fundamental self-definition. Some of the women at the founding convention simply had not been involved for years with the leading men in DSOC in common struggles as Debbie, Ruth, and Liz had.

Indeed some of them had come to our convention in the very first flush of understanding the link between economic and social struggles. And they wanted to be represented as a new and distinct generation, even if their socialist feminism had existed before. They were right.

But then, it also turned out that some of the younger women in our cadre felt the same way. So the intense debate at Debbie's took place within the inner circle. Ronnie Ratner was joined by youth leaders, such as Nancy Shier and Gretchen Donart, but also won the support of Ruth Spitz, a labor economist and longtime Socialist activist, the representative of a feminist impulse that had never disappeared from the movement. People such as myself, alas, were shocked and uncomprehending. Hadn't we committed ourselves to all the political goals of the feminist movement? Hadn't we slated a good number of women for the national committee?

The fact was, we were profoundly insensitive to the demands of women wanting to play a major role in the organization *as* women, *as* feminists. We were more than willing to acknowledge and respect those women who had achieved leadership under the old, male-dominated rules of the game. Debbie Meier was, after all, a leader with a moral authority at least as great as my own. But precisely because we were thus declared opponents of sexism, supporters of the Equal Rights Amendment and all the other political demands of the feminist movement gave us a righteousness that ignored the demand for new rules of the game within our own world.

For the feminist movement was a combination of the personal and the political. That is, it was not simply concerned that *x* or *y* percent of the committee be women, nor even that women should pick their representatives in terms of their feminist values. Those things were important, of course. But the movement also wanted the men to change, to recognize that those feminist values were as basic to socialism as the commitment to workers or minorities. Feminism was not simply one more good "issue" but a challenge to the most primordial form of human domination and exploitation.

Once that massive hole in our theories was pointed out to us— as Chesterton once remarked, it is sometimes necessary to show scholars that earthquakes happened or nations fell—we could accept it easily enough. Internalizing that theory, making it as instinctive as our visceral reaction to class exploitation or racism was something else, however. And the feminist insistence that we recognize that fact in the daily life of our own organization raised even more difficult issues. Those can be located within a historic socialist debate about whether the movement itself should be "prefigurative," living out the new values even within the old order (Rosa Luxemburg's position) or whether that was an impossibility when radical organizations existed within the corruption of capitalism (Leon Trotsky's position).

Of course, Trotsky was right: it is silly to think that Leftists, subject to all the pressures of the system, are going to be ahistorical saints much as if they had been "born again" in a religious sense. Indeed, for some of us, it was an understanding of this complexity that led us to the wrong attitude. We saw feminists as just one more expression of a utopianism in which the kingdom of freedom was to be built immediately, even if within the wretched confines of the kingdom of necessity. But on questions of gender and racism, Luxemburg was right: if the movement could not attain perfection in this world (or, I would add, in any world I can imagine), neither could it practice the most outrageous forms of repression. It is simply impossible to be honestly and effectively committed to human liberation if you practice sexism or racism within the liberation movement. To understand that hardly requires adopting an impossible stance of achieving secular sanctity in the here and now.

In *Personal Politics*, a fine book, Sara Evans relates how the new feminism began, precisely, among women activists in the civil rights, antiwar, and New Left movements who discovered that the male leaders used them for secretaries, lovers, and cooks even as they preached total emancipation. One of the first manifestos of that movement was written by a small group of white women in the Student NonViolent Coordinating Committee. They were working in the South and therefore under the constant threat of violence—of rape as well as personal injury or death. And yet when they circulated their document they did so anonymously because they were afraid of hostile responses from the men in their own organization with whom they shared the daily risk of violence and death.

Many of us in the founding group of DSA had been critical of some of the more self-indulgent and counterproductive tactics of the New Left, and that kept us from feeling the full impact of its critically important encounter with feminism. Moreover, our intellectual tradition tended to emphasize class rather than gender, and even though we had corrected the historical errors of our movement with regard to race—the simple-minded notion that the anticapitalist struggle would automatically eliminate the sources of racism and that, therefore, no special program for minorities was required—we now made the same mistake with regard to women.

The meeting at Debbie's had a profound effect. Feminist activists were elected to the national committee, and we began the painful process of re-educating the men, myself most emphatically included. At the DSOC 1975 convention, the women's caucus decided not to run its own slate of candidates because the organization as a whole had learned enough about feminism to be trusted. The problem was, some people were playing regional games, our system of proportional representation was fiendishly complex, and as a result women were woefully underrepresented on our national committee. We had to undo that idiocy by means of some special provisions of the constitution, but the sense of sisterhood and brotherhood was totally shattered. The celebration of our new consciousness turned into a round of bitter recriminations.

There was an even more significant—and difficult—moment at the 1977 convention in Chicago. I was talking with Nancy Shier about the composition of the national committee. It should, she said, be 50 percent women. I replied that for several reasons—starting with the fact that women made up about one third of the organization—there simply were not as many qualified women candidates as men. If we followed her rule, I told Nancy, it would knock out a significant number of males who could make a very real contribution. I triumphantly concluded with what I regarded as a reductio ad absurdum: did Nancy want the size of the national committee determined by the pool of capable women? The answer was yes. Later, I realized she was right.

Most of the concern over "reverse discrimination" in the United States is phrased as if it is based on a deep moral revulsion against any unfair treatment of anyone, yet it is primarily found among those who never bothered about such issues until their own relatively privileged position was threatened. It is not simple hypocrisy, however, for it is true that the reversal of centuries of systematic, governmentally abetted discrimination against women and minorities will involve pain and loss and that some innocents will suffer. That means that attention must be paid to mitigate that suffering, above all where livelihoods are at stake. But it does not justify tolerating injustice on the grounds that it is so entrenched, or that its abolition will cause some people problems.

In the case of DSOC, I am appalled that I even hesitated over the issue. No one was being deprived of a paid job. There were a handful of men who would have been given greater recognition if our feminist commitment had not given priority to gender equality. But those people would survive the experience handily—as indeed they did—and the organization actually became stronger as a result. In 1979 we adopted a procedure whereby women automatically constituted fifty percent of the leadership and, once that was done, everyone forgot the issue. In 1986, when Gro Harlem Brundtland, one of the most effective women leaders in the Socialist International, became prime minister of Norway, she noted that her party required that 40 percent of its leaders be women. So she named a cabinet in which 40 percent of its members were women.

I do not want to romanticize. The activists in the feminist movement were disproportionately drawn from a college-educated stratum with at least a middle-class standard of living. Some of them, even some of the socialists among them, inverted my own error and saw oppression exclusively in terms of gender without any reference to class. It was necessary to point out that an underpaid male worker in a declining industry often suffered more than a college-educated woman, even if women and minorities were much more likely to be found at the bottom of the society.

It would be wrong to pretend that there are "positive sum" solutions to all of the conflicts between gender and class (or race and class, generation and generation, and so on). The ideal answer to many of these problems is, of course, to create a society of such decency that it can meet the needs of *both* men and women. If, for instance, there were full employment, there could be affirmative action with no cost to anyone. Indeed in the sixties I routinely got building trades unionists to agree that, if there were good jobs for all of their existing members, they would be more than happy to agree that the new hires should be disproportionately black to make up for past injustices. But what does one do while waiting for full employment in a period when higher and higher levels of joblessness are being accepted by the society?

In 1974 through 1975, when there were widespread layoffs, some feminist activists urged that there be affirmative action, not simply in hiring, but in firing as well. Rather than follow the seniority principle in determining who gets laid off, there should be two seniority lists, one for men and one for women, and the pink slips should be given out in equal number to both lists.

That proposal infuriated the trade unionists. It was not just because there were still strong sexist currents that resented such a plan within the labor movement, though that was true. But the best of the labor militants, including quite a few women, regarded seniority as a key defense of the very security and existence of their institution. Allow the boss to pick and choose whom he fires—violate that seniority principle in the name of the best cause you can think of—and the company would figure a way to use that new freedom to strike out at the most outspoken people in the plant, male and female.

And yet, the feminists obviously had a point, too. Women had been put into a systematically inferior position in the labor force through no fault of their own. Why, then, should radicals stand idly by while that famous principle of "last hired, first fired" discriminated against them (and against minorities)?

We got together an off-the-record group of trade unionists and feminists, some of the latter from the labor movement, others not. There was more than a little shouting but it was, so to speak, among friends. In fact, everyone knew that, in practical political terms, there was no possibility that the affirmative action plan for firing would go through. Yet everyone, including the least enlightened male trade unionist present, admitted that the issue was compelling and demanded an answer. We finally agreed to work for a change in the unemployment law that would permit the part-time unemployed to get compensation for the portion of the week they were out of work. So if there had to be a 20 percent labor-force cut, rather than laying off the lowest fifth of those on the seniority list, everyone would work four days a week and draw unemployment for the fifth day.

That approach has been adopted by a number of states (not, of course, because of us). It, in effect, partly socializes a kind of work sharing with results that favor those with low seniority, i.e., women and minorities, but gives some partial recompense, through that unemployment benefit, to those who would have had a full-time job under the old rules.

I do not want to pretend that our small success in coming up with a common practical program for the trade unionists and feminists means that all of these conflicts can be neatly solved. There are social class and racial-ethnic differences, not only between men and women, but among women themselves, and they cannot be wished away by pious formulas about unity. Hispanic women tend to be factory workers; white women tend to be clerical workers. There is a greater gap between the average wage of black and white men than between black and white women (though one should immediately add that the reason black women are more nearly equal to their white sisters than black men are to white men is because *all* women are in a systematically inferior position in the society). Above all, white middle-class women have a profound class difference with working-class and poor women of whatever ethnicity.

As a social fact—but not in personal or even organizational lives—the revolution of women in the post–World War II period transcends all these differences. That is, working-class and poor women, many of whom would aggressively reject being called feminist, have probably gained more as a result of the activism of college-educated women than those college-educated women themselves. In the telephone company, for instance, there was a major breakthrough against a sexist hiring and promotion system that permanently relegated most women to the job of operator. Yet, one suspects that the majority of those who benefited from that victory were not ideological feminists.

I remember seeing on television the first two women to become coal miners. The reporter said to one of them, "Now I suppose you're taking this kind of job because you're a women's liberationist." "No way," was the reply. "It beats being a cocktail waitress." Just as the seventeenth-century merchant who unwittingly subverted the feudal order by the very fact of promoting a money economy would have been appalled if someone told him that he was a revolutionary, so millions of women during the past decades have, out of economic necessity and in response to changes in the structure of the family and of consumption, radicalized the entire society but without necessarily knowing it.

I got a sense of these complexities one evening in Chicago in the seventies. DSOC was holding its annual dinner, and Crystal Lee Sutton, a textile worker and trade unionist whose life had been the basis of the successful movie *Norma Rae*, was the featured speaker. That day, most of us had marched in a huge women's demonstration on behalf of the Equal Rights Amendment. After the DSOC dinner, Pam Woywod, who was on the staff of the Amalgamated Clothing and Textile Workers, and I went with Crystal Lee to the party put on by the organizers of the march. I went up to one of them, who was a friend, and told her who Crystal Lee was. That fact was then announced to an audience of middle- and upper-class activists, and it had a stunning impact.

There was excitement, even tears, that a Southern working-class woman was a part of the struggle.

And yet, if the moment was moving, it was also sad. For one felt the enormous gulf that divided the feminine worlds of the activists and the Southern union militant. One also knew with terrible certainty that the moment of unity was a brief, historic accident, that each side would soon go back into class ghettos, which were, and are, even more restrictive than the ghettos of gender.

That said, I think Robert Nisbett, the conservative sociologist, is quite right: the most radical movement of our times has been the challenge to the most ancient form of oppression on the planet. There is a theory, which has considerable merit, that the rhythm of feminist activism has been marked by the militancy of grand-mothers and granddaughters. The first feminist generation in the United States, the Seneca Falls movement of the late 1840s, made its impact; the daughters of this generation enjoyed whatever gains had been made, and the granddaughters became the "suffragettes" of the campaign to get women the right to vote in the early twentieth century. During that latter campaign, it had been widely argued by feminists that the franchise for women would push the entire society to the Left, particularly on issues of war and peace. But that did not happen. Instead, the daughters of the suffragettes had to face the Depression, and economic necessity and sexism were so strong that the Social Security law was carefully designed to discourage women from taking jobs in the paid labor market. In the sixties and seventies the granddaughters of the suffragettes once more raised the banner. This time, however, the pattern had been broken.

As I write, in the late eighties, the ERA has been defeated, most feminist organizations are experiencing difficult times, and the period of movement and change seems to be again over. The past is repeating itself. This time, however, the transformations have been so profound, reshaping both the family and the occupational structure, that, even if an enormous amount of gender discrimination persists, an irreversible and radical shift has taken place.

The daughters of this generation of feminists will be unlike any generation of women the West has ever known.

On a much less cosmic scale, the men, and even some of the women, in our socialist movement and cadre were deeply changed by these events. Our ideological righteousness and unconscious sexism collided with each other. Because we were Socialists, we acted out that conflict in terms of high principle even as we grappled with it on practical issues such as women's representation on the national committee. More than that, we had begun to confront a problem that is still central to the mainstream Left in the United States and throughout the world. Now that it is impossible to define the struggle for justice in terms of the stark polarity between capital and labor, now that gender and race and age and new social strata that had never been imagined in the old scenario are forces in their own right, how does one actually practice the politics of a coalition divided into sometimes warring components?

At the congress of the Socialist International in Lima in 1986, the major political parties of the world—and especially the European Left—had to deal with the same issues that had suddenly confronted me when I went to the party at Debbie Meier's during the founding convention of DSOC. It was a matter of principle for them *and* an utterly necessary response to the emergence of strong feminist tendencies in the European electorate.

Our experience in the very small confines of DSOC and DSA was indeed prefigurative. Alas, it still is.

CHAPTER THREE

Contradictions

*I*n December 1975 in Louisville, Ruth Jordan and I were standing near a window in a convention center when a security guard came up and asked us to move. Someone, he said, might throw a rock at us.

The someone in question would have been a trade unionist protesting against the UAW's commitment to racial integration. Ruth and I and a number of other members of DSOC were in Louisville for a conference sponsored by the UAW, with most of the Democratic presidential candidates in attendance. The conference was intended to give progressives the chance to discuss the issues and to size up the men who wanted to lead them into the 1976 elections.

But members of the local UAW were bitter about the UAW's integrationist politics in general and its actions in some internal disputes involving race in particular. They had been protesting, and there had been some violence. Ruth and I were looking out that window at the police who ringed the building and protected us against . . . union workers. The contradictions of coalition could not have been more in evidence. Both she and I had spent years in the civil rights and labor movements, arguing that the rank and file of both had a profound community of interest. Indeed, Ruth had been an organizer for the International Union of Electrical

Workers (IUE) in the South. And now we needed police protection from the anger of the rank and file.

This was one more moment in the excruciating history of America trying to come to terms with its most perennial injustice, our national crime against black people.

I

Ironically, I had at first thought that the American socialist record on race was even worse than it was. Eugene Victor Debs, I used to say, was totally unconcerned with the specific outrages of racism, seeing them as simply one more manifestation of the misery of capitalism.

I believed that Debs thought that ending capitalism would automatically end racism, so no special programs were needed in the meantime. Some years after Louisville, I learned from Nick Salvatore's fine book on Debs that he had been much better on the issue than I realized, fighting specifically against trade union racism. He had his limits on the issue, but they were of his time and place and he was, in any case, deeply concerned about working-class racism, which made him better than most. But that was small consolation. For the history of American workers was, in fact, shot through with prejudice and discrimination. Our coalition strategy for the mass democratic Left, then, had to struggle with this enormous fact.

This problem did not exist because workers in this country were in some mysterious way morally inferior to those in Europe or Canada. It was, rather, because no other Western nation had such a large minority population within its borders. Given the profound antiunionism of the American employers, they were more than willing to use racial conflict as a means of defeating labor organizing. So it was that blacks, who were even more desperate than whites, were recruited as strikebreakers. In 1917, for instance, the hostility among black and white workers had led to rioting and death in East St. Louis; in 1944, in the midst of a popular war against fascist racism, blacks and whites fought one another on Belle Island in Detroit (though the UAW, to its enormous credit, worked effectively to keep its members out of the battle).

There were labor parties created around the turn of the century on the West Coast for the explicit purpose of fighting Asians, particularly the Chinese. Indeed, that issue had been a difficult one for the Debsian Socialist party: did one support restrictions on immigration in order to keep out the "coolie" workers from China, who would utterly depress the whites' living standard?; or did one honor a commitment to a genuine internationalism? That debate was typical of an entire history.

For if there were always workers who were racists—in a racist society, how could it be otherwise?—that tendency became particularly virulent when it was linked to economic fears. Those anti-Chinese labor parties on the Coast were, objectively, clearly racist. But what motivated their adherents? A notion that the Chinese were inferior, the whites superior? Or simply a fear of the low wages for which the Chinese worked because their poverty was even more desperate than that of the whites?

When Martin Luther King, Jr., led demonstrators through a working-class neighborhood in Chicago and was bitterly attacked, was the hostility toward him directed against a black as a black or against a man who was perceived as threatening the houses and communities of people who had laboriously built both and were only one rung above the blacks on the social ladder?

There were two movements that had tried to respond creatively to the double victimization of black America by the related evils of class exploitation and racial discrimination. They did not, and could not, settle the theoretical debate over where racial hatred ended and economic fear began in the minds of whites who fought against minority workers. But they could try to deal with the economic motivation and see how its alleviation might make the situation better.

A. Philip Randolph was the historic leader of one of the movements taking this approach. Courtly and gentle, but with a magnificent voice and vibrant rhetoric, he was one of nature's noblemen, like his good friend Norman Thomas. He had grown up in Florida and come to New York to be an actor. But then he became a socialist and, early on, was seized by the vision of a united, interracial movement of the working class for an integrated justice. That was not such an obvious tactic at a time when most of the unions in the United States had racial exclusion clauses, mainly directed against the blacks. But Randolph became a key figure in the organization of the Brotherhood of Sleeping Car Porters, for years the central institution of black trade unionism in this country.

In the thirties Randolph encountered the other major proponent of linking antiracism with the broad progressive movement: the Communist party. In the twenties, the Communists had become utterly dependent on Moscow in everything, including tactics. In 1928, a Finnish leader of the Comintern, who knew little if anything about the race situation in the United States, decided that blacks were a nation within this country. American Communists must, therefore, fight for the right of that black nation to create its own state within the territory of the United States. This was the period during which the Comintern also ordered all Communists to treat all democratic socialists and liberals as secret fascists, and this "radical" theory fit perfectly with that strategy.

The notion of a black nationhood was not, to be sure, simply a figment of the Comintern's imagination. It had inspired Marcus Garvey's United Negro Improvement Association, which was then the most effective mass mobilization of black America. It was the militant cry of blacks who had moved in large numbers to the North around the time of World War I and discovered that, if a juridical system of Jim Crow did not exist north of the Mason-Dixon line, economic, social, and psychological racism did—and therefore all of America, the North as well as the South, was the enemy. But the Garveyites had more in common with the Zionists than the Communists. They called for emigration and the establishment of an independent black state in the African homeland, not in the American diaspora.

That nationalist impulse played a significant role among black Americans, and still does. Yet it was always a minority point of view, and the Communist version of it, with its labored attempts to prove that American blacks met all of the criteria for nationhood developed by Lenin and Stalin in a czarist context, was quite bizarre. But that ignorant decision of the Comintern had the very practical effect of making the Communists give major priority to working among blacks. With great dedication and courage they worked in the South and organized in Harlem and Chicago, the first American radicals ever to do so with such single-minded determination. They were behind the massive public campaign to save the "Scottsboro boys"; they helped create the National Negro Congress where, for a time, they cooperated with Randolph, Norman Thomas, and other democratic socialists; and within the party itself they used an authoritarian discipline, sometimes quite unfairly, to strike out at "white chauvinism."

That had a very real effect. Indeed, during my years as a civil rights activist, I assumed that a really trained black militant of a certain generation had probably been in, or around, the Communist party. But ultimately, the Comintern, which had first turned the Communists toward American blacks, subverted their influence with them. When Moscow changed its line in 1935 and declared that socialists and liberals were friends, not fascists, that abrupt shift had to be communicated on the streets of Harlem and the South Side of Chicago, where it meant the end of attacks on the hypocrisy of white liberalism. If supporters of the Roosevelt coalition were now part of the Popular Front decreed in Moscow, then it was necessary to end some of the demonstrations on 125th Street in New York.

A little later on, when the line changed again, the National Negro Congress, perhaps the most effective single institution to come out of the Communist strategy, was destroyed by the Hitler-Stalin pact. There is an unforgettable (but earlier) image of disillusionment, which resulted in Richard Wright's description of how he, a party member who had found a sense of worldwide solidarity in his struggle against racism in Chicago, was expelled and then physically ejected from the line of march at a May Day parade just as the crowd began to sing "The Internationale." And sometimes, as one can see in Harold Cruse's angry book *The Crisis of the Black Intellectual*, that process led to anti-Semitism, since the white Communist organizers were disproportionately Jewish.

There was, however, a brief period in the thirties when it seemed that the Communists and Randolph had the same idea: a class movement of black and white workers. Norman Thomas, Randolph's comrade, was playing a critical role in organizing an integrated union of sharecroppers and poor farmers in the South, and Randolph himself had emerged as a key black trade unionist. But when Randolph organized the March on Washington Movement and forced Roosevelt to decree an antidiscrimination measure in the war industries, the Communists, now supporting World War II with a fanatic intensity since the Soviet Union was under attack, denounced him as a "fascist." After World War II, the Communists were viciously persecuted by Democratic liberals, such as Harry Truman and Hubert Humphrey, as well as by Joe McCarthy; the crimes of Stalin were partially acknowledged by Khrushchev; and the party lost almost all of its previous influence, in white America as well as black.

Randolph, of course, continued as a major leader in the struggle until his death in 1979. When I became deeply involved in the civil rights movement in the fifties and sixties, I was a conscious Randolphite, dedicated to the program of an integrated class struggle against both exploitation and racism. And when I began to work with Martin Luther King, Jr., I discovered that he, too, had much the same view. After the first time that we were able to talk together at length—which was over several days in Los Angeles in 1960 when we were hiding him in a hotel room so that the representatives of the various Democratic presidential candidates could not pester him for endorsements—I concluded that he was a democratic socialist, like Randolph.

It did not even occur to me to ask King to proclaim publicly those beliefs since I understood that he had troubles enough without adding to them an ideological commitment, which would be inevitably misunderstood. But I was delighted when *Bearing the Cross*, David Garrow's brilliant biography of King, recently documented the truth of my conviction about him, revealing that King actually called himself a democratic socialist in private conversation.

In any case, the Vietnam War imposed new burdens on King and made the Randolph strategy extremely difficult. It split the civil rights coalition itself as the labor and liberal hawks—and Randolph himself—backed Lyndon Johnson and the war while King rightly opposed that insanity. It shifted political attention and funds away from the struggle against poverty at home and thus embittered the younger and more militant blacks who had thought that economic and social deliverance was finally at hand. So there was a completely understandable recrudescence of a militant nationalism as some of King's own youthful followers turned against him, mocking him as "De Lawd." The riots and the militancy, which were a part of the same process, then played a major role in stimulating a racist backlash, and George Wallace received about 13 percent of the vote in the 1968 elections (he had been at around 25 percent in the polls not too long before the vote).

This was the context in which we organized DSOC. Every one of the founding members old enough to have done so had been active in the movement of the fifties and sixties. Many of us had worked for years in the ghettos, fighting shoulder to shoulder with blacks of every social class. Yet the militant black mood of the late sixties and early seventies would not let most black activists join an organization that was primarily white, as ours was. Worse, our political strategy of working within the Democratic party and reaching out even to those trade unionists who had supported the unconscionable war was seen as a cop-out.

I put all of this in macropolitical terms. But on the personal level, what was involved was one of the greatest disappointments of my life. During those years in the civil rights movement, I felt I had at least begun to transcend the racism that is tragically the birthright of every American white. In the first phase of my activity—from about the time I joined the Harlem branch of the NAACP in 1954 until the beginning of the hostility between whites and blacks in 1965 and 1966—I felt at home in the ghettos. In

New York, we worked out of the Brotherhood of Sleeping Car Porters' office on 125th Street, the very center of Harlem; in Los Angeles, I spent six weeks based at the Brotherhood's office while organizing the civil rights demonstrations at the Democratic Convention in 1960. I routinely found myself the only white in black restaurants. As a sophisticated urban white, I became apprehensive in New York late at night if I found myself on a street alone with young blacks; but in the South, I felt the identical emotion with young whites and only felt secure when I was in the ghetto.

The problem was not just that suddenly I had the wrong skin color but, worse, that I understood why a black person could rationally come to such a conclusion, which meant I could not respond in anger or righteousness. I opposed black nationalism as such, yet I was profoundly sympathetic to the desire to replace white activists, like me, with blacks. To one degree or another, that was true of all of the whites of my generation in DSOC. There were just a few blacks in the founding cadre, and when we reached out it was to other blacks who had known us in the movement. Many of them—Julian Bond, Jim Farmer, John Lewis—either joined or worked with us out of a historic sympathy and shared politics, but did not really participate in the life of the organization. Inevitably their main focus was elsewhere.

Take Bill Lynch. He joined in good measure because of his personal ties in CORE with two of our activists, Bill Gellermann and Marjorie Phyfe, and because he agreed with our "Randolph" approach to racism. And he loyally participated as the only black member of our resident committee in New York for two years. He didn't quit but eventually drifted away because he saw no point in being the one black in a leadership that simply could not reach out to his own brothers and sisters. We worked with him on various campaigns, and he played a key role in helping to elect Major Owens to Congress in Brooklyn and then in making David Dinkins borough president of Manhattan. In a way he then drifted back toward us. But we have not yet created an organization in which a thoughtful, talented black like Bill could feel really comfortable, even though he shared all of the essentials of our politics.

So we suffered from a catch-22: because we had only a few blacks, we could not recruit many blacks, and our miserable situation merely repeated itself over and over.

This often led to attacks of white guilt. Some member, or members, would say: we have not done enough, we are adapting to this racist culture. In some ways, that was true enough. But what were we to do about it? It was easy for the critics of the leadership to get up at a meeting and denounce us for our admitted failure and make everyone feel even more unhappy than before and to get all of the emotional consolations that come when a sinner publicly proclaims his or her guilt. But I never met one of them who had a solution to the problem.

I exaggerate, but only a bit. During the seventies, there were three groups in black America with which we were able to work effectively: the politicians, the trade unionists, and the intellectuals. But even this modest success had its bitter irony: we developed a relation with a black elite at the same time that its own relation to the black masses was becoming problematic.

I I

One of the enduring accomplishments of the civil rights movement of the fifties and sixties—and of the antiwar movement, which was related to it—was the emergence of a stratum of black elected officials. Indeed, during that decade the Congressional Black Caucus (CBC) became the most imaginative and radical single constituent of the Democratic party. Early on in the decade, Bertram Gross, one of the drafters of the original full-employment bill of 1944 (it was downgraded into the much more conservative Employment Act of 1946, the Republicans having decided that "full" employment was too Leftist a concept), began to work with the Caucus. At some point in that period, he also joined DSOC.

The result of Gross's collaboration with the Caucus was the original Hawkins bill, which then became the Humphrey-Hawkins bill and finally, in a completely gutted version, the Humphrey-

Hawkins Act. In its first draft it was the most radical piece of legislation proposed since the thirties, creating, among many other things, a legal right to a job and giving an unemployed man or woman standing to sue in court because no work was made available to them. That, of course, was along the lines of our basic thinking and strategy and we began to make Humphrey-Hawkins a central agitational concern very early on. I had met Augustus (Gus) Hawkins when I was doing civil rights organizing in Los Angeles in 1960, so we asked him to come to a meeting in New York in 1974.

We had decided that we didn't want to hold one more meeting where black and white intellectuals would berate one another for not being sufficiently militant. We involved our trade union friends in New York and told them that we wanted them to get shop stewards and militant activists to attend a conference in a hall on Union Square.

Not too many rank and filers showed up, and those who did came mainly from unions such as District Council 37 of AFSCME and Local 1199 of the Hospital Workers, where our members and friends in the leadership strongly encouraged them to participate. One of the chief reasons we failed to reach out was simple enough: the meeting was held on a Saturday and most workers, even dedicated trade unionists, don't want to give up a day off to a political meeting, no matter how well intentioned.

Still, Hawkins spoke, and we began to make his bill central to everything we did, particularly in the Democratic party. Through that activity we came into much closer contact with two leading members of the Congressional Black Caucus, John Conyers of Detroit and Ron Dellums from Oakland-Berkeley. Conyers is one of those people whose appearance belies his temperament. The son of an autoworker who had been a Communist activist, he is a nattily dressed, soft-spoken man with a gentle and humorous manner. Because of his quiet demeanor I was a bit taken aback a day or so before Reagan's inauguration in 1981 when John suggested that perhaps he and I could go over to Capitol Hill and sit in, or make some kind of outrageous fuss, in honor of the event.

Dellums's family was deeply involved in the Brotherhood of Sleeping Car Porters. (In Los Angeles in 1960 I had worked with an uncle of his who was a leader of the union.) Tall, eloquent, and with more than a touch of the rhythms of the streets, he had come out of an extremely militant West Coast Left, and his moving toward us, and then joining, surprised more than a few people. When he was first elected, I suspect that Ron was not an untypical Left member of Congress, more adept at a ringing speech than at the intricate, difficult work of the legislative process. But over the years he became a much deeper person and eventually developed a real expertise on defense and—I am sure to the utter consternation of the Pentagon—rose to become a subcommittee chair of the House Military Affairs Committee. In 1986 he was the principal author of the House bill for sanctions against South African racism—and the only card-carrying member of the Democratic Socialists of America on Capitol Hill. In 1986 he lost that distinction when Major Owens, an extremely thoughtful black congressperson from Brooklyn, doubled the ranks of the socialist caucus on Capitol Hill by joining DSA.

David Dinkins was another of the new breed of black politicians. Like Conyers, he is the very model of a moderate and respectable gentleperson with a will of iron and a deep commitment to social justice. He identified with our coalition politics and our insistence that full employment was a key to both black and white justice, and became a dynamic and important ally in our work in the Democratic party in New York. Significantly, I first met him when Victor Gotbaum, the leader of the major public employee trade union in New York, invited both of us to dinner at the Democratic miniconvention in Kansas City in 1974. That is to say, the Randolph connection between labor and antiracist struggles brought us together.

Let these three men stand for a whole stratum of black politicians, from district leaders in Harlem to members of the House, with whom we worked and whom we sometimes recruited. Ironically, black politicians were somewhat exempt from the general rule that any identification with socialism led to electoral defeat.

Their constituencies were either desperate or, even when there had been upward mobility, excluded, and the charge that a black was some kind of a Red didn't have the resonance it did in the rest of the country. I don't want to exaggerate: in 1960, when I appeared on behalf of Martin Luther King, Jr., before the Oakland, California, ministerial association to ask for support for our demonstrations in Los Angeles, the first question I was asked was whether we were Communists. Still, a Dellums or a Conyers or a Dinkins was simply not under the kind of pressure on this issue that a white politician felt.

But the catch-22 surfaced again even in this privileged area. Men like Conyers, Dellums, and Dinkins were committed to our issues and shared our strategy. Yet their working with us was more a sign of their decency than their *realpolitik*. They were members of a generation that had participated in the same civil rights and antiwar struggles as our founding cadre. Yet, even as we developed excellent working relations with such impressive leaders, we were still unable to reach out to the black rank and file in any significant way.

There was another group of blacks, closely related to, and politically involved with, the new political leaders: the trade unionists.

In the late sixties, many militant blacks and most New Leftists regarded the established trade union movement as a bulwark of racism. In Detroit in those years there were some "revolutionary union movements" that did indeed manage to reach out to black discontent in a city where minorities constituted a very high percentage of autoworkers. Those initiatives did not last too long—some of the most capable leaders were elected to office in the UAW and, in any case, the period changed. Still, when DSOC was founded in 1973, our commitment to labor in general and to the antiwar wing of the AFL-CIO in particular, was one more reason why many people of the more intransigent Left regarded us as sellouts.

We argued that the class institutions of the American workers were the best single arena for the struggle of blacks, who were disproportionately either members of the working class or part of an "underclass" (we would have said privately, a *lumpenprole-tariat*) that had not achieved the status of workers. Yes, we con-ceded, there were outrageous racist practices that still existed in a minority of unions. But, we added, there were more black elected officials and executive board members in labor organizations than in any other institution in the society. The unions—and particu-larly the industrial unions, which organized every single worker in a jurisdiction—were actually much more integrated than the government, the churches, or the schools. We were, in my retro-spective opinion, right, as a fair number of our critics came to realize.

In the mid-seventies, for instance, I spoke, along with Coretta Scott King, at a day-long conference in Detroit sponsored by the South Eastern Michigan regions of the UAW. The leaders of several of those regions—who were members of the International Exec-utive Board by virtue of that fact—were black, and at least 50 percent of those in the audience were too. We had just published a DSOC pamphlet on full employment and every delegate received it. I don't want to paint the event romantically. Everybody there was getting paid time off to attend, but when I spoke in the last afternoon session, a good number had already gone home. That fact was denounced from the floor by several militants, but it reflected a reality in which workers, including black workers, had achieved sufficient economic gains through union action to make them less responsive to union events.

Still, this was a major area where we were able to reach out to black leaders. In the American Federation of State, County, and Municipal Employees Union, for instance, we constantly worked with Bill Lucy, the secretary-treasurer in Washington, and Lillian Roberts, for many years the second in command of the huge New York District. They were labor intellectuals, as were many of our members and friends who had come up through the Auto Workers in the thirties and forties. That is, they had a command of the issues of their union and of the economy that was superior to most Ph.D.'s, but they had acquired it through struggle more than in the classroom. And one reason why we could relate to them, personally and politically, was that we spoke the same language.

In Selig Perlman's enormously influential book about the twenties, *A Theory of the Labor Movement*, most of the failures of the working-class movement are explained as the result of the unfortunate influence of intellectuals, with their utopian yearnings and schemes, in unions that should have focused on the very specific issue of jobs. Perlman did not realize—as the great Italian Marxist Antonio Gramsci did—that trade unionists without advanced degrees became intellectuals; they became reflective, analytic, thoughtful commentators on the conditions of labor life without necessarily having gone through formal academic training. And that was, and is, quite true with regard to black union activists. And even though the whites in DSOC and DSA had come to their first socialist conclusions through books rather than immediate experience, they had a shared language, as well as shared concerns, with those who had become intellectuals on the shop floor or as welfare workers. So it was possible to have a meaningful, and even comfortable, exchange across the racial barriers.

That same ease did not exist with the rank and file, and particularly the black rank and file. To be sure, when I talked at a union convention or educational meeting, I got a respectful, often even an enthusiastic, hearing. But the barriers of class and racial difference are extremely difficult to transcend in personal life precisely because, in most cases, there is simply not that shared language. So even here, in the project of uniting black and white trade unionists around a political program—in this most "Randolphite" area of American life—we could work with the leaders, but had deep problems in relating to the ranks.

We shared a language and many insights with the more traditional black intellectuals, who proliferated as a result of the spread of mass higher education. But there, it seemed to me, another problem surfaced. The talented black man or woman who went on from college—sometimes an elite college—to graduate school was entering a white (male) world light-years distant from the ghetto. Yet they themselves often came from that ghetto—but not, as I think of my friends and acquaintances in this group, from the lower depths of the ghetto—and felt ambivalent, or even guilty, about their own success. When they encountered people such as myself, with my well-known ties to some labor leaders (leaders!) and my insistence on working in the Democratic party, they were often deeply suspicious or even hostile. They were, so to speak, frightened that they might turn into someone like me and thereby lose their connection to their own origins. Yet, at the same time, in so far as they were intellectuals, they *were* like me.

In 1983 and 1984, for instance, these contradictions played a role in defining positions with regard to Jesse Jackson's presidential candidacy. As I marched in the twentieth commemoration of the August 1963 March on Washington, at which Martin Luther King, Jr., made his famous speech, a black socialist-intellectual candidly told me that he shared all of my doubts and hesitations about Jackson inherited from my days in the King civil rights movement, but that he had to commit himself unambiguously to the candidacy. I understood, of course. That kind of defensive solidarity has marked every new class and ethnic force in a society during the period when that class is establishing its identity and was particularly powerful among blacks who had suffered from more misery and discrimination than any other group in the country except the American Indians.

In 1988, my attitude toward Jackson changed and I supported him for President, drafting several of his speeches in the process. Even though I was not completely satisfied with his account of why he had accepted the support in the 1984 campaign of Louis Farrakhan, a genuine racist demagogue and anti-Semite, I was profoundly impressed by the changes in Jackson's strategy. It was not only that he was advocating a social democratic program with which I essentially agreed, but that he was trying to build a Populist, multi-racial coalition on the Randolph model. I was—and am—hopeful that this pointed to the creation of a true "rainbow" movement of all colors, albeit with blacks playing a more significant leadership role in their own name than ever before. In 1987–1988 Jesse Jackson was making a significant contribution, not only to black America, but to all of America.

Sometimes, then, the distortions that racism imposes on any white and any black in this country vanish, if only for a while. In conversations with Cornel West, for instance, I sometimes felt that the national racist heritage, which I participated in even as I fought against it, had been put in parentheses. Cornel is a marvelously complex man, the son of a preacher, with a deep commitment to the religious sources of black revolt—which is the theme of his fine book *Prophesy Deliverance!*—who is utterly fluent in the language of scholarly Left abstraction. Still, those exchanges with Cornel West did not define my (white socialist) relation to black intellectuals, or blacks in general. Neither, alas, did those years in the movement sharing work and danger with black militants of every class.

For the sad truth I have learned from more than thirty years of involvement in the antiracist struggle is that it is impossible to flee this country's historic crimes against people of color even if you dedicate a good part of your life to fighting them. Even those whites who try to give total acceptance to the struggle—who suppress their own egos and doubts and even come to hate themselves— end up by mimicking blacks without being black, achieving a fraudulent, self-deceptive peace by simply inverting the viciousness they deplore. "White is bad" is, in our society, not as destructive as the traditional racist "black is bad," but it is still grotesque and an impossible solution for the society as a whole.

But then, these tensions were not simply a matter of black and white psychodrama. At about the same time that we were organizing DSOC, a major change (obviously unrelated to our minimal existence) was taking place in the black world. The rising unemployment rates and the deindustrialization of smokestack America hit minorities very hard. They had just established themselves in the blue-collar, unionized jobs, which had been the way out of poverty for so many of the immigrant generations, when those jobs began to disappear. So in the Reagan Recovery of the eighties, poverty in general and black poverty in particular showed the ability to persist despite relatively high growth rates.

That set the stage for a certain disorganization of life in the black ghettos as the successful workers and then the middle-class left, and there emerged, through no fault of their own, a society of the rejected. That is, it was not simply difficult for a predominantly white organization to find a toehold in such a world—it was hard for blacks to do so as well. And that fed the frustration and guilt of the activists and intellectuals who had succeeded in leaving this world but were still bound to it by ties of solidarity and guilt. It is no accident, in my opinion, that Jesse Jackson has had such an impact. For the authoritative voice of the pastor, of the black church, gained a resonance in this context that merely secular politicians did not have. It spoke to the heart and desperation of the ghetto, not just to its class interest.

And then in 1987 I got to know William Julius Wilson, the brilliant black scholar at the University of Chicago whose book, *The Truly Disadvantaged*, documents and analyzes the problems of the underclass better than anything written before it. To my delight, Wilson identified himself as a "social democrat" and joined DSA. It made me feel that with all of the frustrating problems of trying to deal with America's racist heritage—and with all of my own particular imperfections—my ideas were still as relevant to the struggle as they had been when I had worked with Dr. King. I was again convinced that whites could transcend the color of their skin and the ambiguities of the privileged racial position that it imposed, willy-nilly, upon them, if they could work with people like Bill Wilson.

I I I

All of these problems became even more complex when we became aware of another huge minority group in America during the seventies—the Hispanics.

Obviously, we all knew about Hispanic poverty in the United States, and many of us had been activists in the grape boycott initiated by Cesar Chávez as part of the struggle for farmworker organization in the late sixties and early seventies. But in the seventies, the huge immigration wave—documented and undocumented—of Latinos and the emergence of a new militancy meant that we had to try to develop a relation with a massive stratum of the society in which we had few ties.

I suspect that many of us first became really conscious of the issue at a board meeting of DSOC. Michael Rivas, a Cuban exile who had supported Fidel but had then broken with the regime over the issue of capital punishment and the treatment of dissidents, was a respected member of the organization. A theologian, Mike was very sophisticated about both liberation and traditional theology and therefore spoke our "language" quite well. Yet, during a discussion of Hispanics at the DSOC meeting, he suddenly began to speak in Spanish to the bewilderment of almost all of us. After a brief while, he went back to English and pointed out that our discomfort would be felt by many Puerto Ricans, Cubans, and Mexicans in the United States if they came to one of our meetings where everyone was speaking English. So we organized a Hispanic Commission, composed of our Spanish-speaking members, and started trying to reach out to this unknown world within the borders of the United States.

On a summer's day in the mid-seventies, I drove down to the Little Havana section of Miami to meet with a small group of Cuban socialists who had become a part of DSOC. They were, they explained to me in a crowded apartment, "exiles among the exiles," that is, Leftist critics of Castro in a community totally dominated, and even terrorized, by Rightist foes of the regime. They were, among many other things, drawn to us by the fact that my analysis of the Cuban Revolution in my book *Socialism* coincided very much with their own. Yet even then, they were primarily defining themselves, in the historic mode of exiles from every revolution, in terms of the politics of their lost homeland. We were not simply biographically and linguistically from different countries; their political frame of reference and mine were located in different geographies.

Eventually, and sadly, that relation broke down. Some of our Cuban members in Florida developed close relationships with foes of Castro who were, from our point of view, Rightist opponents of the regime. There was a brief flurry of unhappy communications on both sides and then we parted company.

In New York, one of our most important centers, we sought to develop ties with the Puerto Rican community. I was trying to learn Spanish at this point and had discovered that the Puerto Rican style of speaking it was the most difficult to understand, at least for me. Still, we worked with José Rivera in the Bronx, and at one point Jack Clark played a key role in a political campaign in that borough's huge barrio. Rivera was a labor organizer as well as a Puerto Rican militant, and I spoke to a group of the rank and file at his storefront on Tremont Avenue in the South Bronx. But, once again, we encountered the double problem of national and class culture. The workers at that meeting agreed with most of what I said, yet we inhabited quite different worlds. José was elected to the state legislature in Albany and we continued to work with him, but it was impossible for us to establish any real and ongoing presence in the Puerto Rican community.

That was true even though we developed a very warm and cooperative relationship with one of the most charismatic politicians in Puerto Rico itself. Roger Baldwin, the venerable founder of the American Civil Liberties Union, had told me that Rubén Berrios, the leader of the Puerto Rican Independence Party (the PIP or *Independistas*), was my kind of socialist, and when I read Rubén's pamphlet on his party's ideology, I was in total agreement with it. The *Independistas* had emerged out of the original Puerto Rican political movement led by Muñoz Marin. When the "Commonwealth" relationship with the United States developed, Muñoz became, in effect, a New Deal Democrat, and only a minority of his followers remained true to the goal of nationhood for the island. Berrios's *Independistas* were antiterrorists sharply critical of Communist dictatorships such as Fidel's and deeply committed to democratic socialism. But they had a major, and very frustrating, difficulty. Rubén and I talked of the problem often, not the least because it was routinely, and sometimes maliciously, misunderstood by Americans and Europeans. The Puerto Ricans were, and are, desperately poor, with about a third of the population dependent on welfare programs financed in Washington. That poverty is hardly their individual fault and persisted long after the "Operation Bootstrap" program—an attempt to develop industry on the basis of subminimum wages—had failed to work its announced transformation. It meant, however, that when Puerto Ricans were asked, in elections or opinion surveys, whether they wanted independence, two questions were answered at the same time with a maximum of confusion. Do you, as a person proud of your heritage and living on an island ruled by a government on the mainland, which does not even speak your language, want self-rule? Do you, through independence, want to lose the food stamps and other benefits that keep you alive?

If, Rubén felt, that first question could be posed independently of the second, the answer would be different. So he argued that any referendum on the issue should provide for a phasing out of the welfare benefits as part of the independence process, a proposal which I found quite persuasive. So it was, for instance, that at the Socialist International I played a small role in helping the PIP become a consultative member, even though the State Department made its displeasure known to all of the major European socialist movements. And this relationship with Rubén—who is now a senator in Puerto Rico—also led to our most romantic and bizarre failure.

In 1979 we decided to hold the DSOC convention in Houston, Texas, in part because it would allow us to reach out to a huge Chicano and Chicana population. Rubén agreed to speak, and we imagined a mass meeting in which he would speak Spanish. Only we mainly saw the Holiday Inn out by the airport where we held our sessions. We had to threaten cutting down on our payment to force management to put WELCOME DEMOCRATIC SOCIALISTS on the roadside sign for the Inn, and our nightly parties were carefully monitored by gun-toting security guards. Rubén's speech took place in a Mexican-American church, which was fine, but almost everyone there was an English-speaking member of DSOC. Berrios, a handsome, incredibly elegant orator, was marvelous, but our hopes were utterly dashed.

This "failure" was not totally our fault. As time went on I realized that it was an oversimplification to talk about "Hispanics" as a coherent group. Most of the Cubans and some of the Chicanos-Chicanas were Republicans; most of the Puerto Ricans were Democrats; and the internal differences within the Spanish-speaking community were enormous. I had dinner with Cesar Chávez in 1985 and quite tentatively and rather apologetically developed this thesis, and he agreed, sadly but emphatically.

These, then, were but a few of the contradictions of coalition in America that grew out of the extreme heterogeneity of the people. When one adds all of the complications that arise out of social class to those stemming from racial and ethnic identity, our effort became extremely difficult, if not impossible: create a multi-racial, multi-class organization. But then our problems were those of the nation writ small. That is, in the thirties, when unemployment was an issue so overwhelming that it defined its own primacy, the working class was a majority of the nation, and the issues of race were secondary, in fact at least, to those of economic survival. It was possible to define a struggle of "us" against "them." But in the post–World War II years, the class structure became more differentiated, and there were new strata of college-educated activists, a mighty surge of racial and ethnic consciousness, and the emergence of the women's movement. We struggled with these new complexities within our own tiny socialist organization. But the larger society and the liberal and labor movements faced the same issues.

At the same time, we were trying to redeem the promise of our founding convention to put an end to the Left's quarrels in the sixties.

I V

My own personal history was a major barrier to that reconciliation, which I earnestly sought, of the entire nonsectarian Left. In explaining this I must of necessity evoke an entire social history: that of the left-wing youth movements of the sixties and seventies.

At the founding meeting of Students for a Democratic Society (SDS) in 1962, I had distinguished myself by a rude insensitivity to young people struggling to define a new identity. I had, as I admitted within some weeks of the event, treated fledgling radicals trying out their own ideas for the first time as if they were hardened faction fighters whose lives were perversely dedicated to principles I abhorred. I then compounded that stupidity by making an alliance with the old guard of the League for Industrial Democracy, the social-democratic and trade union–based parent organization of SDS, against my former protégés. When I came to my senses, the damage had been done and, as far as many in the New Left were concerned, I was one more horrible example of the untrustworthiness of people over thirty.

This situation was made even more complex because, even when I realized how wrong I had been, I continued to think I was right on the substance of the issues debated at that SDS meeting in Port Huron, Michigan, in 1962. We argued into the night over Stalinism, the American unions, and liberalism. For the young activists, anti-Communism was identified—purely, simply, and exclusively— with McCarthyism and the Bay of Pigs invasion of Cuba. I had, of course, opposed both, yet I defined another anti-Communism, which spoke in the name of the Left—only it had nothing to do with the actual experience of the SDS generation. Emotionally, I felt myself in solidarity with the Russian oppositionists, the Left Socialists and anarchists in the Spanish Civil War, the Hungarians invaded by the Red Army in 1956, and the Poles in their endless struggle for freedom and decency in the shadow of Soviet power. For most of the new young radicals all of that was a vague, antediluvian past that played no role in their political emotions.

Secondly, I was painfully aware of the limitations of the American unions. But I also knew many militants who were trying to build a truly democratic and social labor movement, and I thought that the established union leadership itself played a progressive role, particularly on domestic issues (this was before the AFL-CIO's down-the-line support of the Vietnam War split the unions on international issues). I argued that American liberalism, for all of its flaws, was the mass Left of the society, and that radicals had to speak to what was positive in it and what made it possible to move liberals to the Left—not simply focus on its inadequacies.

In 1985 Todd Gitlin, one of the leaders of the first generation of SDS, interviewed me for a book he was writing on the sixties and casually mentioned—to my surprise and delight—that in going over the debate at Port Huron he had concluded that on the issues I had been more right than wrong. That was the problem. My egregious error had not been to champion the views I have just outlined—which I hold to this day—but to respond to criticism of them by having a middle-age tantrum and making a political bloc with people who did not really share my basic attitudes.

What is more, the very evolution of the New Left in the sixties further complicated my problems. SDS, which had begun with a marvelous commitment to an undogmatic radicalism, became more and more dogmatic as the Vietnam War turned uglier and fostered an "us" against "them" psychology in which the enemy of my enemies must be my friend (i.e., the Viet Cong and Ho Chi Minh must be good if the United States is so very bad). The founding generation of SDS had actually responded to my arguments even if they rejected them (and an accidental misunderstanding had something to do with my personal debacle at Port Huron). But now, a new generation of leaders of SDS—the generations shifted almost yearly—was much more intransigent and was moving in the direction of a Maoist version of Marxism-Leninism. The rank and file was much more reasonable and was happy to discover that I was not a monster when I appeared on campuses.

Thus when DSOC formed, with its announced intention of ending the bitter splits of the sixties, the omens were hardly propitious.

On the one hand, Irving Howe and I, two of the most visible leaders of the new organization, were seen by the New Left as veritable antimodels of what a radical should be: middle-aged, adapting to the powers that be, anti-Communists who were, willy-nilly, tied in with the McCarthyite version of that creed. And on the other hand, SDS itself had self-destructed in an orgy of self-righteous radicalism, with rival factions chanting the name of Ho Chi Minh or reciting from Mao's little red book. How could these differences be bridged? And worse, was it even worth the trouble now that the revolutionaries of the sixties were turning into the Yuppies (I anticipated the label but not the concept) of the seventies and eighties?

That second question was, and is, easy to answer. The young radicals of the sixties had never been as numerous as they, and both their friends and critics, thought. They had indeed put their stamp on a generation, but the overwhelming majority of that generation had done nothing more radical than go to a demon-stration or two. There was, for instance, abundant evidence that most of the students involved in the great upheavals at Berkeley in the mid-sixties were, even then, liberals, not revolutionaries. But then, that is always the case. The Communists of the "Red Decade" of the thirties were a thin stratum, yet they played a critical role in a number of mass movements and seemed much more powerful in their own right than they ever were.

The corollary error of overestimating the radicalism of the six-ties was wildly exaggerating the way its activists sold out in the seventies. There were some prominent cases—Jerry Rubin, the semianarchist Dadaist of the sixties, did indeed turn into a cele-brant of capitalist greed—and it was easy to overgeneralize such cases exponentially. But a solid majority of the people who had been really committed to the movement of the sixties became trade union staffers, community activists and organizers, radical aca-demics, and the like, in the seventies. The founding cadre of DSOC understood that fact well. Which was one of the many reasons we wanted to reach out to this group.

We discovered after our first convention that some of those

New Leftists were indeed taking a wary look at us. Ron Radosh, who had been in the Communist movement and then in the New Left, wrote an article in the review *Socialist Revolution* in which he took us seriously, if critically, and even noted that some militants of the sixties had been at the convention, if only because we seemed to be the only game in town. And then we came into contact with Harry Boyte, a civil rights militant who was now playing an active role in the New American Movement (NAM), the chief successor organization of SDS. Harry has a kind of tolerant, open, even Quaker, personality and he has since become a major exponent of grass-roots organizing, of the "neighborhood revolution." He was one of the first of the New Left generation to understand that it was important that we talk to one another.

So it was that DSOC and NAM held a joint conference in 1975. We came together—and in many cases, we discovered how distant we were from one another. Few, if any, of the New Left veterans were pro-Soviet, but they did tend to be Third Worldist, i.e., uncritical of any liberation movement or ex-colonial government, too ready—from my point of view—to accept the claim that the regimes of the wretched of the earth were "socialist." That testified to the decency of their hearts but not to the clarity of their concepts of socialism. While we were meeting, Cambodia celebrated its independence, and some of the NAM people greeted the event with a totally uncritical joy.

That same mind-set also led many of them to accept all of the claims of the Palestine Liberation Organization and Yasir Arafat and to effectively reject the actual right of Jewish self-determination in the state of Israel. And they thought that our strategy of working within the Democratic party was just one more example of our congenital reformism. Since Irving Howe and I were quite visible leaders of DSOC, such conduct was the result of self-evident causes.

Gradually attitudes changed. When in 1975 through 1976 we organized Democratic Agenda, the broad labor-liberal coalition around programmatic issues, there were those in NAM who realized that we were indeed carving out a radical niche in the mainstream of the society. One of them, Richard Healy, later told me that he had said to his comrades in NAM that this was the kind of thing they should be doing. NAM did come to endorse Democratic Agenda not too long afterward—a sign of the waning sectarianism of the sixties graduates.

One of the reasons for that transition had to do with an ironic consequence of a psychological difference between the NAM and DSOC leaders. NAM had felt at home in—and some of its people had led—the great demonstrations of the late sixties and early seventies. Filled with optimism, they began their new organization in 1972, assuming that the return of the days of mass protest was imminent. Many of us in DSOC had attended those same demonstrations because we were viscerally opposed to the war, yet we were more than a little unhappy with some of the ultra-Leftist rhetoric we heard. We later concluded, after a rather serious discussion, that we had been quite wrong to demand small group standards of political correctness in what must inevitably be the ideological sloppiness of a huge mobilization. We should have acted, we realized, like everyone else: speaking our mind from the podium even though we differed, sometimes significantly, from those who talked before and after us.

But such retrospective wisdom did not change our feeling that the great mass potential of the sixties ended with the murders of Martin Luther King, Jr., and Robert Kennedy, i.e., with the collapse of the mass movement of the broad democratic Left. We were therefore pessimistic when we began DSOC and surprised when we achieved some modest growth. NAM, as I see it, had to get over illusions about the inherent radicalism of the United States before it could face up to the task of movement building. We had been deprived of our illusions much earlier, which turned out to be something of a liberating experience and a tactical advantage.

That was one of the reasons why in the mid-seventies DSOC, presumably an organization of old fogies, began to recruit significant numbers of young people. Our open, antisectarian realism, our determination to take socialism from the margin of the society into the Democratic party, the unions, and the social movements, had a considerable appeal. Strangely, at least some of the New Leftists were now making my own, earlier error: they were looking for new movements that would behave exactly as they had done in their own youth, only the times had changed. Our skepticism and lowered expectations, our insistence that idealism be practical, turned out to have considerable appeal.

Our first youth organizer, Cynthia Ward, came from an extraordinarily energetic group of that younger generation at the University of Chicago. Joe Schwartz, who began his militant career as a high school militant against the Vietnam War, was a brilliant, voluble young man who "advanced" an enormously successful tour for me in California in 1979. Mark Levinson, who had grown up in a Socialist family, was both intellectually subtle and gifted with an optimistic, unhostile temperament. Jeremey Karpatkin, the son of liberal activists, was a tireless organizer. And Penny Schantz, one of my few students to join the movement, had a particularly passionate commitment to trade unionism, in theory and practice.

These, and the many others who cannot be named, were an enormous hidden resource for us. They slept on couches and took buses as well as planes when they were on the road; they worked for starvation wages and put in impossible hours. They had, they all understood, "movement" jobs. All of them are active today, and it is indicative to see where they are. Ward is a university administrator; Schwartz a Harvard Ph.D.; Levinson is also a Ph.D., on the research staff of the Auto Workers union; Karpatkin joined the presidential campaign staff of Paul Simon in 1988; and Schantz is a union organizer and president of the Santa Cruz Labor Council.

At our regular youth camps in the summer, our organizers and the new recruits would spend three or four days listening to lectures, arguing their politics, and consuming enormous quantities of beer (under the sponsorship of the Rosa Luxemburg Caucus). We always had one session where veterans from different generations would teach history simply by telling their own stories. There were socialist union organizers from the thirties, like Millie Jeffrey; one-time Communist leaders who had broken with the party but kept their idealism; black leaders, like Jim Farmer, the founder of CORE; graduates of the "thin" class of the fifties, like me, and of the new class of the sixties, like Nancy Kleniewksi.

We lived off those generations when our deepest organizational-financial crisis hit in 1983–1984 (it coincided with the demoralizing landslide re-election of Ronald Reagan, which made it all the worse). Maxine Phillips, a gentle, extremely able woman who had never belonged to a political sect and came from the religious socialist movement, became executive director. At the same time Gordon Haskell, with a radical pedigree that went back to socialist organizing as a railroad worker and who had been a functionary of the Independent Socialist League when I made my youthful contact with that group, took on a critical role when he officially "retired" from the labor force. And a crisis or two later, two youth section graduates became leaders—Guy Molyneux, a shrewd and extraordinarily gifted workaholic, and Patrick Lacefield, a native Arkansan with a marvelous midwestern manner who, among many other things, had spent almost two years working with a medical team in rural Salvador. Thus it was our historic continuity, and not just the young people alone, that allowed us to survive against impossible odds.

Probably the most dramatic single moment in this development of a new socialist youth movement took place in March 1980. We had opposed both the outrageous Soviet invasion of Afghanistan and the overreaction to it by Jimmy Carter. I was particularly appalled that Carter said he was "shocked" to learn the Soviets could do such a thing, as if he had never heard of Czechoslovakia in 1968 or Hungary in 1956. In particular, we felt that the decision to reinstitute registration for the draft was either an idle gesture or a dangerous attempt to play on a visceral, hysterical anti-Communism. So we took the lead in organizing a major antidraft demonstration in Washington, D.C.

Suddenly our tiny office was flooded with volunteers and the phones rang off the hook. At the Ellipse, just behind the White House, on the day of the march, my heart sank. When I arrived, the only people there were the sectarians of every stripe, some of them with vivid banners and posters, all of them pushing ideas that would repel, or infuriate, at least 99.9 percent of the American people. But as time passed, thousands and then tens of thousands of students showed up, and it was clear that we had struck a very real chord. When I spoke, Joe Schwartz told me, "Five minutes, Mike. We don't know how long we can hold the perimeter." That was a reference to a small but energetic and tough group of Rightists who were trying to fight their way to the microphone and disrupt the demonstration. But we held out against them.

Events like the antidraft demo helped convince NAM that we were not the staid, Cold War social democrats they imagined. As far back as 1977, we held a meeting with a group of NAM leaders, including some former Communist activists who had played a major role in the party. DSOC decided that there was no point in dissembling, so Irving Howe, who excited great hostility on the part of the New Left veterans, was very much part of our delegation. Although we later learned that some people in NAM found this a difficult fact to accept, all of us survived the experience and continued talking to one another.

Meanwhile, people in and around NAM were going through a sea change. The experience of the Pol Pot regime in Cambodia had dealt a brutal, but not completely fatal, blow to some of the Third Worldist illusions; Democratic Agenda prospered and convinced more and more people that we had found a way to present a "transitional program" to significant forces in American life, ideas well to the right of our full socialist vision and very much to the left of all of serious American politics; and some of the Jews in NAM and its periphery, who had proved their commitment to the movement by trying to "rise above" their own ethnicity, rediscovered that ethnicity and questioned their previous attitudes at about the same time.

One of the people who drew some conclusions from all this was Jim Chapin. A professional historian, Chapin had been in the antiwar movement of the sixties but had not participated in the bitter faction fighting. A WASP descendant of a radical family, which included the critic Kenneth Burke, he was a very innovative and imaginative thinker who knew each election district around his Queens apartment. Chapin decided that the time had come to unite DSOC and NAM. He broached that daring proposition, and major leaders on both sides accepted it. So DSOC, after some fairly serious internal disputes, endorsed this idea at its 1979 convention in Houston. The three years of debates and negotiations that ensued are of intrinsic interest only to the historian of American sectarianism, but the broad themes that were broached in the process are symptomatic of a significant change in the culture of the entire American Left.

Three points were central to our negotiations. First, there was the issue of working within the Left wing of the Democratic party. There were nuances to be cleared up, hypothetical questions to be explored, but basically we had already come to a practical agreement there. Second, and of great ideological moment, we also specified that however one might theorize the reality, actual Communist states were not socialist as we defined the term. Some might call them bureaucratic collectivist, as I did, or state capitalist, or even a terribly deformed result of the attempt to build socialism, but all of us rejected the model. Even more to the point, we stood for the rights of free speech within the Communist world, including free speech for the reactionary critics of the regime, like Solzhenitsyn.

That left the question of the Middle East. I rightly predicted that it would be the most difficult to resolve. DSOC was officially committed to a "two-state" policy, i.e., support for the right of self-determination for *both* the Jews in Israel *and* the Palestinians in a state of their own creation. But within that magisterial formula, some of us were Zionists and others more critical. There were now Zionists in NAM, but the majority felt—and I think feelings were more important than analysis in this case, which made discussion difficult—that sharp criticism of the PLO was somehow the betrayal of a colonial liberation struggle.

We eventually worked out a "two-state" position in which every word and comma was subjected to careful scrutiny. But even as we moved toward agreement, tensions increased within NAM. For this was not simply a unity between two organizations, it was a reconciliation of generations, and that had powerful emotional overtones. DSOC had been founded by people such as myself who had had a bellyful of socialist sectarianism, of endless splits in pursuit of perfect "positions," and we had always insisted on being a broad organization with disparate points of view. After a very heated discussion about the merger with NAM, the 1981 DSOC convention typically agreed to the proposition, with about 80 percent for, none against, and 20 percent abstaining. Our opponents wanted to indicate that they were unhappy—and that they were staying.

NAM did not have the same "broad church" tradition, so there was one last internal battle, and a minority seceded rather than join up with the "social democrats" of DSOC. Our unity convention was held in Detroit in 1982 and was addressed by George Crockett, a member of the Black Caucus in the House, and by Bill Lucy, the leading black trade unionist. I gave a keynote which, like the opening speech at the DSOC convention in 1973, had been circulated in advance to all of the leaders of the new organization, Democratic Socialists of America. There was enthusiasm and applause, and unity balloons were released at the proper moment. There we were in the ruins of what had once been bustling downtown Detroit, the architects of a unity that created a new organization of around 6,000 members. It was the largest democratic socialist group since about 1935—which testified both to our success and its modest character.

For me, the moment was a kind of a homecoming. Some of the people whose trust I had forfeited at Port Huron in 1962 were now members of an organization I chaired, and so were many of their heirs. On a personal level, I had finally expiated my stupidity in SDS. In terms of the United States of America, we had either created an important bridge to a future Left or mobilized an ineffective remnant. Only time will tell.

CHAPTER FOUR

The Nonparty Party

I had been active, as a socialist, in the Democratic party for almost a quarter of a century when I realized that it was not a political party at all.

That notion came to me in Paris in 1983 when I was teaching at the St.-Denis (formerly Vincennes) campus of the university. I was trying to explain American politics to my students when I suddenly realized that I could simplify their lives and mine by telling them that there were no political parties in the United States. The Democrats and Republicans, I said, were not parties in any European sense of the word. They were undisciplined and periodic coalitions, which came together on the basis of electoral opportunism every two years—and in a national sense, only every four years. They had no real program, and the platforms adopted by party conventions were, by the common consent of all, simply consigned to the wastebasket once they were voted.

The institution of the primary, I continued, was a marvelous, and uniquely American, example of this organized anarchism. In Europe, the parties of the Left tend to name leaders on the basis of a political viewpoint and, in any case, only dues-paying members of the party have the right to elect delegates, who in turn select that leader. Even conservative parties such as the British Tories have some kind of a mechanism whereby leaders "emerge." Moreover, in the parliamentary system it is quite common for victorious parties to enact their entire electoral program. That happened in the 1945 Labour government in Britain and as a result of the Socialist triumph in France in 1981–1982. But in the United States anyone who declares himself or herself a member of a party can, without the payment of dues or the affirmation of a single political principle, help determine the leadership, program, and policies of the party.

Indeed, it was only in my own lifetime that the custom of cross-over voting in primaries was largely eliminated. That is, it used to be quite easy for voters to select the party to which they "belonged" on primary day itself. This meant that Democrats could vote in the Republican primary to select the worst possible candidate from the Republican point of view, and that Republicans could return the favor. Under such circumstances, I told my students, it was all but impossible to have a serious, disciplined party—indeed to have a party in any sense of the word—since elected officials responded to their amorphous, unorganized base and not to any institution.

This puzzling fact was one of the reasons why generations of American socialists had committed political suicide. They had attempted to create a party and movement in the United States on the European model—only that model didn't apply. It took a long time for American socialists—and for me—to grasp this home truth. We righteously pointed out that the Democratic party contained a good number of the most reactionary people in the United States: not just crooks and swindlers, which was obvious enough, but union busters, militarists, racists, sexists, and just about every single variety of political undesirable. What we did not notice was that, *at the very same time*, the Democratic party had, since the New Deal, also contained the clear majority of the progressive forces. That was, and is, a blatant contradiction. A very American contradiction.

I began to try to deal with this impossible reality in the late fifties. Given that I was then in my most intense period of political sectarianism, it is surprising that I did so for eminently practical, empirical reasons. It led me to become a part of the liberal wing of the New York Democratic party and to become involved with some fascinating political figures, such as Ed Koch, Bella Abzug, and Ruth Messinger. My experience, I think, might help illuminate a political period.

I

As a fierce socialist sectarian in the mid-fifties, I would have nothing to do with a bourgeois institution like the Democratic party. But I did go from time to time to dances at the Village Independent Democrats (VID). The VID had been organized as a Stevenson-for-President club in 1952 and then continued its independent existence as a staunch member of the Democratic reform movement. The latter was the political creation of young middle-class people—lawyers, advertising executives, and pioneers of a new and still inchoate sector of the economy called "communications"—who wanted to challenge the regular Democrats who had been so tepid about Adlai Stevenson. They were liberal on most issues, but their overriding concern had to do with process: how to challenge the Tammany Hall style of boss-dominated politics, of duchies and baronies, that was the New York Democratic party.

The most famous villain in that Democratic party was Carmine De Sapio, the leader of the Tamawa Club, which was based on the political power of the Italian community in the south Village (which is the part of Little Italy that formed the southern precincts of Greenwich Village). De Sapio was a most untraditional political boss and had gone out of his way to cultivate a progressive image. But fate was not kind to him. He had some kind of eye trouble and wore tinted glasses, which gave him a positively sinister public persona through no fault of his own. Long before he did, in fact, run afoul of the law, he had the air of being a petty criminal.

In the late fifties, however, De Sapio's fall from grace lay far in the future. He was at the height of his power and authority, and *Time* magazine ran a very complimentary article on how he was bringing the Regulars into the modern world. The Tamawa Club, located just south of Sheridan Square, was a center of power and influence; the VID, which occupied a shabby loft on the Square itself, was a gathering place for the idealistic, ideological Left as well a good place for women and men to meet. I first entered this curious outpost, which I then regarded as just another capitalist party, for the high moral purpose of going to a dance with a woman friend (who is now a judge).

In the fifties I had been an enrolled member of the Liberal party. It had been formed out of a split in the American Labor Party (ALP), which had been founded as a haven for trade unionists, Communists, and Socialists who wanted to back Roosevelt but remain independent of Tammany. The Socialists and liberals in the ALP eventually had a showdown with the Communists and fellow travelers, and the Liberal party was born. Since it was organizationally independent of the Democratic party and based on unions, our sectarian faith allowed us to belong to it. We simply ignored the fact that by the mid-fifties it was tightly controlled by two union leaders, David Dubinsky of the ILGWU and Alex Rose of the Hatters. Indeed, it was much less internally democratic than De Sapio's Democratic party, but what was such a detail to a committed ideologue?

Around 1959 the spell of all those abstractions began to weaken. The VID was now engaged in a very serious fight for the lowly office of district leader (male and female) of the Democratic party in the Village. Such posts were usually the very first rung on the political ladder, or else a place of retirement for the party faithful. But De Sapio's organizational legitimacy in the party was technically a result of his being the district leader (male) in his own neighborhood. If Tamawa could be beaten on that insignificant political level, there would be consequences at the summit of New York politics. In that first challenge in 1959, though, the reformers lost. The VID then set its sights on an even lesser post: they would try to beat Tamawa in the race for state committee.

I knew some of the activists in that campaign socially, one of whom was Sarah Schoenkopf (later Sarah Kovner), the female candidate for state committee. She and James Lanigan, who had failed to take the district leadership from De Sapio, were to be the first VIDs to win over Tamawa. But not before there was a small civil war within the reform movement itself—the first of many.

There were three reform clubs in lower Manhattan, and two of them did not go along with the VID attack on De Sapio. The Tamawa leader had shrewdly exploited this split and named two reformers, Eleanor Clark French and Charles Kinsolving, to be *his* candidates for state committee. Sarah and Lanigan won and became part of a tiny reform minority on the state committee which was—Sarah swears it was literally true—called "Commie" and told to "go back to Russia" by their regular colleagues. One of the unintended consequences of this development was that, to the bipartisan disgust of all the regulars at the polling place, I switched my registration to Democratic. I was now an enrolled member of what I still regarded as a bourgeois party—and what I now knew to be the only game in town. That was how I got to know a man whose demeanor clearly marked him as an amiable nonentity, Ed Koch, who is now in his third term as mayor of New York.

I cannot give the precise date at which I met Ed. When I encountered this unassuming, if enthusiastic, man I had no idea that he was going to play a major role in the political history of New York City. Koch was a young lawyer who had been quite briefly a member of the Tamawa Club. That was hardly a port of entry for an aspiring young Jewish politician, since Tamawa was primarily an Italian-American institution. One election night, Stephanie Gervis, the *Village Voice* reporter whom I later married, was sent up to Tamawa, and I went with her. We were asked to leave rather quickly—the *Voice* was a center of the anti–De Sapio movement—but not before we took in the room, where the women sat in chairs against the walls while the men milled around the center. The ethnicity was as unmistakable as that at Our Lady of Pompeii on Bleecker and Carmine streets.

That ethnic description has to do with a fact, not with a prejudice. At the time that we made our brief visit to Tamawa, Stephanie and I were living together just down from Our Lady of Pompeii in the heart of the Italian Village. Our neighbors were easygoing and tolerant, much more so than the concierge of our apartment in "liberated" Paris who continued to regard Stephanie as a fallen woman even after we were married. We were not, then, unsympathetic to the ethnics who thronged the Tamawa Club that night. The simple reality, however, was that the Tamawa was as Italian as the Democratic party of my youth in St. Louis had been Irish. And the VID, like the entire Manhattan Left of that period, was heavily Jewish. So Ed Koch rather quickly found his way up to the VID loft on Sheridan Square.

I simplify. When Sarah Schoenkopf took her place on the state committee, there were eleven reformers out of a total of some three hundred members. That little band included WASPs of considerable wealth and family such as Marietta Tree, as well as Jewish reformers such as Sarah. Indeed, the progressive wing of the New York Democrats at that point was something of an alliance between wealthy, patrician reformers on the Averell Harriman model and liberal upstarts, who were usually Jewish. I had political reservations about the latter group, not the least because I had never participated in the cult of Adlai Stevenson in 1952. The reformers had proclaimed him the first real "egghead" in American politics, and all but idolized him. I thought of Stevenson as an aloof aristocrat who was really not at home in the party of the American working class and as a Churchillian conservative who would have made a marvelous Tory candidate for British prime minister—which put him on the Left in the United States.

When I got to know Ed Koch he was in the process of becoming the VID's candidate for district leader (male). He had the look of a diffident, somewhat lovable schlemiel and was utterly lacking in the overweening self-confidence he acquired as mayor. I liked him immediately, particularly when I discovered that his retiring, modest manner concealed a political maverick. There was a split in the Reform movement between the purists and those who understood that they had to become politicians—a new and different kind, to be sure, but politicians nevertheless. At the VID, for instance, there were those who didn't want to get involved in the struggle over naming judges, on the grounds that the whole process should be taken out of politics (they rarely tried to specify how that impossibility would be achieved). Koch was in the realist camp and would make funny but acidic comments about his co-workers, who were utterly dedicated to losing and who insisted on impotence if by some chance they won.

By a not surprising dialectic, once I had decided to enter the unprincipled precincts of the Democratic party, it never occurred to me to be opposed to compromise. How could one be pure in an institution that was unprincipled on principle? So it was my radicalism that made me something of a realist. If, I thought, you were going to play piano in a whorehouse, you might as well do so with gusto and flair. Thus, I found Koch's witty cynicism quite congenial.

This is not to say that, at that time, he was simply a disappointed apprentice from Tamawa who had made his way to the VID for opportunistic reasons and therefore took the side of *realpolitik*. He was then a deeply committed and gutsy liberal. In 1964 he went to Mississippi in a summer that saw three civil rights workers murdered. That he was quite visible and quite Jewish was not something to endear him to the racists of Mississippi (of the three civil rights workers killed, one was black and two were Jews). In 1965, he had staked, and almost lost, his political career when he broke ranks and endorsed John Lindsay, a liberal Republican, for mayor. Stephanie remembers him mulling over that decision in the *Village Voice* office, talking about it to Dan Wolfe, the editor of the *Voice* who was his mentor (and who became his confidant at City Hall more than a decade later). He was, she remembers, extremely nervous and very much aware of the danger of what he was doing. He was right to be afraid.

There were those who wanted to purge the handful of liberal Democratic officeholders that made the same courageous switch, but Koch survived his very principled decision. Later, when he ran for Lindsay's old congressional seat, Lindsay endorsed the Republican candidate against him, an act that Koch bitterly resented. And rightly so.

Even in those early days Koch was working out a position that turned out to be shrewd politics but pitted him against many in the VID. There was more than a little of the town-gown relationship between Tamawa and VID: the Italian community, which was an ethnic bastion of the world of south Village tenements, and college-educated, mainly Jewish reformers with little or no relation to the world of working Americans who lived in those tenements. I don't want to romanticize the former. When Howard Moody, the pastor of Judson Memorial Church on Washington Square—an officially Baptist institution that probably had more atheists, gays, lesbians, and political radicals in its congregation than any church in New York—tried to get some of the leaders of the Italian community to support an antidrug program, they resented his Protestant poaching and told him that their youth were not in any danger. A little later, a young man died from an overdose in a doorway just across from Our Lady of Pompeii.

There can be no doubt that the hostility of the Italian-Americans to the interracial scene in Washington Square was partly motivated by racist attitudes. But Ed Koch understood, rightly, I think, that racism was not the whole story. The traditionalist Villagers who lived in the tenements along MacDougal Street—a central artery of the Bohemian Village—were hardly being racist when they complained that they were being kept up late at night by the floating party that regularly took place on the sidewalks and streets below. So Koch was one of the first of the reformers to reach out to the Italians, listen to their complaints, and even try to do something about them. That was innovative and intelligent and, it turned out, good politics as well.

All of these actions and attitudes made me admire Ed Koch as well as like him personally. Still, if truth be told, Stephanie and I were convinced that each of his triumphs would be his last. When he did defeat De Sapio, we thought he had had his moment on the stage of history—but he then went on to the city council. That, we thought, would be the climax of a career that had already carried this maverick yet unprepossessing man to heights we had not imagined he would scale. The next thing I knew, Ed asked me if I would chair the citizens' committee when he ran for Congress. I agreed, and one morning Ed came by our apartment on Ninth Street, woke me up, and got me to sign some official paper to that effect—but once again I thought that Koch had set his sights too high. And, of course, he won again.

It was at this point that I began to give him advice, which he carefully ignored. A permanent campaigner, who used to go from his victory party to a subway to shake hands in anticipation of the next election, Koch soon turned his "silk stocking" seat, which by rights should have been Republican, into his private property. Why not, I said to him, become a ten- or twelve-term member of the House? Pick a committee that is of central importance to you, become its chairman, and shape the legislative agenda of the nation in that area. But, as I had known from the time I first met him, Ed Koch wanted, above all else, to be mayor of New York City. This likeable, improbable politician would sit in a Village bar (but drink very little) and tell me how he wanted to be like Fiorello La Guardia. I knew, of course, that that was an utter impossibility.

In the mid-sixties, however, his mayoralty campaigns were far in the future. Congressperson Koch had been one of the first politicians to oppose the Vietnam War. At one of the huge Washington mobilizations at which he spoke, someone who came after him had begun to denounce Israel as a puppet of that same American imperialism, which was acting so unconscionably in Southeast Asia. He recounted with gusto how he, a dignitary on this occasion, a member of the House, had rushed toward the podium and yelled "Fuck you!" at the speaker. I liked that quality in Koch, and I shared his support of Israel, an attitude that was sometimes controversial in the rarefied precincts of the Reform movement.

That maverick spirit was also quite visible during one of the worst moments in New York politics: the school strike in 1968. I have to go a long way around in describing that event. But doing so will identify some of the factors that led to Ed Koch's dramatic political shift in the seventies as well as evoke a decisive, ugly moment in the evolution of the entire New York Reform movement.

I I

John Lindsay, who was elected mayor in 1965 with Koch's support, had decentralized the public school system, creating local and elected district boards of education. In the Ocean Hill–Brownsville section, a black ghetto in Brooklyn, a bitter dispute occurred. Several white teachers were summarily removed and sent back to the central office for reassignment to some other district. The union challenged that action on grounds of due process, an action which I approved. But that move was seen by the blacks and a majority of the Manhattan reformers as an authoritarian, and even racist, policy. A bitter struggle followed that was part Hegelian tragedy, the conflict of two rights, and part ugly farce, which pitted a superficial utopianism against an insensitive emphasis upon formal rights. I found myself in the middle, agreeing with the union on the specific issue, sympathetic to the local black school board, yet profoundly suspicious of some of the absurd claims made on its behalf.

On the one hand, not a few of the black activists and reformers believed that decentralization was the gate to the educational millennium. If only the local community could have control of its own institutions, then the children would miraculously increase their academic performance. But, as I argued in the endless debates at that time, shrewd conservatives, such as William F. Buckley, Jr., and Barry Goldwater, were perfectly willing to let poor blacks have community control of ghettos in Brooklyn and Manhattan as long as rich whites had community control of Park Avenue and Wall Street. That is, a good number of the advocates of a decentralist panacea had forgotten, in the name of a romantic exaltation of the "power of the people," about the power of class structures. White teachers—*Jewish* white teachers, for there was sometimes more than a hint of anti-Semitism in the dispute—were *the* cause of the educational backwardness of so many of the poor. Give authority to a local school board and leave every other social determinant in its unjust place, and all would be well.

On the union side, Al Shanker, the president of the United Federation of Teachers, tended to treat the issue as if it were a simple collective bargaining dispute. He routinely talked on television about the contract but ignored the fact that the actions of many in the black community were a desperate *cri de coeur* over the fate of their children, not an attitude toward labor law. Indeed, the very utopianism of the local militants was more a product of the social agony of their daily lives than of the shallow theories they sometimes espoused. I supported the union, yet I was all but torn in two by my profound sympathies with those on the other side who, I thought, were morally right, legally wrong, and very ill advised by theorists from outside their community.

I was quite friendly with Al Shanker. The first time I met him, in 1964 or 1965, we visited a New Jersey grape importer, urging him to honor Cesar Chávez's boycott of nonunion grapes from California, and he had gone on to play a major role in supporting that struggle of poor—and mainly minority—workers. Around the same time, there was a united front between the United Federation of Teachers and the militant black community in a boycott of the school system which focused on, and linked, both the inferiority of education for the poor and the treatment of teachers. When Shanker was jailed in a union dispute in 1964, he had received a check from Martin Luther King, Jr., to help pay his costs (and had wisely framed it rather than cash it). Shanker was later to move toward neo-conservatism, as did not a few of my comrades of that period. But in 1968 I was unaware that such surprising reversals were soon to take place.

My wife suggested that I go and talk to Al and try to persuade him to articulate the union position more as a commitment to the children rather than on behalf of the sanctity of the contract.

I went to the Gramercy Park Hotel, where Shanker was staying for the duration of the dispute, and was admitted to his room by an armed guard (given the virulence of the dispute, that was not a paranoid precaution). The local board, I said to Al, was presenting its case in terms of the children, and he was talking only about union rights. He was, I continued, committed to the children too, and should make clear that the union's position was not based on mere legalism but was part of an effort to create an educational framework in which teachers would be able to teach. The insistence on tenure rights, I suggested, should be presented—and thought of—as a means to the end of quality education for all and particularly for minority youth. Al was extremely receptive to my message and told me that he would take it to heart. The next night, or so it seemed to me, he was back talking about the contract.

The progressive community was profoundly divided when the teachers went out on strike over the issue. There were reform Democrats who broke into public schools and tried to keep them open despite the strike—an action that the entire Left would have denounced as "scabbing" only a few years before. There were also some anti-Semitic leaflets passed out in Brooklyn. At the same time, the cause of the black community school district was clearly one that commanded moral solidarity on the part of anyone committed to civil rights. And that was true even though the claims for the educational gains to be made through decentralization were clearly extreme. (To his great credit, Kenneth Clark, who was an articulate champion of the local board, later candidly said that he had been wrong in claiming that decentralization would have an enormous educational impact upon the students.) I suspect that this confrontation between two rights in 1968 was to prefigure the split in the liberal-labor-black movement, which was the precondition of Republican presidential power for the next two decades. It was also one of the reasons why Ed Koch was to change so much in the seventies. Of that, more in a moment.

It was during this period that I went with Koch, then running for Congress, to a meeting of the upper-middle-class Left in a comfortable apartment on the East Side of Manhattan. Koch's position was suitably unclassifiable and, I think, quite genuine. He was, he said, opposed to the strike on the grounds that it was a violation of the state law that denied public employees the right to walk off the job. That satisfied those who were, for whatever reason, against the strike. But he was, he continued, in support of the union's basic demand with regard to the teachers who had been summarily removed. That sat well with the union and its backers. Clearly, one could argue that this position was a calculated exercise in political opportunism, that Koch had discovered a way to have his cake and eat it at the same time. I don't think so now and I certainly didn't then. I did not agree with him—I thought the state antistrike law an abomination and favored getting around it legally or "illegally"—yet I found his strange attitude totally consistent with his maverick personality. It was, I thought (and think), of a piece with his opposition to the Vietnam War and simultaneous anti-Communism.

In any case, I continued to regard Ed as part of my own world and, as late as the summer of 1974, he endorsed my candidacy for delegate to the Democratic midterm convention. But by that time, I also had some significant intimations that a change was underway.

In 1973 Koch tested the waters for a mayoral candidacy. He asked Stephanie and me if we would invite a few friends over to our place—we then lived at 85 Perry Street in the Village—so that he could explore that possibility with them. Ed arrived with a small retinue from his Congressional staff; I have forgotten most of those who were there, with the exception of Norman Dorsen. Norman, who lived just around the corner, was a professor at New York University Law School and a major figure in the American Civil Liberties Union (he later became its president). There was a sharp conflict between him, Stephanie, and me on the one side, and Ed Koch on the other.

This was not too long after a furious dispute about a public housing project in the middle- and upper-middle-class area of Forest Hills. There was no doubt in my mind that the actual proposal was ill-conceived: a huge, high-rise building in the midst of houses and apartment buildings that were on a much more human scale. But it was quite clear as well that a good part of the furious opposition to the Forest Hills scheme was not based on objections to a flawed plan, but was motivated by a racist hostility to any public housing that would bring blacks into the neighborhood. The liberal position—to build the project, but scaled down, so that it would fit into the area—was defended by a young Italian-American lawyer from Queens by the name of Mario Cuomo. The opponents of the project engaged in strident, and almost openly racist, rhetoric. Koch took their side.

That evening in the living room of our apartment on Perry Street, Ed talked about the need for a social-environmental impact statement whenever public housing was proposed. When strongly challenged by Norman Dorsen and me, he went so far as to argue that blacks really wanted to stay in their own neighborhoods, that they didn't want to mix with whites (many of whom, in the case of Forest Hills, were Jewish). I was appalled. Still, the debate was civil, though sharp.

As the evening came to an end, Stephanie said—and I agreed completely—"Ed, don't give up your principles as a tactic in a mayoral campaign that you can't even win." We were right on the first, moral count; but in 1977, history was to prove us wrong in our prediction. Ed's switch in position was indeed one of the reasons he became mayor of New York.

Forest Hills was a turning point, both for Ed Koch and the liberal Jewish community. It was, in some ways, a continuation of the civil war that had started within the Left during the teachers' strike of 1968. But it took a while for me to realize that Koch's attitude on Forest Hills was not an isolated exercise in his unique politics but a significant and quite deliberate political move. In 1975 and 1976, as he geared up to make a really serious run for the mayoralty in 1977, he moved to the Right on a whole series of issues. He began to emphasize his support for capital punishment, a position which was totally irrelevant to the office of mayor (who has no life or death powers whatsoever) but had a lot to do with the feelings of the white, middle-class electorate in New York City. So it was that in that 1977 race I found myself backing Bella Abzug against Ed Koch. Therein lies a story.

My early relation with Bella was a disaster, but by the mid-seventies I had changed my mind in a most fundamental way about her. That original hostility had much to do with style—but also with a historic association of style and substance. Bella's manner was, and is, legendary in American politics: forceful, aggressive, sometimes strident (particularly in the sixties and early seventies), and even downright nasty. There is no doubt that she was regularly victimized by a double standard, that qualities deemed abrasive in a woman are celebrated as machismo in a man. But that was not what put me off.

When I first encountered Bella, I interpreted her style as an expression of the Leftist tradition of high-minded viciousness, an ugly inheritance from Karl Marx's dyspeptic, angry attitude toward all opponents. Bella had been a Leftist Zionist as a college student and had learned that lesson all too well. I sensed a certain anti–anti-Communism in her attitudes, and in my personal experience that political position was often expressed vituperatively. My reaction to Bella, then, was historical and political as well as personal.

Indeed, in the sixties one of the bonds between Ed Koch and me was a common antipathy to Bella's manner as well as some questions about some of her positions on the Middle East. But after the 1974 election, I began to become aware that she was one of the hardest-working, most effective members of Congress. A friend of mine, Steve Silbiger, was an aide to Congressperson Steve Solarz of Brooklyn, and he shared most of my reservations about Bella. When he began to tell me, from an insider's vantage point, that she was a very serious liberal who, unlike some of her more mannerly colleagues, did an enormous amount of effective work, my attitude began to change. At the same time, her attitude toward both Soviet injustice and the defense of Israel, whatever it may once have been, was now clearly similar to my own. When she ran against Daniel Patrick Moynihan for the Senate nomination in 1976, I was enthusiastic about her candidacy. It was not just that she would begin to integrate the most sexist institution in American politics, the Senate, but also that I thought she had a capacity to be a truly great senator. In retrospect, I think I was right.

By 1977, then, my political attitudes had shifted radically. My old friend Ed Koch had moved to the Right and was running for mayor in a spirit that, I thought, appealed to some of the worst racist and antiunion emotions in the city. And I was a supporter of Bella, toward whom I had been somewhat antagonistic. Still, I was not one to forget personal links even though political relations had changed. So I called up John LoCicero, a key organizational lieutenant for Ed, and had coffee with him over on Sheridan Square. I still liked Ed, I explained to him, but I now disagreed with him on some fundamental issues and simply could not support him for mayor. I asked LoCicero to communicate to Koch that my backing for Bella was not a personal attack on him but the result of deeply held political convictions.

Later, after Ed was elected, a friend of mine who had stayed with him told me that Ed had been quite angry that I had not, despite our differences, backed him. But even so there were still a few strange twists left in our personal relationship.

In the primary, Koch had come in first, but he had had to win a runoff against Mario Cuomo. By that time, Stephanie and I were living on Mercer Street, a few short blocks away from Ed's apartment on Washington Place. One night we ran into him as we emerged from an Italian restaurant just down the street from his building. Stephanie talked to him with considerable emotion, telling him that she wanted to vote for him for old times' sake, but that some of his positions made it difficult to do so. She mentioned his attitude toward minorities and the unions and said to him, among other things, that he had to promise to talk with Victor Gotbaum, the leading public employee trade unionist in town and a friend and associate of mine. Ed agreed and, after he won the runoff, which assured him of victory, was as good as his word. Ed, his media advisor Dave Garth, Vic Gotbaum, Stephanie, and I had dinner together at Charley O's, a favorite Koch hangout.

There were two striking aspects of that meeting. First, Koch told Gotbaum that, even as mayor-elect, he found it all but impossible to discover what the city finances really were (at this point, New York City was still in a deep fiscal crisis). I had known abstractly that governmental bureaucracies can escape the control of the governors themselves—John Kennedy thought that it would take an entire term as president before he could get the State Department to do his bidding—but this was an absurd example of the fact. And second, Dave Garth was friendly and open as we chatted, yet it was a new development in American politics that the leader of the largest city in the nation, when meeting with the municipality's most powerful trade unionist, would bring his media advisor along with him.

It was a year later—a year of bitter acrimony between Koch and Gotbaum—when Stephanie and I were asked to go to dinner at the Gotbaums' as part of a kind of peace effort on both sides of that dispute. It was a small affair (though the press did check out the guest list): Victor and Betsy Gotbaum and an old friend of Betsy's; Koch and Bess Myerson, the former Miss America who had become a political activist and ally of Koch's; Lillian Roberts, Vic's number two and one of the very finest black trade unionists in the country; and Simeon Golar, a liberal black politician. Everything began on a pleasant, low key.

Early on, I took the opportunity to take Ed aside and talk to him about Ruth Messinger, a member of the city council whom he was crudely attacking as a pro-Communist. So I now will introduce the person who is, in many ways, the heroine of this chapter, the New York reformer who has not been a disappointment in any way.

I'm not sure exactly when I met Ruth. She was an activist on the West Side of Manhattan, which was one of those strange enclaves in which the Left was the hegemonic political power (its spirit and culture have been immortalized in some of the films of Woody Allen). That meant, among many other things, that it was the scene of titanic rhetorical battles over nuances of antiwar or antiracist or antisexist politics, all of which would have been bewildering, not simply to the Midwest, but to the boroughs of Queens and Brooklyn as well. Ruth had managed the incredible task of building a constituency there and yet maintained a high seriousness about political and social issues that soared above some of the petty intrigues with which she had to deal.

I met her at Debbie Meier's house on West Seventy-seventh

Street in the heart of the West Side enclave. One of her most trusted advisors was Paul DuBrul, who had joined the socialist movement when he was a student at Hunter College in the early sixties. She was also quite close to Jack Newfield, one of DuBrul's friends from college and the co-author with him of a fine book on New York City's "permanent government." As an investigative reporter at the *Village Voice*, Jack was a conscience of the New York Left and an intransigent foe of the Ed Koch whom he, like me, had known as a young reformer in the Village. Ruth shared our politics and had joined DSOC, a decision that was certainly facilitated by both Paul and Jack being members.

Over the years Ruth had carefully done her homework with regard to the hard and very specific issues of New York life, becoming a more effective politician, and then city council member. Reformers—and it is certainly not a sin peculiar to them—have a tendency toward lofty generalizations, passionate opinions, and slipshod data. Ruth remained true to the basic principles, but she had learned to relate them to reality better than anyone I know. Indeed, it is fair to say that she translated some of my own abstractions into critiques and proposals of mundane issues, such as municipal housing and transportation policy. At the same time, she had been more giving of her time and commitment to DSOC (and later to DSA) than any of our members in elected public life. And Koch was Red-baiting her.

On many occasions I had talked, privately and publicly, with Ruth about questions of freedom, democracy, and the Soviet sphere, and she was as horrified by violations of civil rights there in the name of "socialism" as I. And though Paul DuBrul, her trusted confidant, was within a socialist movement, he was critical of the very foundation and structure of the Communist regimes and was famous for being a particularly implacable critic of their antidemocracy. He and Ruth and all the rest of us were, of course, also opponents of America's militaristic response to those Communist wrongs, and proponents of disarmament and peace. That hardly made us Moscow sympathizers. Now Koch, who had seemed to have that very same mix of attitudes when he opposed the American intervention in Vietnam in the sixties, was turning on Ruth in a scandalous way.

So I repeated to him at the Gotbaums' what I had said to him earlier in a letter: he was profoundly wrong about Ruth. He was, alas, noncommittal, and his hostility to her continues to this day. The dinner party, however, was to end on an ironic note. Stephanie and Vic Gotbaum engaged in a heated exchange—which ended in a minor explosion—over our decision to move to the suburbs. As Stephanie and I left, hastily and early, Koch seemed to enjoy the moment immensely. It was the last time we were to see him socially.

So have I simply proved one of the oldest and most cynical clichés of American politics: that Ed Koch was somewhat radical as a young and powerless man and then became smart and unprincipled as he got older and serious political power beckoned? I don't think so.

I I I

There is no doubt that "life" plays a conservatizing role in most biographies. Those blinding, all-encompassing radical certitudes, which sometimes are the epiphanies of youth, are not so dazzling any more. Instead, the complexities and shadows come into view. At the same time, marriage and parenthood are indeed two of the great forces making people bourgeois. When I became a father, I discovered a willingness to be selfish—and a loss of some of my Leftist inhibitions about making money—that I would have treated contemptuously when I was in my twenties. And, yes, the actual exercise of power, or even its mere imminence, is often a reason for second thoughts.

But there are at least two basic objections to turning such insights into anything like a complete account of social reality. First, if individuals change in this fashion, the world does not. It may well be that younger people fired with the passion to do something about poverty and war and injustice become more conformist when they grow old. *But that is sad because the poverty and war and injustice do not disappear just because aging radicals are less willing to fight them.* Those people who delight in the theory that says all youthful socialism turns into mature conservatism think they are being "realistic" and congratulate themselves on their own clear-sightedness. They do not even notice that they come to their triumphant truth by blinding themselves to the rest of the world. They exult when they should weep.

And, second, that cynical thesis operates quite imperfectly. It is obvious that my world view is more complicated than it was when I became a socialist at the age of twenty. But I have remained a socialist. And if Ed Koch changed, Ruth Messinger did not. That means that one cannot deal with these matters on the basis of a few scraps of *realpolitik.* It is necessary, for instance, to understand why the sixties contradicted the theory that twenty-year-old socialists inevitably become forty-year-old conservatives. Sometimes that contradiction even proceeded to the point of caricature, as when people in their forties and fifties aped the cult of youth, or the sober *New York Review of Books* printed the instructions for making a Molotov cocktail on its cover. I knew balding "flower children" in those days.

Why did the process of conservatization become so much more pronounced in the seventies and eighties? One cannot account for that on the basis of individual life cycles. It is necessary to look at the social and historical context.

Ed Koch was, after all, not the only Jewish antiwar liberal who moved to the Right. He was part of a social trend that affected many people like him, which is one of the reasons why I reject the simplistic notion that he just "sold out" his principles for a political mess of pottage (if that is how one wants to characterize the office of mayor of New York). Norman Podhoretz, the editor of *Commentary,* who happily printed my articles in the sixties and then moved even further to the Right than Koch in the seventies and eighties—he became an open Reaganite—gained neither office nor money by his transformation. The explanation of Koch's conversion as a mere sellout misses trends that are much larger than the alleged opportunism of a single politician.

There was, after all, a general tendency within the Jewish Left to turn from socialism or liberalism to neo-conservatism. Koch was not an intellectual, yet he was certainly affected by the intellectual trends in the Jewish community. But since there were non-Jews who made the same transition—one thinks, for instance, of the Catholic writer Michael Novak, who as a peace activist considered himself well to my Left and then wound up far to my Right—why insist upon the Jewish dimension of Koch's personal transformation?

Because the issue of Israel played an important role in it, not simply for him, but for a whole stratum of Jews in his generation. With the rise of the New Left in the sixties, there was a simplistic trend to think of the Palestine Liberation Organization (PLO) as just another movement of national liberation that all progressives should support on anti-imperialist grounds. Since it was locked in struggle with Israel, it was illogically reasoned that the latter must be a part of the imperialist system. The notion that the Israelis themselves represented an earlier national liberation movement and that their conflict with the PLO was the counterposition of two legitimate rights to national self-determination, was too sophisticated for some of the youthful activists of the sixties to grasp. And for some of their older comrades as well.

There were similar problems within the United States. During the terrible fight over school decentralization in New York in 1968, there were anti-Semitic leaflets and speeches from the side of those who saw themselves as pitted against a Jewish-led union. That some of the blacks in the community were driven to such racism by the impossible conditions they had to confront in their daily lives—and even more important, in the lives of their children—makes it more explicable even if it provides no reason for condoning what was said. (Poor whites in the South are often racist for reasons rooted in their poverty, which means that one has to reach out to their just woes but not compromise with, or conceal, the horrible racism they provoke.) The whites, and sometimes upper-middle-class or even upper-class whites whose salon radicalism ignored, or even justified, that anti-Semitism in 1968, were intellectually wrong and morally reprehensible in a much less ambiguous sense than those they defended.

Koch, as I wrote earlier, was often rightly critical of some of the superficial and purist Leftism of the early Reform movement. But he, and a part of his political generation, then overreacted to equally grounded objections to the shallowness of some on the Left on issues such as anti-Semitism in the school strike, the right of Israel to exist, or the lyric identification with Ho Chi Minh as a kindly grandfather rather than as a Communist man of power. People like Ed Koch understandably turned their backs on the mistakes of their one-time friends and wrongly embraced the principles of their one-time enemies.

For instance, in 1980 Koch, by then mayor of New York, made it quite clear that he regarded a vote for Ronald Reagan, and against Jimmy Carter, as a decent thing to do. Carter, to be sure, had committed one of his more memorable gaffes in the spring of that year when the United States had wrongly voted against Israel at the United Nations (and then reversed its position in a matter of hours). But was that reason to embrace a man who would cruelly attack the poor, minorities, women's rights, the Third World, and attempt to overthrow the Nicaraguan government, temporize with South African racism, and all the rest?

Koch, and many, many others, was responding to the crisis of liberalism when he moved to the Right. There was a heady atmosphere in New York during the first term of John Lindsay. There was an alliance between an educated and privileged Left and an immiserated, mainly black, mass. The go-go years were in full swing, and it seemed to everyone—businessmen as well as radicals—that an endlessly growing GNP would finance permanent social experimentation. In fact, the experiments were much more moderate than the rhetoric, not the least because none of them dealt with the basic structures of inequality and power that were to take their revenge in the seventies upon the shallow utopias. But when the weather changed—the American economy was internationalized in an unprecedented fashion, productivity dropped, the new jobs were primarily low-paying and unorganized, and so on—many liberals came to agree with Richard Nixon.

The sixties, Nixon had said in an enormously influential interview the day after his landslide re-election in 1972, had "thrown money at problems." That simply was not true, as I have demonstrated in *The New American Poverty, The Next Left: The History of a Future*, and other works. The New York City crisis was not, as Ken Auletta wrote in *The Streets Were Paved with Gold*, the Left's "Vietnam," a function of the overcommitment of John Lindsay and other liberals. It was the consequence of massive national and international trends. That line of analysis, however, points beyond liberalism in the direction of the socialist Left. Nixon's simplistic thesis, which moved back toward conservatism, was dramatic, did not require new attempts at innovation in a period when many people were politically tired, and was therefore quite popular. It was not just Ed Koch who embraced such notions. So did the entire Democratic party.

Am I saying that Ed Koch was totally unconcerned with the political advantages that accrued to him personally when he shifted toward the Right? Not at all. He was not simply the plaything of economic and intellectual trends—but neither was he the pure product of opportunism. He was, very much like the rest of us, a complex man. He did indeed become much too friendly—socially and politically—with the real estate interests that drove the homeless from single room occupancy hotels and built a Manhattan designed for the rich and trendy, and he abetted them in their antisocial work. That, I think, was his most grievous error. And it was a tragedy that a man of Koch's personal honesty should have been unaware of the corruption of some of his political allies that came to the fore in 1986 and 1987. But I still think that in another historic period his self-interest and his very real idealism would have yielded a different outcome.

Finally, Ed Koch's evolution was not a fate, as Ruth Messinger proves. As she matured, she became more serious, more effective, in her basic commitment. She clearly is a long-distance runner.

There was a meeting at the New School for Social Research in the fall of 1986. A group of German politicians and journalists was visiting the United States on a junket sponsored by the Friedrich Ebert Foundation. Michael Bertram, from the Ebert office in New York, had assembled a remarkable group of people, including some city bureaucrats, Frances Fox Piven, Ruth Messinger, and me. At one point, a spokesperson for the city launched into a description of all the things that had been done for the homeless. Then Ruth pointed out that these things had been achieved under a court order and proceeded to analyze the complicity of New York in creating homelessness in great detail, with precise references to laws and policies. She was more radical than when I first met her years ago because she had deepened her values by making them more informed, more politically effective, than ever before.

The complex case of Ed Koch can be cited simplistically by the superficial cynics. But the party of hope has Ruth Messinger.

CHAPTER FIVE

The Democratic Left

*I*n the fall of 1974, I went to various subway stops around Greenwich Village and greeted people going in and out, handing them a leaflet in the time-honored tradition of political activism. "Hi," I said, "I'm Mike Harrington and I'm running for midterm convention delegate." I was utterly embarrassed by the experience.

Most people, of course, brushed past, looking right through me as New Yorkers do when they want to ignore someone weird. A few smiled and took the leaflet and a small minority stopped to talk to me. That latter group all had one question: what, in God's name, is the midterm convention you're running for?

The answer was a fairly well-kept secret, and not by accident. In 1972, when the McGovern forces had an absolute majority at the Miami Beach nominating convention, they were prepared to change the party rules and to institute a regular midterm convention. The idea, championed by one of the most thoughtful and decent members of Congress, Don Fraser, was to try to make the Democratic party into something vaguely resembling a party.

At nominating conventions, Fraser and his supporters rightly noted, platforms and policy discussions are simply means to the end of getting a candidate put at the top of the ticket. Everyone knows that this is the only *real* decision before the delegates and that their choice will, if he (or, the optimists like me would add, she) becomes President, then decide what position to take on the issues. The official "positions" of the party then will be as nothing compared to the power of the White House. That, alas, is obviously true in our unique, partyless system, and Fraser understood that he could not possibly challenge that reality head-on.

Why not, he concluded, mandate an issues convention in the year of nonpresidential elections? Since there would be no nominee to pick, the delegates might even bother their heads about what the nation should do. If, Fraser argued, such an institution had been in place in 1966, then the growing hostility within the Democratic party to Lyndon Johnson's Vietnam intervention could have expressed itself in a way that might even have caused Johnson to reconsider. Then there would have been no need to have the civil war within the party, which did so much to elect Richard Nixon in both 1968 (when many of the peace advocates failed to rally to Humphrey) and 1972 (when the hawks would have nothing to do with McGovern). The McGovernites had the votes to make their proposal party law but, in a gesture of moderation and reconciliation, they simply legislated a single midterm, for 1974, which would then shape the permanent institution.

It was a marvelously rational idea, which is why, I suspect, the party regulars, taking advantage of Fraser's forbearance, subverted it for ten years and then simply destroyed it outright. But we socialists who were becoming active in the liberal-labor wing of the party took the proposal with the utmost seriousness, not the least because we knew and cared about issues. The Democratic leadership, once the McGovern period was past, had to go along—there was a convention resolution binding them—but they supported the idea, as Lenin once put it so well, the way a rope supports a hanging man. The convention was scheduled for December so that it could not have any influence on Democrats in the 1974 elections, and the preparations were carried out with a minimum of publicity and a maximum of gracelessness. Nothing would be allowed on the floor except a leadership proposal for a set of rules that would permit, but not require, future midterm conventions.

We, however, still took the idea seriously, even if the Democratic leadership did not. So I kept my vigil at the subways; I wrote an op-ed piece on poverty for the *New York Times*, which appeared around Labor Day and was designed to coincide with the big campaign; and we even organized a fund-raiser in the fashionable, Left-leaning resort of the Hamptons, replete with celebrity names on the invitation (as I remember, Willem de Kooning was a sponsor and I had fantasies of getting the contribution of one painting from him and thereby financing the whole organization for a couple of years). But since this was New York and the Democratic party in the seventies, life was not quite that simple.

I

The various reform clubs in the Seventeenth Congressional District, where I lived and ran (basically the Village and Staten Island), had decided that rather than having liberal candidates cancel one another out in the elections, the Left would pick a unified slate of three. The largest club in the district, and the most influential in picking candidates, was the club I mentioned in the previous chapter—the Village Independent Democrats (VID).

First, I went to a screening committee meeting at the VID. I passed all questions with flying colors as long as economic and foreign-policy issues were at the center of the discussion. But then a gay activist on the panel asked me if I would promise to lead a floor fight for gay rights on the floor of the convention. I explained that I would vote for a gay rights resolution because I believed in it, but that I felt that my role at the convention should be to unite the trade union, minority, and middle-class segments of the Left around a common economic program. Given that definition of my function, I said, I could not pledge to become a major leader of the gay rights fight. I would speak and vote for it, but if I were able to take the lead on any issue, I thought it should be that of economic policy. The gays were not in the least persuaded and opposed me.

But there were others, including the representatives of District 37 of the American Federation of State, County, and Municipal Employees (AFSCME), who vigorously backed my candidacy, and I was recommended by the screening panel. Then the VID itself had to endorse me. One woman, mindful of my reputation as a fierce anti-Communist, asked me in what year I had decided to oppose American intervention in Vietnam. She thought I would say 1967 or 1968 which, in those days in that club, would have made some people suspect me of being a militarist or worse. I replied, quite truthfully, that I went on my first demonstration against intervention in 1954, right after the defeat of the French at Dien Bien Phu. So I was nominated on a three-person slate that also included one of the gay Democrats and a woman named Marjorie Phyfe Gellermann (who later divorced and became Marjorie Phyfe).

In some ways, Marjorie was typical of the kind of people who were recruited into the socialist movement in the seventies; in other significant ways, as she became one of the best political organizers in the country, she was utterly unique. A graduate of Wellesley, she and her then husband, Bill, had become deeply involved in the civil rights movement in the sixties. She had worked with CORE, the organization that had pioneered the use of Gandhian nonviolent methods in the struggle against racism. Living in Staten Island, she then became active in the antiwar movement and the reform Democrats and, as part of the growing feminist consciousness in the Left, she had been picked as a candidate for the midterm by her political club. Her autobiography is, I suspect, the outline of the life of an entire stratum of the women who were to join the organization: from civil rights and antiwar work to feminism and then to socialism.

When we met Marjorie and Bill they were socialists without knowing it, a political position that is much more common in the

United States than that of being a conscious socialist. That is, their commitment to equality and racial justice had led them to realize that structural change was necessary to make a real transformation in the economy and the society as well as in the political sphere. All we had to do in order to recruit them was to explain why we thought that the structure impeding such a transformation was, in a complex way, capitalism, even its welfare-state variant, and that each individual measure to meet their immediate goals required a democratization of economic and social power. The vision of a society that made such democratic exceptions to the rule of the capitalist economy into the guiding principle of a new system was, we said, socialism. All we really did was to give names to truths they already knew.

By the time the campaign was over, Marjorie and Bill had joined DSOC. I was elected outright, not the least, we figured, because the large and quite conservative Irish Catholic population on Staten Island mistakenly supported me as one of their own. Marjorie just missed being picked as one of the three delegates. At that point, I phoned John Burns, a John F. Kennedy regular Democrat and a very decent man, and suggested that he support her for selection by the state committee as an alternate delegate. He did, and she got the designation.

So it was that Marjorie and I, with Jack Clark and Frank Llewellyn as support staff, arrived in Kansas City in December of 1974 with a huge box of the latest issue of our newsletter, now called *Democratic Left*, which was specifically addressed to the convention. Frank had joined DSOC at the outset—he had been a member of the Socialist party youth at the State University of New York at Cortland—and volunteered indefatigably, becoming the second member of our paid staff, a job which, at that point, required periodic layoffs financed by unemployment insurance. He worked ten and twelve hours a day at a desk whose disorder resembled the Bermuda Triangle, and was one of the shrewdest analysts of Democratic politics in the organization.

We had become a part of the mainstream Democratic party,

just as our theory said we should, and had even won the approval of voters in one congressional district in the process. Our only problem was, we didn't know what to do.

That difficulty was not unique to us. That is, the Democratic leadership had carefully structured the convention so that there was really nothing for anyone to do. To be sure, we chased around to various caucus meetings and worked hard for affirmative action and making the midterm a permanent institution (we lost on both counts and my ex-comrades from Social Democrats USA joined with the party conservatives to help defeat our side). But we were, even in the Left wing, newcomers, relatively insignificant compared to the people who had been Kennedy or McCarthy delegates in 1968 or taken part in the McGovern millennium in 1972. Indeed, we did not even know when we made very important contacts— such as when I met David Dinkins at a dinner with Vic Gotbaum.

Perhaps the paradigm of our innocence and helplessness was our socialist breakfast. We put leaflets in all of the delegation mailboxes, ordered up coffee and Danish for a decent crowd, and then stood, nervously embarrassed, in an almost empty room until the time came to end an event that never should have been begun.

It was not enough, we realized, to be abstractly right and work as socialists in the Democratic party. It was also necessary to have something to do. It occurred to me that in response to the Nixon landslide of 1972, the Democrats, including not a few liberals, had begun to move to the Right. Even before then, the editors of *Dissent* had realized that a neo-conservatism was emerging in the United States, largely the work of disillusioned Leftists who had been our friends and comrades. I was puzzled some years later when Daniel Patrick Moynihan credited me with coining the label *neo-conservative*, since I could never remember whether it was Irving Howe, some other editor, or me who came up with the term. But, whatever the details, all of us had been sensitized to the possibility that a section of the liberal, and even socialist, Left would move to the Right.

Given that I had participated in, and chronicled, the War on Poverty, I was particularly hostile to the myth that the sixties had spent enormous sums of money in the pursuit of glorious ideals that did not work at all. Nixon had said that in a very influential interview the day after his electoral victory in 1972 but, more to my point, it was now being articulated on all sides. The Democrats, one was told from within the party, have to pull in their horns and accept the proposition that government really can't accomplish very much, that one must rely instead on the benign and creative working of the market. I documented in articles and books, which had nothing like the circulation of my analyses of poverty in the sympathetic sixties, that this was nonsense.

The amount of money actually spent on the poor by the War on Poverty and Great Society was distressingly modest and, in any case, most of the programs that had been funded, such as Head Start and job training, had done reasonably well. The really massive increase in Washington's outlays had gone to Social Security and it was rightly so popular that even the conservatives were loath to attack it. When Nixon charged that the sixties liberals had "thrown money at problems"—spent wildly and ineffectively— he was being as loose with the truth as he was during the Watergate cover-up. But if the people, and then the prosecutors, saw through the Watergate lie, they accepted Nixon's mythic rejection of the sixties. And a good number of Democrats were in the van of this utterly inaccurate revisionist history.

Our job, I concluded, was to show how America can solve its problems, that it was not necessary to remain passive in the face of persistent poverty, chronic unemployment, the corporate domination of energy, and so on. Even though we socialists were only a handful of people, we knew how to document these problems better than anyone else. And we had the contacts that would permit us to act as a bridge between the Left's working class, middle class, and "new class." These social and political forces had an objective, common interest in uniting against the drift to the Right, only they didn't yet know it. It was our job to help them become conscious of that fact. In a fit of sterile creativity I decided to call the whole effort the "America Can" movement. Its theme would be: America *can* solve its problems.

There was, of course, a fight over my perspective inside of DSOC. There were those who thought that it was too short-run and not sufficiently socialist. There were long, seemingly interminable discussions, and eventually my point of view prevailed although—fortunately—the project was renamed Democratic Agenda. We hired Marjorie to staff it and geared up for a major conference in January 1976.

I I

It was precisely because we insisted on some unpopular truths that Democratic Agenda worked surprisingly well. We began with what amounted to an ideological monopoly in a period of Rightward drift. Who else would actually defend the sixties? Above all, our modest but significant success was a result of our insisting, in thought and action, that the unions were a critical force in American life.

I was a child of the thirties and had grown up in a prolabor but middle-class home. My Jesuit teachers in St. Louis, members of the most liberal province of their order in the United States, were militant supporters of the unions. When I had my brief stint at a "straight" job—as a writer-trainee for *Life* magazine in 1950—I was told by a friendly co-worker that management didn't like people who joined the American Newspaper Guild. I signed up immediately.

All of this hardly made me a product of the labor movement. But when I went to the Catholic Worker in 1951, and then joined the Socialist movement in 1952, I became more involved with the unions. In part, my transition was simply intellectual. As a young radical under the spell of Karl Marx, I discovered a huge and soaring abstraction, the working class—a sort of imaginary, proletarian deus ex machina that would somehow save sinful humanity from itself. I did not know it at the time, but I was in fact retracing Marx's own path, which began in 1843 and 1844 with the sudden revelation of the workers' movement as a metaphysical concept, and then turned him toward the workers' movement as a movement.

By the early fifties, the links between liberalism and trade unionism, which had been a central characteristic of the New Deal, were frayed. Indeed, one of the reasons I resisted the infatuation with Adlai Stevenson in 1952 was that I could not possibly imagine him talking in a union hall. But since I had become a socialist, I refused to accept the divorce between middle-class and working-class reform. More to the point, in our tiny socialist sects, the Young Socialist League and the Independent Socialist League, we followed, chronicled, and analyzed the internal life of the unions. Since the general public had lost interest in the functioning of the largest democratic institution in this society other than the government itself, that, alas, made us exceptional.

Our information was not simply bookish. We still had a handful of socialist activists in various unions, above all in the United Auto Workers. So I learned my labor history from veterans, some who were still shop stewards or local union officers. When the Fund for the Republic created a Trade Union Project in the late fifties, my friend Paul Jacobs hired me as a writer, notetaker, researcher, and all-purpose utility intellectual. So it was that I wrote studies of the UAW Public Review Board and of the actual functioning of Right to Work laws as well as a small book on the retail clerks' union.

As a result, when modest celebrity descended on me with the success of *The Other America*, I found myself speaking at union functions of the Auto Workers, Packinghouse Workers, the Western Federation of Teamsters, and the like. And when we decided upon the Democratic Agenda project, we naturally turned to the unions, a move for which my personal history had prepared me. Even the right-wing socialists who were carefully spreading the word that I was antilabor, moving in the direction of pro-Communism, etc., helped. For the charges were so preposterous that they made people even more sympathetic than they would have been otherwise.

Democratic Agenda, it turned out, was a living demonstration of a truth we socialists had been articulating for some time. The unions, we said, are rooted in the daily necessities of working life. They therefore have a stability, a permanence, that in this society is denied the other opposition movements, which demand that women or minorities or professionals *add* a voluntary responsibility to their normal, and often exhausting, routine. Therefore, in very practical terms, labor has more money, more printing presses, more organizers, than any other component of a potential progressive coalition. Democratic Agenda was, in fact, financed and politically supported by three major American unions: the American Federation of State, County, and Municipal Employees (AFSCME), the International Association of Machinists (IAM), and the United Auto Workers (the UAW). It would not have even existed were it not for the backing of working-class institutions ignored by moderate liberals and excoriated by revolutionary Leftists.

Jerry Wurf was the president of AFSCME. He kept treating Democratic Agenda as an out-and-out socialist organization when we were carefully trying to disguise how central our role was. At our first conference, in January 1976, he said that he had come to speak because "a meeting organized by Mike Harrington is the only place in the United States, outside of the American Legion, where somebody can call me comrade."* A gruff, sometimes explosive, man whose heart had never forgotten his youthful days as a socialist agitator in Brooklyn, Jerry was the leader of one of the few unions in the United States that was growing. He was committed, by his most basic instincts as well as by his position as a public-sector trade unionist, to fight the lie that government spending was an ineffectual waste.

---

*It is not generally known, but the American Legion has used the greeting "comrade." In Germany, the idea of "comradeship" is deeply implanted in the military, and the word *Kamerad* describes the relationship among soldiers. The Socialists used the term *Genosse*. Even in the United States, when a firefighter or police officer dies in the line of duty, his or her funeral is routinely described by the media as a tribute by their comrades.

The leader of AFSCME in New York—who later was involved in a bitter internal fight with Jerry—was Vic Gotbaum, who had never been a member of a socialist organization but had long moved in a radical milieu that included his then wife, Sarah. He would send a hundred or so of his union activists to conferences of Democratic Agenda. Local 1199 (New York Hospital Workers), a union in which Communists had originally played a significant role and which operated as a social movement of minorities and women at least as much as an economic bargainer, also involved its rank and file in our meetings.

Then there was Bill Winpisinger. A vice president of the IAM when we began to involve him in Democratic Agenda, he later became the head of the union. "Wimpy" is one of the few individuals who went through the stages of political consciousness that were supposed to be the path of the entire American working class. He began as an auto mechanic, then a militant trade unionist, identified with Walter Reuther's version of political and social unionism, and reached socialist conclusions on his own. The first time I met him was in the early seventies when we both spoke at a college program. I had a syndicated column at the time—a once-a-week piece that had declining readership almost from the start but was unique in that it was the only explicitly prolabor commentary to be found in all of the major print media—and had just written about the need to humanize work.

"Your column is great," Wimpy told me. "But only an intellectual who never worked in a plant would talk about humanizing work. The people on the line know that the point is to get out of the shop as fast as possible, not to try to make it a pleasant place." That was the beginning of a friendship, and the IAM did yeoman work on Democratic Agenda. To my consternation, Marjorie Phyfe asked Wimpy to join DSOC at a lunch conference—a sophisticated operative such as myself knew that you didn't push important labor contacts on the membership issue, and I was appalled at her innocence. Wimpy, however, immediately wrote a check to pay his dues.

In the Auto Workers we had many friends and members, both

in Solidarity House, the headquarters in Detroit, and in Region 9A in New Jersey, led by Martin Garber and Ed Gray. Leonard Woodcock had succeeded Walter Reuther as president in 1970 and, as a veteran of some rather esoteric faction fights in the Socialist party in the forties, he was both friendly and suspicious that we might be destructively irrelevant. Our main contact in the top leadership was Doug Fraser. Doug was a high school dropout who went into the plant and applied his enormous energy and intelligence to the work of the union. He, like Wimpy, had not been a member of any radical group but had matured within the left-wing world of internal UAW politics and was deeply sympathetic to our cause.

It was Brendan Sexton, though, who was the very model of the "organic" worker-intellectual described by Antonio Gramsci. A burly man with the map of Ireland on his face, he too dropped out of high school, became a Socialist agitator, an organizer for the Steel Workers Organizing Committee in the glory days of the thirties, and a key figure in the Reuther caucus of the UAW for a good three decades after that. He was the man who designed the imaginative curriculum at the Auto Workers' Educational Center at Black Lake, Michigan, and he—and his wife, Pat, who went from an assembly line to a Ph.D.—were with us from day one in DSOC and DSA.

Those biographies are, in some ways, the background of the present crisis of the American labor movement. For there was no generation that followed in the path of these men. Most bright, idealistic sons of the traditional working class, even if they might have had some contact with the socialist movement, went to college after World War II and left the working class. Precisely because of the early struggles of such leaders, the next generation had new options. That is one of the reasons I believe that minority and women workers, as well as professionals who have learned that they too have to organize, will have to become the dominant leaders of a resurgent trade union movement. In the seventies, however, we did not think such long thoughts. With the aid of our trade union allies we got the support that made it possible to turn our theories about building coalitions in the Democratic party into some kind of reality.

We reached out beyond the unions, of course. Feminists, such as Gloria Steinem (who was incredibly loyal and committed to our project) and Bella Abzug; liberals, including Leon Shull, the head of Americans for Democratic Action and a key progressive lobbyist in Washington; religious activists; and an entire stratum of sixties veterans who had not sold out, joined in. At the 1979 Democratic Agenda conference in Washington, largely organized by my old friend and comrade, Ruth Jordan, there was an opening session in a huge church, which had a black congregation, with Robert Georgine, the head of the AFL-CIO building trades unions, and Barry Commoner, the environmentalist, sharing a platform with Wimpy, Barbara Mikulski, then the most dynamic woman in the House and later to become a U.S. senator, and Bill Lucy, the secretary-treasurer of AFSCME, who was also a key leader in the Coalition of Black Trade Unionists.

However, the real high point of the whole effort took place at the Memphis Democratic party midterm in 1978. It was not just that we had traveled light years from our aimless, frustrating experience in Kansas City in 1974; we actually played a role that was catalytic in a serious national movement.

I I I

Our success at the 1978 midterm had to do with Jimmy Carter's failure.

Carter came out of nowhere in 1976 and had the nomination wrapped up before the unions and regulars knew what had hit them. Ominously, he lost just about every primary after he had captured the votes for the nomination, a trend that prefigured a very poor campaign in the general election and almost resulted in a victory for Gerald Ford a mere two years after Watergate. Be that as it may, when we went to Washington to lobby the platform-writing committee for the convention, the Carter forces were in complete charge. Fortunately for us, an old friend from the antiwar movement, Joe Duffy, was running the platform process for Carter. So it was that the 1976 platform was probably the most liberal in the history of the Democratic party.

We did not know then that Carter was going to ignore almost all of the fine planks we had given him to run on. We did, however, have some portents of this. Carter was the last candidate to endorse the Humphrey-Hawkins full-employment bill and he did so with evident distaste. And Marjorie and I were deeply bothered at the drafting sessions in Washington that the whole procedure was evidently regarded as unimportant. I complained about that to the columnist David Broder, and he pronounced one of the most chilling judgments on American politics I have ever heard: "You people," he remarked, "are just too sane." Were we flamboyant Leftists making impossible demands, on the model of some of the sixties' agitators, there would have been endless media discussions of our nonideas. But since we were concentrating on mundane issues such as full employment and national health, neither the candidate nor the press particularly cared.

There was an incident at the convention in the summer of 1976 that dramatized this profoundly anti-ideological bias of American politics. Some of the liberal delegates were concerned that the whole event was simply designed to ratify Carter's victories in the primaries. His forces were in control on all issues and the only question was the identity of the vice-presidential candidate Carter himself would pick. So the liberals floated the idea of having debates on the three issues, which the delegates would decide by signing petitions, that were the most important for the party and the nation. But the Carter campaign was terrified that this would lead to a prime-time airing of the question of abortion. They therefore moved to quash the proposal.

A high-ranking Carter official came to see me. If I would agree to oppose the liberal procedural motion in a speech of one minute, I would then be given nine additional minutes to address the convention on the subject of the Democratic Agenda program. "But," I objected, "I am not a delegate and have no right to speak." That,

I was told with a smile, could be taken care of, and, in any case, the credentials that would take me to the podium were already being typed. I, of course, refused the offer, which I took as something of an insult (the notion that I would betray the liberal caucus) but also as a kind of backhanded tribute to the effectiveness of Democratic Agenda. It was also a sign of the ideological vacuousness of American politics. For the Carter people, it was less dangerous to have a socialist speaking to the nation on economic policy for nine minutes than to have any kind of a debate on the issue of abortion.

By the fall of 1977, our worst fears about the Carter administration were confirmed. In economic and social policy, it was timidly liberal, which satisfied no one. So at the Democratic Agenda conference we marched over to the Democratic National Committee offices late on a gray afternoon, carrying candles and making the radical demand that the Democratic President actually carry out some of the planks of the platform on which he ran. By the fall of 1978, when the midterm convention had been reluctantly scheduled for irrelevance in December, the hostility of the liberal and labor forces was intense. Carter was now in the process of becoming a timid conservative, which outraged the Left (and failed utterly to convince the Right).

The Democratic National Committee had decided to deal with the problem of liberal opposition at the midterm in characteristic fashion. To get a resolution onto the floor without the prior approval of the National Committee, it was necessary to get 25 percent of the delegates to sign the appeal and to file it three days *before* the convention opened. Since it was all but impossible to contact a quarter of the delegates, dispersed all over the United States, before they even began to leave for Memphis, the Democratic leadership assumed that it had guaranteed a conflict-free, resolutionless convention that would meekly listen to Jimmy Carter, rubber-stamp the official documents, and go home. The meeting envisioned in this scenario made the rigidly structured Kansas City convention of 1974 look like sheer anarchy.

Democratic Agenda, however, managed to collect the signatures of more than 25 percent of the delegates and to file them on behalf of a series of resolutions more than three days in advance of the convention. There was a "boiler room" in the DSOC office, with Marjorie Phyfe in charge and Skip Roberts, a socialist, trade unionist, and leader of the Vietnam vets as her number two. It turned out that all of those meetings, from January 1976 through November 1978, had put us in touch with—or rather, created—a network of party activists all over the nation. In 1976, for instance, Marjorie had testified at all of the regional platform hearings for the convention, and I had presented our point of view at the national meeting in Washington. At each one of those events, and at the various conferences, we had, in effect, turned ourselves into a communication center of the liberal-labor wing of the Democratic party.

For instance, we got a lot of signatures from New England because Roget Hare, a machinist staffer from that region, was able to call the delegates. We also had built up a significant base of support in the New Mexico Democratic party. Our forces were not confined to the traditional Leftist centers of Boston–New York and San Francisco–Los Angeles. They were grass roots and they were national.

So it was that the caucus of the liberal delegates at the Memphis convention, jointly organized by Democratic Agenda and Americans for Democratic Action, was co-chaired by Doug Fraser and me. And once we had opened the floodgates by qualifying our proposals, the Democratic leadership more or less threw up its hands and allowed us to put yet another resolution on the agenda, this one specifically attacking the domestic budget priorities of President Carter. The Carter operatives at the convention sent out instructions to their whips in the various delegations, telling them how to vote against our resolutions. For the most part, the misrepresentation of our point of view stayed within the normal limits of permissible distortion and lying that are standard in American politics—an energy resolution that called for the establishment of one, publicly owned energy corporation, to act as a yardstick for measuring private-sector policy, was summarized as a call for the nationalization of the entire energy industry.

A few of the Southern delegations picked up on those cues and began to mutter the wheezing, decrepit charge that Socialists were menacing the party. I suspect that they said such things by rote and that they might have been astounded to discover that, for once, there was a grain of truth in their old-fashioned Red-baiting.

I was the one who moved the energy resolution. The chair had recognized Ruth Jordan, a delegate from the District of Columbia, and Ruth, with an amused elation in her voice that only our close friends would have picked up, yielded to Michael Harrington from New York. Meanwhile, the White House staffers were negotiating with Marjorie on which resolutions the administration would accept. Their principle was simple: as long as a document did not attack Jimmy Carter or his administration specifically, they would accept it. That was, of course, a sign of the contempt they felt for the whole process, and it caused me to propose privately that we introduce the Communist Manifesto as a resolution. The Carter people, I argued, would accept it since it did not say a word against the President.

But all was not harmony. The leaders of the gay and lesbian caucus asked me to put Democratic Agenda behind their resolution. I told them that I agreed with their assertion of the right of consenting adults to act on sexual preferences that did not do physical harm to others. But, I said, I could not on my own commit a coalition—organized around an economic program—to give support to proposals that had never been discussed. I offered to check out the issue with Doug Fraser, Jerry Wurf, and Wimpy, but said that I doubted that they would suddenly bring such a resolution to their caucuses. My position was interpreted as hostile to gay rights and I had some contentious conversations with leaders of that movement later on in New York.

Then there were the blacks. One would have thought that the resolution attacking the Carter budget's priorities—whose austerity would fall most heavily on the poor, who were disproportionately members of minority groups—would have had the universal support of the black delegates. In 1978, however, some of the most important centers of black political power were to be found in city halls in places like Detroit, Newark, and Gary, Indiana. Coleman Young, the intensely political and very effective black mayor of Detroit, was backing Carter. He had every black leader he could find brought to the podium for a little conversation. Whatever happened in Memphis, he explained, Jimmy Carter was going to be President of the United States until January 20, 1981, and his agents would decide who got what in the cities of America. They were the ones who were going to divvy up the pie, whether it was larger or smaller.

So most of the black delegates voted against the resolution attacking the Carter budget's priorities. And yet, even with the brilliant show of pro-Carter politicking by Young, we got about 40 percent of the votes against the policies of a sitting Democratic President at a Democratic convention. In that sense, the event, despite the efforts of the National Committee to rig it, had fulfilled the function defined by Don Fraser in 1972: to alert the party to the existence of a major rank and file revolt against the leadership.

It also served another function. Ted Kennedy came to Memphis and gave a speech on the need for a national health program. It was delivered with passionate effectiveness and ended with a favorite Kennedy peroration. The senator said, Most people know the medical problems my family has endured: a retarded sister, Jack's wartime injuries, my own problems resulting from an airplane crash, and so on. All I want, he continued, is that every man, woman, and child in America should have the same kind of quality medical care that the Kennedys have received. By the time he finished, the audience of delegates was so pumped up that I think it would have followed Kennedy into the Mississippi River if he had led them there.

I do not believe it is an exaggeration to say that the entire event, including the role of Democratic Agenda, was a factor in Kennedy's decision to challenge Carter in the Democratic primaries of 1980. And it certainly brought Democratic Agenda more attention than it had ever received before. Ben Wattenberg, the Hubert Humphrey liberal who had moved to the Right but insisted on defending his past, told one of our most effective operatives, Harold Meyerson, who was from Los Angeles, that we had put ourselves on the map. The columnist Rowland Evans bought me a drink, a sure sign of our new status in the mainstream.

Not so incidentally, Meyerson was to go on from his involvement in Democratic Agenda—he organized one of its last conferences in Los Angeles in 1982—to become a professional political consultant and organizer in California. For all of his analytic brilliance, he also remains one of the wittiest people on the American Left.

Harold wrote a triumphant article about our exploits in Memphis for the *Nation* and, for a while, it seemed that we were indeed on a roll that would finally take socialists out of their irrelevant ghetto in American politics. The 1979 Democratic Agenda in Washington, D.C., was the largest ever. *Business Week* wrote a story, headlined on the cover, that socialists were now being taken seriously within the American trade union movement. Leftists of almost every stripe, some of whom had denounced us as sellouts only a few years before, began forming liberal-labor coalitions on the Democratic Agenda model. There was a Big Business Day, largely organized by members and friends of DSOC, in which there were media events and teach-ins all over the country on the role of the corporation. Harold Meyerson organized an Academy Awards ceremony for the corporations in Los Angeles, handing out prizes— the statue of a pig—to the star private-sector offenders against the public good.

And then, in the fall of 1979, Ted Kennedy announced his candidacy. We had tried to get the senator to come to the 1979 Democratic Agenda conference, and it was a portent, though we did not know it, that he refused. Had he attended, he would have been able to recruit a good portion of the 2,500 activists to his cause. And the people there, it must be emphasized, were not a random slice of the American population, but an assembly of the most committed politicals of the broad Democratic Left. But Kennedy at that point was running for a coronation rather than a nomination. His campaign was not focused on the specific sins of the Carter administration, which had so outraged the liberal constituency, and it completely lacked that passion for social justice, which was so evident in the speech on national health at the Memphis midterm. Given that game plan, a Democratic Agenda conference was the wrong place to go.

The Iran hostage drama at first helped President Carter and allowed him to take the high road of staying in the Oval Office working to free the captured Americans. Without saying a word, that permitted Carter to depict Kennedy as a divisive man who placed his own ambitions above the needs of the nation. It was only in February 1980, when the nomination had effectively been lost, that in a speech at Georgetown University Kennedy came out fighting. Several months later, in June, I ran into the senator's sister Eunice Shriver at a celebration of the domestic Peace Corps, Volunteers in Service to America.

Why, I asked Eunice, didn't your brother begin his campaign with the Georgetown speech? If he had, we might be on the eve of the nomination. She answered that, just prior to the Georgetown speech, the advisors who had designed her brother's timid campaign had told him that he should simply give up, that he should not insist on raising issues since all was lost. As I look back, I suspect that Kennedy would not have won the presidency under any circumstances in 1980 (even though I remain convinced that he was the best person for the job). That judgment has to do with a complex history, which includes Chappaquiddick and its impact on the electorate. But he might have become the Democratic candidate and he certainly could have given much more prominence to the issues that he only defined when he had already lost. It is the supreme irony that the most powerful and moving speech of the entire Kennedy presidential campaign of 1980 was made to the convention that was convened to nominate his opponent.

There was one last development in the Kennedy campaign that attested to the relevance we had achieved in the party. I was scheduled to be a Kennedy candidate for the platform committee—the seats were apportioned on the basis of the New York State vote and the Kennedy forces had six, the Carter delegates five. But at the last minute the Kennedy and Carter campaigns cut a deal to allow Senator Pat Moynihan and Assembly Leader Stanley Fink to go on the committee as joint nominees of both caucuses. As the lowest person on the Kennedy slate I had to go.

At a packed caucus meeting of the delegates for the convention, Ruth Messinger put me in nomination for the committee anyway. He is, she said, one of the best socialist organizers I have met, a remark that caused consternation among the Buffalo delegates with whom I happened to be sitting. The Kennedy people all proclaimed their respect for me but urged their people to go along with the compromise. In an election that required signed ballots to be deposited at the office of the Secretary of State, I got about a quarter of the votes against Moynihan, an incumbent Democratic senator.

Pat was not amused, for the incident showed that his neoconservative stance had opened him to a serious challenge in the 1982 senatorial primary. His people called every delegate who had voted for me to ask why. (Jim Chapin simply replied, "Because I agree with him.") And there is no question that during the next two years—and indeed to this day—Moynihan moved to the Left on a number of significant issues. We were, in short, part of a liberal wing that had some serious political clout in the Democratic party.

Even when Reagan became President, we thought that the nation's misfortune might turn out to be our good luck. Our natural constituency was even more furious than under Carter, and there were people who paid their dues on the grounds that it had become an urgent moral necessity in the America of Ronald Reagan. That 1982 Democratic Agenda conference in Los Angeles was an ebullient, militant event, in part because the economy was in a shambles by then. Reagan's popularity had dropped to a historic low for that point in his presidential tenure, and many of us thought that the Right-wing interregnum was nothing more than an interlude.

Those same conditions, however, led to the undoing of our

whole project. When the Democratic National Committee convened a midterm *conference* (not a convention) of mainly appointed people in Philadelphia in late 1982, there was a mindless euphoria, in large measure the product of the significant Democratic gains in the off-year elections. I went to the labor caucus—by accident I was sitting next to Al Shanker, one of the most hawkish members of the AFL-CIO Executive Council. Many people were surprised to see us chatting together, though they did not know that we were not talking politics but discussing student theater at Mamaroneck High School, which both our sons attended. The union line was simple: no one should disturb a unity built on simple opposition to Reagan by bringing up policy issues that could divide the party.

This attitude was pervasive at an event that was the reductio ad absurdum of the kind of democratic, grass-roots consultation Don Fraser had had in mind in 1972. There were, for instance, two resolutions on foreign policy, one by the hawks, the other by the doves. An *and* was placed between them and the resulting contradiction was solemnly adopted as Democratic policy. In part, this farcical caricature of party debate occurred, I suspect, because we had done our job much too well at the 1978 midterm. We had convinced the official leadership that it would be intolerable if the Democratic party actually became a party.

There was a tragedy, which also affected us. Harry Chapin, the popular singer, was Jim Chapin's brother. But much more than kinship was involved. Harry was one of the most thoughtful and committed entertainers of his generation, a man who gave away roughly half of his income, which usually reached a million dollars a year. He was not, however, the "star" who identifies with a noncontroversial issue just slightly to the Left of the Community Chest. His passion focused on world hunger, and he created an organization to deal with the issue, personally and effectively lobbying Republicans as well as Democrats.

I got to know Harry through his brother Jim and found him both engaging and talented. Finally, he agreed to assign us $75,000 of his concert income over fifteen months so that we could put

Democratic Agenda on a regular footing. The last time I saw him, he was in the DSOC office talking about world hunger issues and suggesting that he and I immediately fly to Germany to talk to Willy Brandt about the problem. The next thing I heard, this utterly decent young man was killed in an automobile accident on the Long Island Expressway.

Meanwhile, life became more difficult for us in 1983 and 1984 when the limited, uneven economic recovery that occurred not because but in spite of Reagan's policies convinced people who had lost their jobs because of the President in 1982 that they should vote for him in gratitude for getting a job back in 1983 or 1984. At the same time, DSA did run into a host of financial and personnel problems, but our underlying difficulty was in large measure political.

In the eighties, America became a "society at three speeds." The upper 20 percent—which includes disparate elements such as people with real wealth, those who have very high incomes, and upper-class apprentices more commonly known as Yuppies—were doing very nicely. The middle stratum—50 percent to 60 percent of the nation—was not in danger of poverty once the recovery occurred, but was justifiably nervous about a changing economy. The feeling of security and optimism that had prevailed in the fifties and sixties was simply not there. Finally, 20 percent of the country was either poor or in the magnetic field of poverty. Disproportionately it consisted of minorities, women, and children.

In short, the times were either ambivalent or bad for the majority, which describes a social setting in which militant movements are rare. It was, for instance, of some moment that the feminist organizations, which had been created by one of the most significant social movements in twentieth-century American history, all lost members once Reagan made his comeback. And the unions were not simply declining because the percentage of the organized work force, above all in the manufacturing sector, was declining. They were, because of that fact, forced to cut back on staff and political contributions.

There was another factor at work, which was particularly difficult for DSA. We did not know it at the time, but in the seventies we lived off the inheritance of the sixties. The youthful cadre that did so much of the work on all of our projects, such as Democratic Agenda, had aged. That generation of activists turned into parents, union and public-interest staffers, tenured professors, mortgage holders. Some simply got tired of banging their heads against the brick wall of corporate power in the United States. Every marriage, every birth, was a joyous event for us as a community of comrades—and a further complication for us as an organization.

All of which is not to announce defeat or my own imminent departure from the trenches. Far from it. In 1986 and 1987 we launched, with union help, Democratic Alternatives, a reprise of Democratic Agenda. Jo-Ann Mort, a poet and graduate of Sarah Lawrence, turned into a solid labor organizer (and is now on the staff of the Amalgamated Clothing and Textile Workers), and we mobilized around three thousand Democratic party activists in conferences to discuss programs and strategy in Washington, D.C., Albany, N.Y., Kansas City, and Chicago. Even as I write, I have been making phone calls for a national day of consciousness about poverty in the United States entitled "Justice for All." Yet I do think that the next phase will be new, that it will not simply be a continuation of what I have been describing in these chapters on DSOC, DSA, and Democratic Agenda. I therefore propose to look backward for a moment, to see where we have come from.

I V

In the late fifties—when some of us democratic socialists began to break decisively with the sectarianism of our past, particularly our refusal to work electorally with the progressive forces in the Democratic party—we had a rather simple explanation of what we were doing.

We were particularly impressed by an analysis made by James MacGregor Burns, a Kennedy Democrat and political scientist. America, Burns said, was a four-party nation: the presidential (mainly liberal) Democrats and the presidential (mainly moderate) Republicans; the congressional (mainly Southern and conservative) Democrats and the congressional (mainly midwestern and traditional) Republicans. Since 1938, Burns argued, Congress had been under the control of a coalition of the congressional Democratic and Republican parties. All of the Presidents in the intervening years had been liberals or (Eisenhower) moderates, but the real power was located in the Dixiecrat-Republican coalition and institutionalized, above all, in the conservative domination of the standing committees of the United States Senate.

So we came up with a "realignment" political strategy. Defeat the congressional Democrats within the Democratic party, either by replacing them, forcing them to change, or, if necessary, driving them to the Republican party. In Texas, for instance, our friends took this analysis so seriously that they publicly backed John Tower, a Republican Neanderthal, against a Democratic Neanderthal for the Senate. If, they argued, Texas has to have a reactionary in that house, then let it be one of *their* reactionaries, not one of ours. We envisioned a new party in the United States that would, in all likelihood, be called the Democratic party, but would be a relatively coherent instrument of the country's progressive forces.

There was considerable truth in that analysis, but the sixties made us significantly amend it. The student and youth movements of that decade marked the arrival of the baby boom in the center of the society and were a precondition for a whole series of social movements: the participation of whites in the civil rights struggle, the antiwar campaigns in the streets and at the ballot box, the feminists, the environmentalists, and all the rest. The society, we realized, was becoming much more complex in its class structure and politics, and if the working class continued to be a quintessential component of any democratic Left coalition, the "new class" of the college-educated employees and hired professionals had to have significantly more weight. Democratic Agenda was, of course, specifically designed to create a bridge between the sometimes hostile components of the mass Left.

In a sense, the Democratic convention in San Francisco in 1984 was exactly what we had sought. Jesse Jackson and Gary Hart accepted the victory of Walter Mondale and backed him for the presidency; Geraldine Ferraro became the first woman to be nominated for Vice President by a major party. At a socialist caucus meeting of delegates at that convention—which was as popular with the Democratic National Committee as the bubonic plague—Harry Britt, a DSA vice-chair and member of the San Francisco Board of Supervisors, made a shrewd comment. The rhetoric of this convention, he said, is social democratic: a celebration of working people and minorities, of women and immigrants, the language of a "peoples' party." Harry, of course, made the point in part to contrast the rhetoric with the reality.

Still, the Mondale campaign united all of the class and social forces we had deemed essential—and went down to ignominious defeat.

There had been, we and others realized, a certain *dealignment*. In America, which was in an even more individualistic mood than usual, organizations per se were less important than political commercials on television that treated candidates like breakfast food. Computerized polling data about public attitudes had become much more compelling than the candidates' political instincts or reports from the precinct captains. We had based so much of our work on the assumption of the emergence of a quasirational party system.

It is possible that America will become a nation, not simply without parties in the European sense, but without parties in the American sense as well. Arthur Schlesinger, Jr., described what then might happen (or what has already happened in part): "Political adventurers might roam the countryside, like Chinese warlords, building personal armies equipped with electronic technologies, conducting hostilities against some rival warlords, forming alliances with others, and, if they win elections, striving to govern through ad hoc coalitions. . . . Without the stabilizing influence of parties, American politics would grow angrier, wilder and more irresponsible."

Could that happen? Of course. Is it inevitable? I think not. The accumulated structural problems of the American economy and society, as I argued in *The Next Left*, are so serious, so fundamental, that if the trend described by Schlesinger were to prevail, it could well precipitate a profound crisis of the entire system. I do not suggest—or exclude—that such a development would mean a new "1929" in which the roof caves in on the economy. It could take the form of what a French writer has called "the slow 1929," a disaster in installments. The Wall Street "meltdown" of October 1987 suggests that it might also take the form of a sudden financial disaster. But whichever variant of our underlying problems prevails, the event might shock American politics into at least a semblance of rationality and decency.

There were two developments that made me think that when that change comes, we can play a real world role.

Jack Sheinkman, who became president of the Amalgamated Clothing and Textile Workers in 1987, was one of the trade unionists who worked with us regularly. He is also one of the most thoughtful men in the American labor movement. In the mid-eighties, Jack headed up the group of AFL-CIO leaders who were opposed to American policy in Central America and even pushed the issue to an open debate at a Federation convention. Working through him, we conceptualized, and helped to organize, a major march on Washington in the spring of 1987. The anti–Vietnam War alumni and alumnae and the religious activists were there, en masse, of course—but so were large delegations of workers marching under union banners, and the emphasis was on the patriotic shame we felt with regard to American policy. It was our dream, 200,000 strong.

And then, starting in 1982, we had worked with my old friend Stanley Sheinbaum—a subtle and brilliant analyst often unfairly seen as just another wealthy California Leftist—in bringing together the new generation of radical, but practical, economists. In the 1988 campaign our ideas were visible in a number of campaigns.

There are signs, in short, that we democratic socialists might even become relevant again.

CHAPTER SIX

Life I

I became a professor of political science in 1972 because I wanted
to get health insurance. The experience changed my life.

Until 1971 my wife, Stephanie, was on the staff of the
Village Voice, and we were covered under their medical plan. But
that year, when Teddy was born, Stephanie decided she would
free-lance, largely because she wanted to spend more time with
the children. I had managed to avoid the regular nine-to-five routine all my life, and even though the success of *The Other America*
in the early sixties took me out of the Bohemian poverty in which
I had lived for fifteen years, I still did not have a "job." To be
sure, I worked harder than most people—and had done so even
when I must have seemed to be just another Greenwich Village
wastrel—but not in the context of any institution.

I had written for years about the anti-individualistic, bureaucratic, and impersonal trends of contemporary society. Now, as a
parent, I encountered them as a fact of my daily life. The price of
individual medical insurance was absurdly high and the coverage
minimal, but with two young sons we had to have that protection.
I concluded that I would finally have to find regular employment
not so much for the pay but for the fringe benefits. Had America
not been the only Western democracy without a national health
system, I would not have been pushed to that absurd conclusion.

I obviously wish that such health care had been available, but I also know that if it had been, I would have missed an enriching involvement in higher education.

I decided to look for my fringe benefits at a university. After all, I had published four books and had spent years lecturing at colleges all over the country. There was only one problem: I was an analyst of society in ways normally classified under social science in the academy; yet my highest degree was a master's in English literature from the University of Chicago.

True, I had been a visiting professor—indeed, occupied an endowed chair—at the University of Illinois in 1970. But I had been nominated to that post by the law school and had lectured in almost every department of the university without teaching a single course. I was an irregular, an exotic star brought to campus precisely because I did not fit into the standard academic slots.

My idea of becoming an academic might seem to have been utterly arrogant because I had none of the formal qualifications for the post. But though the calendar said 1971, when I started looking for a college position with health insurance the sixties were still alive and well in the groves of academe. The expansion of the faculty and the student population were proceeding apace and no one dreamed of the budget cuts that were to come. More to the point, there was a spirit of innovation, of new departures, as campuses responded to the upheaval of the sixties by instituting courses on Marxism, Zen Buddhism, and the women's movement. No mistake about it, there were dilettantish idiocies committed in the name of the cult of Youth and the New, yet on balance the transformation of higher education was positive.

That enormous institutional change comes up indirectly at the beginning of every course I teach. I carefully tell my students that I am a socialist and if I am given a semester to define what I mean, a democratic Marxist. I will not soapbox, I explain, and in any case all of the faculty who pretend to be "value free" in their attitudes toward society are fooling their classes and probably themselves since there is no neutral perch from which to view a question as contentious and emotional as power and wealth. And,

I add, it had not always been possible for people like me to teach at Queens or in the City University. That, I argue, is one of the gains of the sixties.

It was, then, not all that preposterous for a free-lance intellectual, at that time in our cultural history, to look for a professorship. Ten years before, or three years later, it would have been preposterous. Still, even in 1971 it took an incredible piece of good luck to make it happen. A friend of mine from the years when I was a thinker-in-residence at the White Horse Tavern in the Village, Joe Bossom, was on the faculty at Queens College. He told Joe Murphy, the president of the College, that I was looking for an academic post, and Joe seized on the idea.

Seventeen years later, I am still a professor of political science at Queens. In the process I have learned much about an idea that I had long advocated—mass higher education—and been taught by both my students and colleagues.

I

Joe Murphy is a fluent, charming, brilliant, and utterly maverick academic politician. He was also a perfect ethnic mix for a president of a senior college in the City University of New York: the son of an Irish father and a Jewish mother, he had lived in public housing as a youth, gone on to a Ph.D. and a high post in the Peace Corps, and become the president of Queens College. (He was named chancellor of the entire City University in 1982.) A shrewd social scientist, he understood that his job was political as well as intellectual and attended every major function of the Democratic party in the borough. When the New York City crisis broke in 1975 and threatened the college, he was accompanied by practically all of the elected officials in Queens when he defended his institution before higher authority.

It was hardly surprising that an innovative, left-wing Kennedy Democrat would be sympathetic to me. But when Joe and I had lunch I realized that we also shared a common vision. He believed that there was no reason why a public university could not be as good as an elite institution like Harvard. In pursuit of that ideal, he had aggressively sought first-rate scholars, attracting them to Queens with salaries that were—prior to the city crisis—as good as any in the nation. His reasoning for wanting me to teach there? He felt it would enrich the students to have contact with an extramural political intellectual who did not fit into any of the standard academic categories. I immodestly think he turned out to be right.

That positive concept of mass higher education was basic to my socialist convictions. I was obviously aware that elite institutions produced more Nobel Prize winners as well as millionaires, that the Ivies were centers of intellectual excellence as well as of monied power. Yet I thought—I still think—that the antiegalitarian character of American society is not the consequence of the inherent inferiority of the bottom half or the superiority of the elites, but of the class and cultural structures that distort the rough genetic equality of the human race. Intelligence, as it is problematically defined in this society, is distributed along a "normal curve," i.e., one sixth are exceptionally gifted, one sixth are problematic, and two thirds are in the middle, a formula that describes shoe sizes and many other things. But wealth and power follow an abnormal curve in which one half of 1 percent occupy a pinnacle, 20 percent inhabit the depths, and the rest are in various stages in between.

If that is so, it is possible that education can be a major force for fostering genuine equality by opening up the possibility of excellence to those who cannot attend elite universities. It is not *the* answer, but it is part of it. Thus going to Queens was not simply, or even primarily, a means to a personal end, even if my first impulse was the mundane one I have described. I was undertaking a journey to see if my ideals were serious.

Shortly after that lunch with Joe Murphy, I was invited by Henry Morton, the chair of the political science department, to deliver a lecture so that the faculty and students could observe me. Not too long after, I was appointed visiting professor of political science, and within a couple of years became a tenured member of the faculty. It is to the enormous credit of the college and the board of higher education that no one mentioned that I had never taken a course in political science.

My start in academe was not without problems, as I later learned. After all, as my first job I was being made a full professor, a rank traditional academics strive for throughout an entire career. And I was not being hired as a writer-in-residence but as a normal member of my department. Small wonder that a few colleagues originally questioned whether the college should make a lasting commitment to me. But then, after my first semester my book *Socialism* appeared, not simply to very positive reviews but also with a formidable apparatus of footnotes. Since a Ph.D. is really only a formal certification that a person is capable of independent research, it was clear that I was qualified in substance, if not in form. There was no dissenting vote when I was given early tenure in 1974.

When I arrived in the spring semester of 1972, the college was about what I imagined it would be. (I had talked there in 1960 as an activist in the civil rights movement, but my expectations were based on a general knowledge of colleges and New York City, rather than on that brief encounter.) Most of the students were from working-class or lower-middle-class families, the first generation to go to college, and hell bent for the middle class. The Italian-Americans were the largest single ethnic group, but the Jews tended to be more visible in terms of student politics and activity. And there were fewer blacks and Puerto Ricans than on most of the other CUNY campuses.

When I arrived, there was still some activism; the sixties were not quite over. One day, for instance, I spoke at an antiwar protest out on the campus (typically, Joe Murphy had canceled classes so that everyone could attend). And there were Leftist students in my classes who thought that my socialism was insufferably right-wing. One of them came to my office and said to me, with respect but passion: "The problem with you, Professor Harrington, is that you don't understand the equations on expanded reproduction in Volume II [of *Das Kapital*]." Put less esoterically, he was accusing me of playing down the structural tendencies toward capitalist crisis in my analysis. And the political students were a leaven in the classroom, particularly when they were critical of me and challenged my analyses. That was also true of the occasional Rightist as well as the Leftists.

I said that the Jews tended to be most involved in the life of the college. But even though my first years at Queens were still influenced by the sixties, there was relatively little student activism because virtually all the students worked. That is, they came to the campus, tended to choose courses on the basis of the times when they were scheduled, and left as soon as possible. Because most faculty members did all of their teaching on two days, and office hours were minimal, there was very little sense of an academic community at Queens. When I was at Holy Cross College, there was a tradition actually honored in practice that everyone said hello to everyone else. At Yale Law School I have lived in a charming pseudomedieval building with gargoyles of cops and robbers, a wood-burning fireplace in the living room of the suite I shared with Dick Fitzsimmons, and on a number of occasions I discovered a faculty member sleeping on the couch after a particularly memorable party. At the University of Chicago there was an intellectual intensity that permeated the bars and lunch counters as well as the classrooms; every waking hour was part of the university experience.

Indeed, I had a love-hate attitude toward Harvard, in part because of the very atmosphere of the campus. I was jealously hostile toward it as an undergraduate, seeing it as a citadel of that WASP privilege and arrogance that had so often tormented my forebears. But even when I was bitter because the Harvard band played the Holy Cross songs better than we did, all I had to do was walk into Harvard Yard and I would be humbled by the hallowed peace of that magnificent space, by an almost physical sense of tradition and learning. Yet I was torn, for I knew that what I sensed was not simply tradition, but the tradition of the American upper class.

Queens, on the contrary, had a marvelous view of Manhattan on a clear day, but it was mainly an unmatched assortment of unimpressive buildings. There were no amenities, no Gothic nooks of the kind one would suddenly discover at Chicago, and the classrooms tended to be scruffy and functional. When I complained to Andrew Hacker, one of the prestigious political scientists Joe Murphy had brought to Queens, that our college was utterly lacking in community, he told me of the obtrusive, unavoidable intimacy of Cornell, where he had taught before.

Hacker also gave me some very good advice. "Don't just refer to 'Merrill Lynch,' " he told me. "Your students have not spent their lives around a dinner table with their fathers complaining about their brokers. Say: Merrill Lynch, a brokerage house that trades in stocks and bonds." That was not simply sound, practical counsel; it also gets to the heart of the problem of mass higher education.

One time when he was still chancellor of the University of Chicago, the irrepressible Robert Hutchins was asked by a reporter if his school were truly great and why. It is great, he said, and the reasons are: we have a magnificent Chancellor, a mediocre faculty, and a wonderful student body. The comment about the faculty was as sardonic as the brazen avowal of his own very real excellence. But the point about the student body was true. At Chicago I learned as much from the endless intellectual conversations and the infectious spirit of irreverent inquiry as I did in class. Perhaps more.

I found something of that spirit at Yale in the mid-seventies when I was a Chubb Fellow. In that program, the fellow eats all his meals with the students, drinks beer late in the night with them, and in general participates in a total immersion in the academic community. After several years teaching at Queens, I was struck by the way in which the Yalies would speak to me almost as to an equal. One student even challenged my interpretation of a bit of left-wing history in which I had personally known most of the participants.

I was not surprised or shocked by the contrast between Yale and Queens. Above all, I did not attribute it to the inherent genius of the students in New Haven. In the sixties, when it had been thought that education would solve many social problems, I had been a dissenter. Following David Riesman and Christopher Jencks, I had argued that in a class society in which the roles and opportunities were distributed in a fundamentally unfair way, the ability of education to correct injustice was limited, for it was itself part of the system of injustice. The wealthy alumni of Harvard and Yale do not, after all, support those schools out of an abstract love of the truth. They are class-based institutions—with scholarship students, of course, since the intelligent men and women of power always want their mandate renewed by the most talented children of the lower orders—with a sophisticated conservative mission in the society. And even when very decent people, some of my friends included, tried to make them responsive to race, poverty, and gender, the progress that could be made was limited.

Moreover, I knew that I participated in these injustices personally. My older son, Alexander, began to read Dostoevsky on his own when he was about fifteen and once told a college professor who was explaining Hegel's dialectic in terms of thesis, antithesis, and synthesis that Hegel didn't use those terms and that he should read the section on the Master and Servant in the *Phenomenology of Spirit* for the real theory. And my younger son, Teddy, is an enthusiastic jock, but with a remarkable vocabulary and a talent for writing. It is clear that these intellectual virtues are, in part at least, a result of the family in which they have been brought up— with both parents writers—and that they have, therefore, a certain advantage over the children of shopkeepers from Queens whose table talk did not include Hegel.

Clearly, the average student at Queens was not the product of the sophisticated backgrounds that predominated at the Ivies. And yet the exceptional ones were just as good. I think, for example, of a young black woman, Dona Macfarlane, who took my regular courses and then three tutorials, the latter in Volumes I, II, and III of *Das Kapital*. The tutorial consisted of the two of us drinking coffee and simply talking over what she had read the previous week. Later Dona was to become a part of the planning department under the democratic socialist regime of Michael Manley in Jamaica—I ran into her when I was on a left-wing junket in Kingston—and the last I heard, she was taking a Ph.D. There was also a young man named Jeff Issacs who currently teaches at the University of Indiana after having taken a Ph.D. at Yale. Jeff understood a fact that eluded many of the students: the Queens social science faculty contained a number of scholars who were as good as, and much more accessible than, the "name" professors at the Ivy League schools. Indeed, we eventually formed a Monday Group, which met for lunch and discussion at a private room in a campus restaurant every Monday. Those men and women were not simply academics; they were also passionately concerned about ideas and about teaching. We regularly debated issues of high theory on Monday—but we also talked about the particular problems of our work at Queens. Jeff shrewdly picked his professors and later, when he was in graduate school at Yale, discovered that he was as well prepared as any of his fellow students. I recently received a copy of his first book, *Power and Marxist Theory*.

Then in the late seventies that very important stratum of undergraduates preparing to go on for doctorates—and, in the social sciences, more often than not, politically involved—disappeared. That had little to do with Queens and much to do with the American economy. Indeed, I have long argued that the GNP trends have done more to determine the curriculum of higher education in the United States—at Harvard and Yale as well as at Queens—than the students and the faculty. The only difference was, the impact of a downturn was most destructive at a public university.

The sixties decisively ended on the American campus during the recession of 1974 to 1975. The repercussions were especially strong at City University because this was also the period of New York City's near-bankruptcy. The first signs of change had surfaced during the recession of 1969 to 1970, but now a basic transformation was underway. The students of the sixties had believed, like everyone else, that affluence would continue forever. Thus one could take "impractical" courses or even drop out for a while. The infinitely wealthy, infinitely tolerant, society would always be there to take care of its rebels. It is easy to caricature the radical tantrums that sometimes resulted from this mood. But, in fact, the economy did permit a greater sense of experimentation, of intellectual searching, in the colleges than at any time before or since.

When the crisis hit in the mid-seventies, when it became clear that the Keynesian utopia of the previous decade had ended with a whimper not a bang, the students drew practical conclusions from the fact. Attendance in courses devoted to theory or literature declined; the accounting department thrived. That was more the case at Queens than at an elite campus because Queens—and mass higher education in general—was, even in its glory days, a trade school for apprentice members of the middle class as well as a center for the dissemination of culture and learning. It was no accident that in the sixties the student rebellion began at places like Harvard, Ann Arbor, and Berkeley and only later filtered down to the state and community colleges. More recently, the anti-intellectual impact of the malfunctioning of the American economy hit first at those universities where economically insecure students felt that they had to be "practical" about their studies.

It was during the mid-seventies that the *New York Times Magazine* asked me to write an article on open admissions, the policy that provided every high school graduate in the city with a slot on one of the campuses of CUNY. (The campus a student attended was determined by grades and class standing, and Queens College, which was the first choice of a large number of students, was affected somewhat less than other campuses, such as City College of New York—CCNY—the famous poor students' Harvard of the thirties.) In the late sixties, civil rights militants had noted that the City University, which was financed by municipal tax funds, had a student body that was much whiter and more middle class than the taxpayers themselves. There were militant demonstrations at CCNY, which is located in the middle of Harlem, and a building was burned. The politicians then made the right decision in the wrong way: overnight they decreed open admissions, without thinking through or preparing for the consequences.

It was then widely believed that the main beneficiaries of this change were poor blacks and Hispanics. In 1970, when this process began, a much higher percentage of nonwhites than whites in New York had not completed high school. The evidence was clear that the white working class had gained more from the new policy than the blacks who had effectively won the political struggle for it. The New York City AFL-CIO, under the leadership of the disproportionately white building trades, certainly understood this fact. It was a very vocal exponent of open admissions.

There were indeed some horror stories about open admissions when students who had graduated from high school without being able to read or write well arrived on college campuses. Did one then indict the students? The open admissions policy? Or the educational system which, often because it was a way of getting government funding, allowed young men and women to participate in an educational farce at the high school level? Later, when the statisticians began to analyze the impact of both Head Start and federal aid to education, it turned out that both these programs had a positive impact.

Still, there were faculty members who had spent years preparing for an academic specialty and in some cases—particularly at CCNY, which had a very high percentage of students who would not have been accepted under the earlier rules—wound up teaching remedial English. I understood their anger and frustration. But what about the anger and frustration of the poor and minorities in New York who saw their taxes financing education primarily for the nonpoor and the white? On balance, I wrote in my *Times* article, the experiment had worked, warts and all.

I had hit a nerve. The liberal middle class in New York, personified by the *Times*, was in the process of moving away from its commitment to effective civil rights. I was told at the very last minute—after correcting the final galleys and making the interminable corrections that a piece for the Sunday *Magazine* always entails—that the article would not run. I engaged in some rather uncharacteristic shouting and threatening, and finally it did appear. But I knew that the times they were a-changing.

By the eighties, the faculty members of the Monday Group were themselves debating whether there had been a decline in the quality of the students. The latter now included a good number of Asians, Greeks, and Iranians—Main Street in the Flushing section of Queens had by now more signs in Korean than in Hebrew—but the mood of "practicality" dictated by the imperious economy was pervasive. Because of the city's financial crisis and the imposition of tuition in 1975, not only had the student body declined from about 25,000 to 16,000, but some of the brighter candidates had probably decided to go to a private college since they had to pay at Queens.

There were other indefinables. Our students were part of a generation that had known television from infancy on, and they suffered from that historical and cultural amnesia which seems to be a permanent feature of our national life. ("America," Irving Howe once wrote, "is about the destruction of memories.") John Kennedy and Martin Luther King, Jr., were now historical figures, and sometime in the late seventies, when lecturing about Jim Crow, I discovered that the students did not know precisely what I meant. So I went back and described pre-1964 America, those years before the Flood, and notes were carefully taken, even by some of the blacks in class.

When I first experienced this phenomenon, and even as I was writing this book, I assumed I was describing something either new, or uniquely American, or both. But then, rereading the last volume of *Remembrance of Things Past* as a noble background for this more prosaic memoir, I found Proust describing the same reality in the Faubourg St.-Germain in Paris just after World War I. The young fashionables, he said, had no memory of the Dreyfus Affair, which had racked France only a few decades earlier. High society had utterly forgotten that the woman who was now the Princess of Guermantes, the bearer of a name illustrious under Louis XIV, had been Madame Verdurin, the center of an apparently second-rate salon during those Dreyfus years.

Perhaps Proust is right. Perhaps time inexorably makes each generation an amnesiac. Even so, there is, I think, something new taking place within the Proustian cycles: fewer people read now, and we professors at Queens are less demanding of our students today than we were a mere ten or fifteen years ago. Are we then participating in some kind of secular decline in the quality of education and thought in America? I cannot be sure, and neither can anyone else. These matters will be decided when we have the profound wisdom of hindsight; in medias res one has only impressions. But I do have some conclusions from this experience of mass higher education.

First, I was educated by becoming a professor. When I arrived at Queens, I was an autodidact, with all of the strengths and weaknesses that implies. I could discuss some of Paul Samuelson's scholarly critiques of Marx's labor theory of value, but I had never paid too much attention to Economics I. My knowledge of the political classics was primarily a result of my socialist and Marxist culture, but I was shaky when it came to what a conservative like Leo Strauss thought of Machiavelli. When I first took the job, Irving Howe told me that I would discover that teaching a regular class was utterly unlike the experience of parachuting onto a campus as a glamorous, one-day lecturer. He was absolutely right.

In order to teach, I had to learn more. As time went on, I became daring, giving seminars on Hegel or Marxist philosophy, and that required not simply that I master the subject matter but that I be able to present it in an intelligible form to undergraduates. No mistake about it, there were students who simply tolerated my excursions into deep theory in the hope that, since I was known as an easy grader, they would get an *A* and then be able to forget the obscure intricacies of the *Phenomenology of Spirit*. But there were also those whose eyes lit up as they began to grasp a portion of their own cultural inheritance.

But all of this also accentuated a personal problem. I have never been able to decide whether I am primarily an agitator or a thinker. I love giving rousing speeches—*and* being a pedant. Typically, I was led from a practical immersion in Marx to reading Hegel and Kant, and then Fichte and Schelling—indeed I taught myself German in order to be able to do so—and in some moods thought I would like to spend another lifetime studying German classical philosophy, from Kant to Marx. But at the same time, it gave me at least as much pleasure to speak to a group of steelworkers in

Canada or machinists in the United States as it did to trade scholarly small talk with fellow academics.

Second, and much less personally, more than fifteen years at Queens has convinced me that the vision Joe Murphy and I shared is a good one. The world of culture should indeed be made accessible to every citizen of the society who has the innate capacity to respond—and that innate capacity is not at all defined by the apparent distribution, which is the product of social injustice rather than genetics, of intellectual talents and skills. I also know, more than ever, that the notion that education at any level can fundamentally change an unfair society is wrong. I am for full employment and egalitarianism, among many other reasons, because I think it will make it possible for more people to read poetry, listen to good music, or even study Hegel.

Often when I spoke on campuses around the country in the seventies and eighties, I would conclude by saying to the students: "You think I've been talking about 'them,' about the poor, the unemployed, the people of the ghettos and barrios. But I'm also talking about you. How many of you are taking courses you don't really want in preparation for leading lives you really don't want to live? You are adapting to the same cruel economy that is vicious to the poor and only—only!—stunts your potential and distorts your life. If you don't solve 'their' problems, you will never solve your own, for you are really part of them."

Practically every time I said such things there was a shock of recognition perceptible in the audience, and at times a trickle of nervous laughter, which signals awareness of an uncomfortable truth. There is also a similar response, but it comes from a completely different group.

As I write, I have just finished teaching a course in a new labor study curriculum at Queens. It was held in the evening, and most of the students were labor activists who came to the campus under a program financed by the contract at work or by the union itself. Many of them lack traditional academic skills; a fair number make grammatical mistakes when they speak or write. And yet they have been some of the most alive and challenging students I have met in all these years. They do not take what I say as gospel; they argue and counter my theories with their experience. Many of them are black and many are women and some are intellectuals who do not know that they are. Meeting them—or talking with a student on the last day of class who tells you that the course has really made a difference—puts all problems and doubts into perspective.

Years ago Antonio Gramsci, one of the greatest Marxists since Marx himself, pointed out that there are intellectuals who have never been to college, reflective people who have come to a profound understanding of society by their participation in, and thinking about, the tasks of a union or a political movement or a community organization. In my class, I met some of those people, and it was, for this rather old-fashioned, Jesuit-trained intellectual obsessed with German classical philosophy in all of its intricate manifestations, yet another learning process, and by no means the least.

I never dreamed that the need for health insurance would turn into such a deeply enriching experience.

II

It was a hot July day in 1979. We were in the throes of one of the most wrenching of experiences: moving. I went into a luncheonette not far from our new place to get a Pepsi, bought a *New York Post* and discovered a story on its gossip page. It was headlined: SOCIALIST LEADER FLEES TO LARCHMONT.

The story did not draw a moral. It reported, in somewhat distorted fashion, how I had told a *Post* reporter that I felt that I had been all but driven from New York City. But the point of the article was, of course, to show that I was just one more left-wing hypocrite, a "man of the people" and opponent of the system who, as soon as he had a dollar or two in his pocket, fled the poor and the working people of Manhattan and sought a comfortable refuge in a Westchester suburb from which to proclaim his moral opposition to oppression. The *Wall Street Journal* editorial page joyously reprinted the revelation; so did a Boston newspaper.

Reading that attack, I had no moral regrets about what I was doing. Not only had I long known that it is impossible for a radical to find any easy way to live in an antiradical society; I had publicly proclaimed all of my hesitations and contradictions in my book *Fragments of the Century*. To be sure, I was deeply saddened to be leaving Manhattan, but that was not because I was betraying my principles. More to the point, I felt sick at the cheap and predictable way that a once-great newspaper, which had become a scurrilous rag, had reduced a complex ethical and social issue to a dirty little piece of nasty gossip.

For that matter, when I had been most "pure"—living for two years at the Catholic Worker House with its third-rate food, bedbugs, and rats—I had always said that clean sheets and fine dinners were good and desirable. I was fundamentally opposed to the way in which they were distributed in our society, but not to the decent pleasures of life. Voluntary poverty as a way of freeing the spirit from its obsession with material things is a noble ideal, and I had lived it in a modest way for two years; but I thought then, and think now, that such an ideal does not mean exalting bad food, bedbugs, and rats. That would be the road to spiritualized masochism. In any case, the house into which I was moving was a very ordinary, middle-class place, not a mansion. So I could dismiss the *New York Post* easily enough, but that did not ease the pain—the sense of defeat—in leaving Manhattan.

I had come to that city as a twenty-one-year-old in 1949 and had instantly fallen in love with the place as only a would-be poet from St. Louis could. But by 1979, when we moved, I knew that the New York I had found had disappeared from the face of the earth. The towering buildings and the sense of raw energy remained, of course. But that was only the decor; the spirit had flown. I had come to a Greenwich Village in which there were cheap apartments and impoverished writers and artists, and now that area had become one of the premier high-rent districts in the city. Once upon a time there had been perhaps ten bookstores that

I would tour, particularly the morning after a night of excessive drinking when I couldn't work. Now almost all of them were gone.

I wrote about that disenchanting experience long before I came to the conclusion that it was necessary to leave my adopted city. Looking back with the wisdom of hindsight, I knew that it was not just Bohemia that had vanished, but the New York City that had existed in 1949: a place with a stable working-class population in a period of exceptional nonviolence.

I don't want to romanticize. One of the reasons for that relative calm was that the blacks in Harlem and Brooklyn endured an intolerable injustice in silence. When they became angrier in the sixties, it led to both real gains in decency *and* an attitude that even rational laws could be broken. As usual, the blacks themselves suffered most from that breakdown of order—they are the victims of most black crime—but one of the by-products, particularly when the chronic high unemployment rates took over in the seventies, was an increase in free-floating hostility throughout the city. I certainly did not want to go back to the days when things were more quiet because, among other reasons, blacks stoically accepted the outrageous. But I could not accept the facile radicalism that saw each black crime as a protest against racism, particularly when so much of that crime was directed against blacks. I was, in short, hoist on my own principles, and afraid as well.

For now New York, and above all Manhattan, had become the home of the rich, the poor, and the childless; a refuge for uprooted and displaced minorities but without jobs for them; the plaything of real estate speculators who made tax-subsidized fortunes by destroying the housing of the impoverished and building the condominiums of the wealthy. The *New York Post* and the *Wall Street Journal* thought it hilariously hypocritical that I should say I felt pushed out of the city, a genteel victim of a process that was infinitely crueler to those much less fortunate than I. But that was indeed the case.

One reason for leaving had to do with the schools.

Alexander, and then Teddy, attended PS 3 on Hudson Street. It was a Village school in more than just its location. It had come into existence as a result of a faction fight over educational theory and values in PS 41 on Eleventh Street. One group wanted an experimental school and held a charrette—a sort of endless encounter session—to hammer out its philosophy. There was, for instance, no Parent Teacher Association but rather a School Community Council with representation from people in the neighborhood who had no children enrolled in PS 3 (or, for that matter, no children at all). The meetings of that council were often contentious debates on educational policy, spiced with copious references to the hallowed principles of the charrette. (Stephanie and I referred privately to the founders as The Pilgrims.)

On paper, it was a great place for experimental education, with an emphasis on the arts and nonstructured classrooms. And with good teachers—known, of course, to all the insiders—it did work to some degree. With teachers who were not so good it was an invitation to chaos. When the city crisis hit in 1975, faculty was fired on the basis of a seniority principle, and those with seniority could, if necessary, move to a new school and "bump" those with lesser tenure. As a result, the PS 3 program, which was designed for a staff deeply committed to the principles of open education, was sometimes implemented by traditionalists who could not care less.

Still, we felt that Alec, and to a lesser extent Teddy (who entered the school just as the situation reached a crisis), was learning, and we were committed to public education. The school did try to live up to its responsibility, actively insisting, for instance, that black students from Harlem be bused in. The moment of truth came when Alec was about to graduate—there were only five grades—in 1979. In the normal course of things, he would have gone to an Intermediate School where some of his slightly older schoolmates had already encountered violence—being shaken down for lunch money, blockades of the toilets, and the like.

I was committed to public education—but not if it meant that my sons would have to cope with physical fear in order to learn. If we stayed in New York, that meant sending Alec, and then Teddy when he graduated from PS 3, to a private school. Thus part of the price for our staying in Manhattan was that we would have to put our children into elite institutions. At that point, the cost of such a move was about five thousand dollars a year per child. That did not strike me as a radical life-style for us or the kids.

Alec's graduation from PS 3 was charming. As it ended, the graduates ran down the aisle, happily singing "Let the Sun Shine In" from *Hair*. But the vision of that countercultural musical, which was not particularly profound to begin with, had long since turned into the ashes of the sixties.

We were also disturbed when we had to take Teddy to his baseball games in a taxi. He and Alec used to take the Eighth Street crosstown bus to PS 3 every day, but the subways were another matter. They had become much more violent and surly than ever before, and we simply did not want the kids to use them alone. For that matter, one afternoon when Alec, Teddy, and I were going to an ice-skating rink on Thirty-third Street, a young black simply punched me in the chest for no apparent reason as we were leaving the subway car. It didn't hurt my body very much, but it sorely wounded my spirit. It was one more reason for concern about raising a family in this environment.

And then there was the problem of rent. For the last three years in the Village, we lived in a high-rise building on Mercer Street, just east of Washington Square. Our children could play in Washington Square—which had once been the haunt of poets and folksingers—and watch the ubiquitous pushers sell their dope. Or they could be mugged in front of their own home, as they were. It also meant that, had we stayed another year, we would have paid seven hundred and fifty dollars for five rooms that were not big enough for the four of us plus the newest member of the family, Humphrey, an utterly wonderful dog. We were contemplating nine thousand dollars a year rent, the possibility of five thousand dollars for Alec's school, and another five thousand dollars for Teddy in a couple of years. With normally abnormal rent increases, the prospect was for well over twenty thousand dollars in outlays for housing and school in order to live a merely middle-class life.

We had spent some years trying to beat the rent problem by joining with friends to buy a brownstone. At one point we even made an offer, but it was refused. By the spring of 1979 we were actively looking for a house in a number of Westchester communities with good school systems. Ironically, Stephanie would not even consider Scarsdale on the grounds that the town's affluent reputation was too posh for America's "foremost socialist." (I was once introduced as such before a debate with William F. Buckley, Jr., who commented, "Being called America's foremost socialist is like being the tallest building in Topeka, Kansas.") Still, the *New York Post*, et al., found Larchmont sufficiently fashionable for its character assassination attempt.

Larchmont itself is a small (mile-square) middle-class village with a handful of rich people and borders on the "outer city" of New Rochelle to the south, with a ghetto and poverty, and part of the town of Mamaroneck, with a large, predominantly Italian-American population of artisans and skilled workers. It is home to a fairly large number of diplomats and foreign executives, many of them French. Ethnically it is, I discovered after I moved in, perhaps a third Irish as well as a third Jewish, and the rest are from assorted backgrounds. Once I became a resident, I remembered that at Holy Cross the Larchmont Yacht Club was considered the acme of "making it" in the Irish Catholic world. But we were looking for schools, not yacht clubs, and in nine years have managed to remain uninvited to the latter.

Some malicious people thought that the idea of moving to Larchmont was Stephanie's—that she had corrupted my pure, radical soul. That was not true: it was a joint, if sad, decision. Ironically, once we arrived I liked the place much more than Stephanie. Freelancing was hard enough when she was living in Manhattan, but now, even though we were a thirty-six-minute commuter train ride from Forty-second Street, she had to get to the station on time and at night could be stuck for an hour in Grand Central if she just missed a train. So Stephanie found that she was isolated as never before.

I on the other hand kept up my full travel schedule around the country and the world and went into our socialist office in Manhattan on most days when I was home. For me Larchmont was a deeply relaxing place where you could walk at night without fear. The trees were a burst of New England color in the fall, I can tell you which bushes and trees bud first in the spring, and after months of going from plane to plane I enormously enjoyed the local tennis courts and bad television in the summer. Even now, as I write, the trees outside my window are filled with squirrels, which fascinate me. Strange, but when I thought I might die considerably earlier than I had planned, one thing that saddened me most was the realization that I would miss the seasons in this place.

We did not seek to reach out to people nor, as far as I can figure, did they seek us out. Larchmont has had a liberal Democratic majority since we arrived and the mayor, Miriam Curnin, is a "Commonweal" Catholic, as are a fair number of the Democrats. I go to one or two political brunches every year and make a very modest contribution to the local cause. There is also a Westchester chapter of DSA, and I have spoken a couple of times at a community church in White Plains.

But it has been through school and sports and Teddy's soccer team above all that we have made friends and acquaintances. The soccer team was an all-star group chosen from among the best players in the regular leagues and represents Larchmont Village in competition in Westchester and nearby counties. The parents were a particularly determined group, cheering loudly at every game, and I enjoyed being a rank and filer among them. The coach of the soccer team, John Lee, was a former Yale basketball all-American and a self-made millionaire. Once during an all-day soccer tournament some parent mentioned to John that I was a socialist, and everyone waited for the fireworks. But both of us turned out to be quite reasonable, and I grew to admire John, even though our values remained worlds apart.

That soccer scene reminded me of a happy experience in Florida during the seventies. We were priced out of the Eastern Long Island summer beach scene and began to take the children to their grandmother Gervis's place in Bal Harbour, Florida, for the summer.

For many of our friends, it was bad enough that someone would want to go to as déclassé a place as Florida in the winter, but enjoying it in the summer was an act of militant boorishness. But we did. Starting in 1973, I became part of an informal group of tennis players who showed up at eight o'clock every morning at the Haulover Park public courts. I was the worst player of the lot, but they were very tolerant and I was delighted to get the daily chance of playing over my head. None of those people—most of whom were small businessmen and Republicans—knew who I was. I was simply an affable hacker and I kept silent about politics because I wanted to play tennis. The parents of the Larchmont soccer team knew who I was, but that was not my primary identity in the group. I was simply a father, albeit with a particularly loud and enthusiastic voice (developed in union halls, classrooms, and street meetings). There is, I realized, a sense of solidarity based on the mundane aspects of daily life, such as a soccer league, that resembles the bonds you feel in larger political struggles.

But the suburbs were not simply a middle-class Shangri-La, as my son Alexander dramatically reminded me one spring. In a bizarre series of events in 1986, I became "Alec Harrington's father" and he ceased to be simply the son of the author of *The Other America*.

Alec is an actor and a socialist (thus far, Teddy has been un-interested in my politics, except as a subject for raillery). As part of his high school acting program, he had to direct a play. He chose *Sister Mary Ignatius Explains It All for You* by Christopher Durang. It was a very controversial work, attacked by various Catholic institutions and some Catholics as being anti-Catholic. It had also been defended by the American Civil Liberties Union and, interestingly, opposed by the Anti-Defamation League of B'nai B'rith. Since Alec is political as well as a connoisseur of drama in life as well as on the stage, Stephanie and I wondered if he had not chosen that play to set off a few fireworks. But he convinced us that he had simply liked it—we had seen it together off-Broadway—and found it the right length for his senior project.

His drama teacher was not amused and refused to let it be put on; the principal and the superintendent of schools concurred. These rulings were made despite Alec's offering, almost from the outset, to invite opponents of the play to discuss it as part of the production. The matter then came up at the Mamaroneck Board of Education, which complimented Alec on his cooperative spirit and decided that he could go ahead with the project.

He did so with great style and intelligence and, without any help from me, lined up a panel composed of the lawyer for the archdiocese of New York (a Larchmont resident), a representative of the Anti-Defamation League, a spokesperson for the ACLU, a Jesuit scholar whom I had known when he was an editor at *Commonweal*, and one of his favorite high school teachers. Finally, he was able to bring the playwright himself to the play. There was a discussion before the performance about whether the play should be staged at a public high school; and after the play a further discussion about whether it was anti-Catholic.

When we had first seen it off-Broadway I was hardly looking at it through the eyes of a Catholic, or even an ex-Catholic. For me it was just a very funny play that evoked memories of my childhood years at St. Rose's School in St. Louis. But suddenly it was in a context, and I looked at it politically. It was still very funny and very true, but there was one scene in which a little doll, as Christ, was nailed to a cross in the re-enactment of a grade-school play. My mother (long since dead) was my litmus test, and I realized that she would have been as horrified as the woman in the audience who cried out "Enough!" But that did not change my mind on the civil libertarian principle involved, since I do not think that my mother's sensibility, or that of any group, should define the forms of permissible speech and art.

During the discussion, I identified myself as "Alec Harrington's father"—which guaranteed maximum celebrity for me on that evening—and argued with the lawyer from the archdiocese. He had particularly attacked the notion of having the play produced in a public, tax-supported place, and I responded that such a point of view would make public schools inherently inferior to private institutions. And indeed, I might have added, the theater was packed (normally there would have been a corporal's guard composed of the student producer's parents, reluctant siblings, and close friends), the atmosphere electric, and the event was probably the outstanding educational experience of the year.

In a broader context, New York suburbia—and I do not know how exceptional it is in this regard—is not the brain-dead center of mediocrity excoriated in the popular fiction and sociology of the fifties. It is, rather, the home of many of the antiwar generation of the sixties, liberal in its politics, and capable, as in the case of Alec's play or local Democratic debates, of being concerned with, and even fascinated by, serious issues. And, ironically, living in Larchmont and going regularly to New Rochelle, I probably spent more time in poor and minority neighborhoods than when I was in Greenwich Village.

For the fact is, in Manhattan a "radical" life-style is increasingly possible only for those with an upper-middle-class income, which insulates them from the very reality they insist is a value to them. The *New York Post* and the *Wall Street Journal* notwithstanding, I was indeed driven out of the city by trends which I had fought; above all, by the polarization of classes and races because of the dominance of wealth over property and housing.

I am intellectually and morally satisfied with the move to Larchmont, yet I cannot suppress a yearning for earlier days when things were simpler. In the summer of 1986 I gave a speech at a state program for selected high school students in Charleston, South Carolina. One of the students, who must have been primed by a faculty member, got up during the question period and asked why, if I were such a radical, I was getting a substantial honorarium for talking. I did not go into the fact that I was having to borrow money to pay bills, but I did explain, aggressively and without apology, that a socialist in a capitalist society has to play by capitalist rules whether he or she likes it or not. I was, and am, absolutely right—and uncomfortable.

In some ways, the happiest days I spent in the radical movement were those two years at the Catholic Worker, when there was total consistency between my ideals and the way in which I lived. But I could not have stayed there for the rest of my life, certainly not as a husband and father. I had to confront all of the contradictions and problems of being a reasonably well-paid critic of the society that paid me.

Whatever my moral hesitations, the squirrels are a joy to watch.

CHAPTER SEVEN

Arise Ye Wretched of the Earth

Arise ye prisoners of starvation,
Arise ye wretched of the earth,
For justice thunders condemnation,
A better world's in birth.
　　　—The Internationale

When the history of the last quarter of the twentieth century is written, the Socialist International will take up less than a chapter and considerably more than a footnote.

It is a consensus organization without the power to bind any of its more than seventy-five member parties to action. Its decisions and resolutions have only a moral authority. To the *realpolitikers* who dominate the Left, Right, and Center of the North and South at century's end, this means that the International is a pious irrelevance. They are often quite right.

Still, there are men of power—indeed, of *realpolitik*—who have taken the International seriously in recent years: Willy Brandt, François Mitterrand, Olof Palme, and Felipe Gonzalez, to name but a few. For a Swiss conservative, Wolfgang Hopker, the International was worthy of a book-length denunciation in 1982 as an anti-American nest of left-wing socialists; for Jean Ziegler, a Swiss Socialist writing in 1986, its revival had the negative importance of a "failed resurrection."

More prosaically, it is clear that the International played an important role in the Portuguese Revolution of 1974–1975, that it helped Felipe Gonzalez and the Spanish Socialist Workers Party (PSOE) establish themselves as *the* party of post-Franco socialism in Spain, that it was a significant factor in both Nicaragua and El Salvador in the late seventies and early eighties. Indeed, under the Reagan administration the International's involvement in Central America earned it the tribute of having a "desk" at the State Department assigned to monitor its work.

My own knowledge of some of these matters is personal. By an accident of history, I began to attend the International's meetings in 1976, the year that Brandt took over as president of the organization and a moribund Old Boys' association of European socialists began to turn into a somewhat serious organization. By 1983 I had become the principal author of the major political resolution adopted at the SI's congress in Portugal, a role I continued to play in 1986 in Peru. This was not so much a tribute to my astuteness as a recognition that I was the only professional, English-speaking writer who was the leader of an affiliate in an organization whose official language was English.

I am unfair to myself and the International. The European socialists who dominate it are politician-intellectuals in a mode that is utterly foreign to America. Indeed, one of their qualifications for power within their own parties is the ability to handle serious political ideas with a certain familiarity. They were therefore more respectful of a powerless American intellectual than my fellow countrymen would ever be. Moreover, most of them had been exiles or lived for a while in the underground, so they knew, and empathized with, isolation.

More important, I am an American, and even though the movement I represent was, and is, a historical failure, it is a failure that continues to have some meaningful influence in the world. In 1969 I was a delegate to the pre-Brandt Old Boys' International at its congress in England. I amended a resolution on disarmament— only later did I learn that mere delegates were not supposed to amend resolutions—to include a reference to the danger of Multiple, Independently Targeted, Reentry Vehicles (MIRVs), America's contribution to the escalation of the arms race at that time.

Fourteen years later I was having dinner in Stockholm with Bernt Carlsson, who had been secretary general of the International from 1976 to 1983. I didn't even remember that he had been at the 1969 congress, but it had made quite an impression on him. It was, he told me, the first time that he had heard of MIRVs. "That is why you Americans are so important to us," he said. "You live where the future is always beginning." Perhaps that was another reason why I was able to get an inside glimpse of events that were, and are, less than a chapter but much more than a footnote to the history of the last decade or so.

I
_____

The Socialist International, reconstituted in 1951, was the heir of two high-minded failures in internationalism.

I do not even take into account its first predecessor, the International Workingmen's, founded in London in 1864 and sent by Karl Marx to New York to die in the early 1870s (it actually expired in Philadelphia in 1876). The links with the Socialist International of 1889 are, however, quite direct, for there are present member parties that helped to form that "Second" International. Its central political mission was to see to it that the workers of the world not fight one another but rather turn upon their own ruling classes when war was declared. That noble hope was totally shattered in 1914 when the European proletariat split along national lines and workers slaughtered one another.

The Labor and Socialist International, which was formed after World War I from the remnants of that debacle, was even less effective. It helplessly contemplated the Communist break in the working-class movement and the related rise of Fascism, and was completely incapable of intervening in the Spanish Civil War, even though the socialists were in power in France during the decisive period of that tragedy of the Left. The workers of the world, it had become quite clear by 1939, were much more patriotic than the capitalists.

And yet, even during World War II, there were those who looked toward the creation of still another International. Harold Laski, the intellectual who was also a serious activist in the British Labour Party, argued that if the Socialists and Communists could cooperate, the continent of Europe itself would go socialist in a matter of years. There was, of course, a Cold War instead, and when the Socialist International finally was re-created in 1951 in Frankfurt, Germany, it had taken sides with the West. The Italian Socialists (PSI), who were then in an electoral alliance with the Communists, were not even invited to attend.

There were some tentative moves to break out of the Cold War definitions of socialism during the late fifties, many of them coming from the German Socialists. But at the Amsterdam congress in 1963, held right after the conclusion of the Test Ban Treaty between the United States and the Soviet Union, most of the delegates probably agreed with Paul-Henri Spaak of Belgium. Spaak, who had been a Left socialist before World War II and the secretary general of NATO after it, was thus a living paradigm of what had happened to the movement. During the Cold War, he said at Amsterdam, we had to forget about socialism and do what was necessary for the defense of the West. But now that Kennedy and Khrushchev are inaugurating the era of détente, we can finally go back to our basic convictions.

The problem was that by the time this change of heart occurred no one cared. The Socialist International, said the Leftist wits of the fifties, was only a "drawer in the desk" of a British Labour Party leader. At that Amsterdam congress, the first I attended (representing the Socialist Party of the United States, the historic party of Eugene Victor Debs and Norman Thomas), there were convivial dinners and even dynamic speeches by rising socialist politicians such as Harold Wilson and Willy Brandt. But Wilson and Brandt were joined on the stage by Guy Mollet, the French leader who had led his party against the Algerian struggle for independence and eventually into oblivion. The mood was one of *Gemütlichkeit* and irrelevance.

Since the organizers of the 1969 congress in England had to telex to London to get the words of "The Internationale" for the open plenary, they were probably unaware that we were meeting in Eastbourne at the place where Friedrich Engels's ashes had been scattered in the sea, an ominous precedent for a half-dead organization. There was much British banquet etiquette—at one luncheon, when the resplendent toastmaster gave us "the Queen," a left-wing Labour MP muttered, "to Winstanley," and at least a few of us drank to the memory of the most radical general in the Revolution of 1640. But I did witness the outbreak of a dispute over the Middle East, which was to become perennial when the International became a serious organization. George Brown, the truculent, hard-drinking Labourite who was then foreign secretary (he later quit the party), had invited all the ambassadors in London to observe the congress. The Egyptians showed up with a representative of their Socialist Union and asked that he be made a fraternal delegate, a move vociferously opposed by the Israeli Labor Party. The first thing I heard when I arrived was Brown bellowing, in the presence of the press and anyone else who wanted to listen, about how he didn't understand what "the Jews" wanted.

In retrospect, the 1969 congress was not the charming anachronism it seemed. Willy Brandt, the impressive leader of the German party, gave a serious speech on détente, which was not well received by the British. Actually, Brandt's success with this policy led him to the Chancellorship of the Federal Republic of Germany and, in 1972, to the greatest socialist electoral victory in his party's history. But then, in 1974, Brandt was the victim of an espionage scandal and had to resign. At that point he turned to Bruno Kreisky and Olof Palme—both Brandt and Kreisky had spent part of their anti-Fascist exile in Sweden, and Brandt still speaks "inter-Scandinavian" to his Nordic comrades—and decided to apply his enormous energies and talents to the reconstruction of the International.

With the support of Kreisky and Palme, Brandt got the major European leaders to take the International seriously and even to promise to attend its meetings in person. The revived organization, he insisted, must become relevant to the Third World and pursue an independent policy of peace and disarmament. Those were the central themes of Brandt's speech at the congress of the International in Geneva in 1976 when he was elected president, and they were to be implemented in ways that caught the attention of the superpowers as well as the liberation movements. That address was, in its own way, a Socialist Manifesto for the last quarter of the twentieth century, and it was to have global implications. It was my good fortune to become an active participant in the International's work at precisely that historic moment.

II

At first glance, the admission of the Democratic Socialist Organizing Committee (DSOC) to the International in 1976 was a preposterous event. Why were the Prime Minister of Sweden, the Chancellor of Austria, the future President of France, and the director of the European Common Market involved in a dispute over whether the United States, with no effective socialist movement, should have two affiliates?

As Chapter 2 recounted, the split in the Socialist party that led to the formation of DSOC refracted significant differences in the mass democratic Left in the United States, which was why the *Wall Street Journal* took it seriously. More to the point of this chapter, those differences, focused on Vietnam, were primarily over international politics. That was, and is, why the involvement of marginal American socialist organizations in the work of the SI was relevant to the struggle of much larger and more serious political tendencies.

When we founded DSOC in 1973, I had no illusions about the International. My participation in the Amsterdam congress of 1963 and the Eastbourne congress of 1969 had made it plain to me that the organization was in its dotage. Even so, we unanimously voted to seek affiliation to it. My contacts with the SI had convinced me that, even in its decadence, it gave us a chance to relate to mass socialist forces and to bask in their reflected glory in the United States. That, I reasoned—quite rightly, it turned out—would help us build our own movement.

The prowar faction in the Socialist party, now called Social Democrats, USA (the SDs), was to make a signal contribution to neo-conservative foreign policy during the seventies. Most, but not all, of the SDs tended to regard me with all of the political affection that Stalin lavished on Trotsky. I was accused of being an egotistical splitter who had gone soft on Communism and turned his back on the very right of the state of Israel to exist. These charges were fanciful, but they were repeated with the passion that marks all sectarian battles. Years later, a trade unionist, who had simply endorsed a dinner we were giving in honor of one of his friends, told me that as a result he was the target of outraged phone calls and had received a huge mimeographed catalogue of my sins.

The SDs had a majority in the split and therefore retained the affiliation with the Socialist International. As a result, for three years I had to carry out a campaign to get us accepted in that organization. Most of the SI parties abominated the SDs' position on Vietnam; that fact, plus my personal relations with Palme and others, got us the enthusiastic support of the Swedish Social Democrats. Fairly early on, the British and the Dutch rallied to our cause. But we were up against one of the oldest and deepest traditions of the European social democracy: that one backs the existing franchise holder in any dispute, even if you disagree with them in a most serious way, because it is wrong to intervene in the internal affairs of other nations. Were it not for the extreme unpopularity of the SDs, we would not have had a ghost of a chance to become members of the SI.

I lobbied everyone I could find. In 1974, when Mario Soares made his first visit to the United States, I had a long, friendly talk with him—in French—in his New York hotel. In 1975, my friend Peter Jankowitsch, then the Austrian ambassador to the UN (and later his country's foreign minister), gave a reception for Bruno Kreisky, the Austrian Chancellor. Peter supported our cause and carefully introduced me to Kreisky. I was not accustomed to speaking to heads of state, particularly about matters of less than world-historic importance, and stood there rather awkwardly. But Gunnar Myrdal, a friend of mine who had known Kreisky during his Swedish exile, immediately came up, slapped the Chancellor on the back and said, "Bruno, let Mike and his friends into the International!" Kreisky agreed to back us.

In 1976, François Mitterrand, the new leader of French Socialism, came to this country. I had followed the French Left ever since I had lived in that country in 1963 and, as a columnist for the *New York Herald-Tribune*, had supported Mitterrand's presidential candidacy in 1965. I met him in Washington when he appeared at the National Press Club, and the fact that I was the only American there who spoke French gave me a chance to talk with him at length. On that same trip I saw him again in New York. The French consul was giving a dinner for Mitterrand, and he arrived with a twinkle in his eyes and the news that *"J'ai porté votre badge à NYU"*—that he had worn a DSOC button I had given him when he had spoken at New York University.

That was only one occasion among many when I glimpsed an aspect of Mitterrand's personality utterly at odds with his image as a kind of Charles de Gaulle—or Louis XIV—of the Left. He is indeed a very private person, yet there is playfulness in the man, a little boy hiding behind the immensely serious President. That evening my wife and I were seated at a small table with Mitterrand, the Nobel Laureate Wassily Leontief, and a member of the *New York Times* editorial board. We rated this august position essentially because we spoke French. This was during the period of the Union of the Left when Mitterrand, in alliance with the Communists, was trying to become Prime Minister.

What, I asked him, would happen if he did win a legislative

majority? Would Giscard, as President, share power with him? He will have to, I was told—which turned out to be a prediction of the "cohabitation" between President Mitterrand and Prime Minister Chirac in 1986. Meanwhile, the man from the *New York Times*, apparently utterly oblivious of Mitterrand's life-long anti-Communism or indeed of the fact that the French Socialists were in the process of completely subverting the Communists, asked over and over about what he would do with them if he became Prime Minister.

Mitterrand would launch into a discussion about economic policy and be asked if he was going to make a Communist minister of the interior. Finally he turned to me in quiet exasperation and said, sotto voce, "Doesn't this man care about *anything* but Communism?" After Mitterrand went back to France, I wrote him and asked his support in our campaign for affiliation with the International, and he agreed. But his party's International secretary, Robert Pontillon, an old Molletist who, I think, believed in the slander that I was anti-Israel, remained hostile to us. And he was the French Socialist who participated on the committees we had to win.

My three years of importuning major political leaders about the fate of a tiny American socialist organization reached a climax in Geneva in the fall of 1976. Jack Clark, the young activist who had taken the impossible job of director of DSOC, and I haunted the hotel where the congress delegates stayed. My old friend Bayard Rustin, now the chair of the SDs, assured me that he did not want to block our membership. If Bayard did not, his comrades who were calling the signals were moving heaven and earth to keep us out. Jack and I talked to everyone we could find, and I spent about half an hour speaking broken German to a man I thought was a member of the SPD delegation and who turned out to be a detective assigned to guard a cabinet minister!

Jack and I stayed at the house of Dan and Liz Gallin in Geneva. Dan and Liz and I had been members of a tiny Left socialist organization in the early fifties, and Dan, a refugee from Romania with only a League of Nations travel document, was expelled from the United States for taking part in our campaign against the Korean War. Now he was the director of the Food and Tobacco Workers' international union secretariat in Geneva, and Liz had worked for years for various religious organizations. Both were extremely knowledgeable about European socialism and international organizations. We spent a couple of evenings sitting around the kitchen table trying to figure out what I should do if I managed to get five minutes to speak at the Bureau of the International, the committee that would recommend action on our application to the congress. What, we asked ourselves, are the arguments that would persuade a group of skeptical social democratic functionaries that they should take the issue seriously and accredit two socialist organizations in a country without a real socialist movement?

We decided upon the truth. I should admit freely that we didn't amount to much—and then point out that our application was supported by several of the most progressive unions, by major black leaders, and by Democratic officeholders. I should even concede that the SDs on their side had their union supporters—including George Meany—and a certain influence in the Scoop Jackson wing of the Democratic party. They should take us seriously, I was to say, because we represented not simply our small membership but a political tendency of the mainstream American Left. And they should admit us into the International for the same reason.

The day before the critical meeting, I had a long and very friendly lunch with David Lewis, the leader of the Canadian affiliate, the New Democratic party. He had spoken at the founding convention of DSOC even though the SDs had used all of their influence, particularly in the Canadian Jewish community, to get him to cancel. Not surprisingly, he was sympathetic when I had lunch with him in Geneva. And when I was allowed into the Bureau, Sico Mansholt, the Common Market leader whom I had met and lobbied through Nat Weinberg, the chief economist of the Auto Workers, was in the chair. But before our point came up on the agenda, someone proposed that no more applications be considered and the motion passed. The representatives of applicant organizations would, however, be allowed to make their statements.

I got the floor and gave my five-minute speech in which every word had been chosen and honed for precisely this audience. Then David Lewis asked me if I would accept DSOC's admission as a consultative, rather than a full-member, party. My heart missed a beat, since that outcome was now beyond my wildest hopes. With as much calm as I could muster, and a show of conciliatory generosity, I said, yes, that would be acceptable. Lewis made a motion to that effect—a lot of people were not paying attention—Mansholt called for a vote, and no one objected. "Congratulations, Michael, we have voted to accept DSOC as a consultative member."

About five minutes later Robert Pontillon realized what had happened. He took the floor on a point of order and pointed out to Mansholt that the motion admitting us was illegal, given the prior procedure against recommending any more applications. "You are quite right, comrade," Mansholt said, "and had you raised your point at the proper time I would have ruled in your favor. But you did not and the motion stands."

There was one last hurdle. The next day when the Bureau's recommendation came before the congress, the SDs asked for the floor to speak against it. While they were talking I raced up to the presiding desk and asked Bernt Carlsson if I could get the floor to reply. Mitterrand was in the chair and, in what seemed to me an almost impish mood, announced that "Michael Harrington has asked to speak. Even though there are some of us who are sympathetic to his cause, I cannot allow him to do so since he has no standing in this congress. I will, then, put the question."

The little boy who hides inside his presidential personality now joined with the sophisticated parliamentary tactician of the Fourth Republic: "All those who want to sustain the unanimous decision of the Bureau will vote yes. All those who want to overturn the unanimous decision of the Bureau will vote no." Put in that way at a European socialist gathering, the outcome was not in doubt for a moment. We were accepted.

III

Brandt's remarkable *tour d'horizon* at Geneva, his insistence that socialism break out of the European ghetto, was taken seriously with uncharacteristic international socialist speed. That the change first manifested itself in the Caribbean convinced the U.S. State Department that the Old Boys' Association of European socialists had turned into a serious organization. And it was in this region that the socialists began to experience some of the ambiguities of their commitment to the wretched of the earth.

One of the first interventions of the new, Brandt-led International took place in 1978 when the candidate of the Dominican Revolutionary Party (PRD) won the presidential election. For a time it was not at all clear if the defeated government, led by Juan Balaguer, who had come to power on American bayonets in the mid-sixties, would turn over power to the victorious opposition. The SI and its member parties engaged in an intense behind-the-scenes effort to convince the American government to urge Balaguer to go. There were, of course, other political forces outside of the International with the same point of view, including important people within the Carter administration itself. Still, the moment marked a shift toward SI involvement in the Third World.

Even before Brandt took over the International, the European socialists had helped Mario Soares and his movement in Portugal at a time when Henry Kissinger, in a Spenglerian mood, was widely reported to have concluded that the Portuguese Stalinists would be victorious. Years later, Brandt reminisced that he had privately told the Soviets at the time that their people taking over a country so distant from the Eastern bloc would simply not work. And the German, Swedish, and other socialists also managed to get some very tangible material support into Portugal to help Soares and his comrades. But then, in the good old—primarily anti-Communist—days of the International it probably would have behaved in a similar fashion. A European country was at stake, and the Portuguese Communists were the most slavishly pro-Moscow party left in the Old World.

But in moving on the Dominican issue, the International was taking sides with a movement that had emerged in opposition to an American intervention in the name of anti-Communism. José Francisco Pena, the leader of the PRD, is not only an incredibly charismatic and handsome black leader; he is also a man for whom the revolutionary concepts and language of the Spanish-speaking Americas are second nature. I once heard him turn a rather routine resolution into a call to the barricades simply by the way in which he read it. And even though the effort to aid Pena and his comrades was brief and diplomatic, it was not at all socially democratic in the classic European sense. Something new was happening.

That new departure was even more in evidence at an SI meeting in Hamburg in 1978. I had gone there to push for full membership for DSOC (successfully) when I met Michael Manley, then the Prime Minister of Jamaica, a man who has increasingly played a critical role within the International as an advocate for the Third World.

Manley is an extraordinary person in every sense of the word. He is handsome, relaxed, and extremely gentle and soft-spoken in private conversation. Yet in his public persona at mass meetings of the People's National Party in Jamaica he is called Joshua and speaks like a prophet of old in a setting of reggae music, turbulent emotions, and the sweet smell of "ganja" (a potent form of marijuana often smoked in cigarettes the size of a cigar).

When I first met him in 1978, and later when he entertained a junket I led to Kingston in 1979, his government was sorely beset by economic problems. The Carter administration had in its early days been somewhat sympathetic—Andy Young, the UN ambassador, knew and admired Manley—but as time went on and Zbigniew Brzezinski's *realpolitik* became more important, Manley had come to feel that the American Right was actively trying to destabilize Jamaica. I had met with Manley's archrival, Edward Seaga, on that 1979 trip—the appointment had been arranged by Manley's staff—and Seaga had tried to convince me that he was a social democrat in the European sense. But the politics he outlined to me involved total subordination of the Jamaican economy to the United States.

When Seaga came to power in 1980, the political violence that had racked the island suddenly stopped and the new Prime Minister was not only Reagan's very first international guest but also received an enormous amount of aid from the United States (though it did not allow him to deal with his country's problems, and he is, at this writing, likely to be soon replaced by . . . Michael Manley). The abrupt end to the shooting on Jamaica, and the rapid and generous support to Seaga from Reagan, made Manley's fears of conscious destabilization from Washington quite substantial. They also related to his strategy within the SI after he lost power. At SI meetings in the early eighties, Manley effectively argued that European socialist talk about the Third World was cheap, but that actual solidarity from Western socialist governments with their socialist comrades in the developing countries had not been taken with any great seriousness.

At the same time, Manley understood that for practical as well as ideological reasons, there was little hope for democratic socialist regimes in the Third World getting assistance from Moscow and its bloc. When I was in Jamaica in 1979 toward the end of his government, there was a kind of gallows humor among his supporters about the Soviet Union. They jokingly fantasized encounters with the Soviets in which they offered them a second island in the Caribbean in return for massive aid. The Russians recoiled in horror, citing the enormous cost of their support of Fidel Castro in Cuba. But if both of the superpowers were off base for a democratic socialist government in the Third World, where should it turn?

Manley's answer: to the parties of the SI in power or positions of influence in Europe. And he lobbied boldly and effectively—with the help of the Dutch Socialist economist Jan Pronk and the British Labourite Stuart Holland—to commit the International to an action program in support of the democratic Left in the developing countries. That perspective has its obvious limits: when Mitterrand came to power in 1981, he made a kind of global Keynesianism a central element in his program. But those excellent intentions did not survive the first rude shocks to his plans in late 1981 and 1982. International solidarity was thus one of the first casualties of the structural economic problems of the French Socialists.

Yet Manley's vision, which was in basic agreement with the central thrust of the programs of both Willy Brandt and Olof Palme, might still have its relevance. If, as I think, the Left returns to power in a number of European countries in the late eighties and early nineties, and if the economic crisis so visible in the deep recession of 1981–1982 returns, it could well be that a proposal for international reflation might turn into very practical politics in the advanced societies. For the Brandt-Palme—and Manley—perspective links jobs and growth in the North to a massive commitment to justice in the South.

Manley was the most effective Third World leader to have seen that their International, for all of its limitations, might be relevant to global issues in a very practical way. But he was by no means the only one. Shortly before he was murdered at the 1983 congress of the International in Portugal, the moderate Palestinian, Issam Sartawi, said that the International had become one of the few places where the representatives of the world's poor could present their cause. Indeed, by the time of the International's congress in Vancouver in 1978—the first time such a meeting was held in North America—the SI had begun to become the target for the lobbying efforts of practically every revolutionary movement in the Third World, the Sandinistas among them. They had been receiving some support from the Venezuelans, then under the presidency of Carlos Andreas Perez, the leader of Acción Democratica, a member party of the International.

By the time the International's next congress convened in Madrid in 1980, the Sandinistas were in power. They sent an impressive delegation, which included their foreign minister, Miguel D'Escoto, a Maryknoll priest who had grown up in the United

States. It was a sign of the times that the congress set up a "Committee to Defend the Nicaraguan Revolution," under the leadership of Felipe Gonzalez, and with almost all of the major leaders as members. To my puzzled delight, D'Escoto specifically requested that I be on the committee.

It was this kind of activity that began to catch the attention of the State Department (the Madrid congress took place after Reagan's election but before his inauguration). Yet Washington obviously failed to understand what was really going on, then and now. All it knew was that the International was lining up with the Sandinistas who, even in the waning days of the Carter administration, were beginning to be seen as Soviet agents in the hemisphere. The truth was, as it usually is, much more complicated.

At Madrid I took the floor very briefly (when I sat down after talking for less than five minutes, Felipe Gonzalez told me that my example should be made mandatory). I urged the delegates to take a strong stand against American intervention in Central America. Brandt, and the other key leaders, did not disagree. But they wanted the motion carefully worded in order to leave open the possibility of friendly negotiations with the United States on the issue.

There was a broader truth behind that attitude. Brandt and the other Europeans had come to leadership in their various national movements during the Cold War, when relations between the socialists and Communists were at their most bitter. Brandt, after all, had been deputy mayor of Berlin at the time of the East German general strike of 1953. At a meeting in Vienna in 1985, one of his close colleagues, Egon Bahr, had, during a discussion of terrorism and the Middle East, remembered the horrified anger that the socialists felt when the Wall first went up and they had had to stand by helplessly while the East German guards killed those whose only crime was the desire to flee a Communist dictatorship.

These men, even when they criticized the United States most harshly, thought of themselves as part of the West. When, for example, at a meeting in Botswana in 1986, the SI endorsed the struggle of the African National Congress, everyone present was perfectly aware of the influential presence of Communists in the

ANC. Brandt commented, somewhat ruefully, that he thought the socialists did know a thing or two about Communism. Given that they had routed the Communists in every country in Europe except Italy—and there the Communist party had become a democratic socialist party—he was quite right.

The Madrid congress voted to help the Sandinistas, but sought to do so in a way that would leave relations with the United States open. In the midst of all this politicking there was also a moment of high emotion.

The Spain where we met had only recently emerged from the shadows of Franco's victory; not too long after we left, a group of army officers had seized the Cortes at gunpoint. But the Socialist Workers Party (PSOE) of Felipe Gonzalez had become *the* party of Spanish socialism, in considerable measure because of the support it had received from the International, starting in 1974. Gonzalez's electoral triumph was in the future, yet we all knew that Spanish socialism was in the process of making a miraculous comeback. So there was a sense of festivity when we met for a ceremonial occasion as the guest of the Socialist mayor, Tierno Galvan (whose Popular Socialist Party had united with the PSOE in 1978). When Brandt replied, in the name of the International, to Tierno Galvan's greetings, my broken German was sufficient for me to understand the feeling of high emotion in that room. The Spanish Civil War had been a decisive tragedy of the thirties, a triumph of fascism over republicanism and socialism, the rehearsal for the Nazi victories of 1940 and 1941. Brandt himself had been in Spain in that period as an exile and anti-Fascist journalist. When he spoke, the emotion that he, and all of us, felt almost overwhelmed him as he tried to explain what it meant for the International to be meeting in Madrid. In Madrid!

The experience was particularly moving and ironic for me. As a child in the thirties, I had rejoiced when the priest at Saint Rose's Church announced that the forces of Christ—Franco—had won a great triumph over the atheists who killed priests and nuns and menaced the Christian West. As a young radical in New York in the fifties, I expiated that sin as executive secretary of the Committee to Defend Franco's Labor Victims and organized solidarity demonstrations for the workers of Barcelona when they went out on strike. Like almost everyone of my generation of the Left, I knew and loved the songs of the International Brigade, and so powerful was my identification with the Spanish anti-Fascists that I responded to them even though I knew of the dark truths about the Communists in Spain that Orwell had described.

"Madrid, your tears of sorrow" I had sung on a hundred beery and sentimental occasions. And now, in Madrid's Retiro Park, there was even an exhibit on the Civil War, with Socialist, Communist, Anarchist, as well as Fascist, flags and a videotape of, among many other things, the last parade of the International Brigade in Barcelona. I cried as I watched it.

I V

As a result of the events at the Madrid congress, I went to Managua in June 1981 as part of a mission of the Committee to Defend the Nicaraguan Revolution. Felipe Gonzalez and Carlos Andreas Perez were the most prominent leaders present, but we also brought an international secretary of the French Socialist party and the reflected glory of François Mitterrand's presidential triumph six weeks before.

I had first met Felipe in the mid-seventies when he came to the United States as the guest of the United Automobile Workers. The UAW had asked me to take over his schedule for one night in New York, and to vary the deadly routine which is so often a feature of such junkets, I took him and a few friends to Rocco's, my favorite restaurant in Greenwich Village (to this day, the older waiters remember that the man who became Prime Minister of Spain dined at the table in the front room by the bar).

Felipe was unassuming, boyish-looking, another one of those leaders whose offstage manner is in stark contrast to his charisma at a rally. The occasion was somewhat stiff, yet I was impressed that this very important leader spoke to me—we talked in French since he did not know English—in the second person singular. But then, that is the rule for socialists in all of those languages that distinguish between the familial and formal "you." Socialists relate to one another as "comrades," not as "Mister," and they are like the members of a family. (In its most radical moments, the French Revolution had simply abolished the *vous* form.)

By the time of the Managua trip, I had gotten to know Felipe much better. I arrived late, in part because an error on my part had led to my being detained by troops at the airport. I felt, and not for the last time, the precariousness of life in a revolutionary society in which peasants, who had never heard of, much less read, my books covered me with automatic weapons.

Strangely, the first Sandinista I had met was the legendary Commandante Zero, Edén Pastora, later to become a leader of an armed, anti-Sandinista insurgency in Costa Rica. That was at an SI meeting in Lisbon in 1979, several months after the Sandinistas had come to power. There was a packed meeting in a sports arena, and the enthusiastic band thundered out "The Internationale" when we filed in. Pastora was wearing his guerrilla fatigues. I didn't get everything he said, but identification with an actual living revolution was a heady enough experience for me.

The SI delegation in Managua was anything but romantic. We had a closed meeting for about three hours with the political committee of the Sandinistas, the Ortega brothers, and Jaime Wheelock. Each of them carefully unstrapped his side arm and put it on the table as we talked. Many things were said, but one theme predominated: every socialist present pressed again and again for free elections. Indeed, the basic SI formula for Nicaragua—mixed economy, political pluralism, nonalignment, and democratic rights— was repeated so often that I wondered if we couldn't refer to it by a number and save our breath. The Sandinistas agreed, but seemingly did not want to be committed to a specific date for the elections.

Carlos Andreas, who had a certain standing in Nicaragua because of his support to the anti-Somoza movement before it won, made an ostentatious visit to Mrs. Chamorro, the widow of the editor of *La Prensa*, whose assassination had triggered Somoza's downfall. She had broken with the Sandinistas quite early. I had no trouble buying that paper and wrote in the *New York Times* when I returned that any society in which you can easily get a publication that accuses the ruling regime of being totalitarian is, by that fact alone, not totalitarian.

There were also some very human moments on the trip; they are the experiences that make dispassionate political analysis difficult, if not impossible. The young Salvadoran woman with whom we talked in the coffee shop, Ann Maria, was quite attractive, and it was hard to believe that she had just come from the guerrilla struggle in her own country. The Sandinista who ran León, the country's second largest city, was also a woman, the daughter of a fairly high-ranking Somoza official (that was common among the revolutionary leaders, since almost anyone who had been able to get an education under the dictatorship, and thereby gain access to radical theory, had been a child of its ruling class).

We ate fish in a charming little restaurant in León; the only thing unusual was that armed guards flanked our table. Later, when we were taken to a battlefield near León, the mayor showed us a tiger cage—a deep hole in the ground with practically no room for a person to move about, open to the weather and covered only by bars at the top. She herself had been confined for over a year in such a cage. When her father learned that she had been captured, he said, according to her: "I have no daughter." When he himself was taken prisoner during the Sandinista victory, she saved him from the possibility of execution.

Walking around that battlefield, we were carefully shown shell casings with Israeli markings, a fact that was constantly cited in debates over the Middle East in the International. (When I visited Israel in 1983, I told my comrades this story, as part of my appeal to end their country's arms traffic with rightist nations like South Africa—and many of them agreed with me.) Riding back to Managua, I discovered that our Sandinista guides, like so many other revolutionaries, had begun their political activity as Catholic youth activists. It was, of course, impossible not to be sympathetic to such people. Yet I had to remind myself of how often "revolutionary tourists" had been seduced by those they had casually—and not always accidentally—met in the Soviet Russia of the twenties and thirties or Mao's China of the fifties and sixties. The naked eye, alas, can never "see" a society.

Our SI delegation in Managua was concerned about democracy and freedom in that country in 1981 and made its position quite clear in the meeting with the Sandinista Political Committee. For the U.S. State Department under Ronald Reagan, such subtleties did not exist. The contrast with the Soviets is quite instructive.

Most of this period was, of course, dominated by Brezhnev's closing years and then by the reigns of his two short-lived successors. That is, we were dealing with Soviet diplomacy at its most unimaginative, even paralyzed, stage. And yet, if the Russian delegation I watched descend the staircase at a palace in Vienna during an SI peace conference in 1985 all but marched in hierarchal lockstep, they were at least always at pains to be "correct." Kalevi Sorsa, later to become Prime Minister of Finland, was practically snubbed when he led a delegation to Washington early in the Reagan administration. The Soviets had welcomed the same group to Moscow as significant political leaders.

At that peace conference in 1985, the American behavior had been surly, contemptuous. The Soviets, Chinese, the United Nations, the Yugoslavs, and the Non-Aligned were all there on time. Kenneth Adelman, the American representative, arrived almost a day late, ostentatiously talked with a subordinate rather than listen to the discussions, and when he did get the floor acted in an insulting way. He commented, for instance, that Neil Kinnock, who had given a conciliatory and very reasonable speech as the leader of the opposition in a NATO country, didn't know what he was talking about. Adelman left hurriedly, and all I could do was to shout at someone from the embassy that I had expected the administration to send a reactionary to Vienna but that, as an American, I was ashamed that he was also an oaf. I apparently disturbed the embassy official enough so that he asked a number of the leaders present what they thought of Adelman's performance. My friend Don Grimes, a minister in the Australian Labour government, told him that had Adelman been his subordinate, he would have fired him for his conduct.

That performance was, however, of a piece with the policy of an administration that tended to see every issue in a polemical, East-West context and thus to view events in Nicaragua and Salvador as a Soviet- or Cuban-inspired plot. Ironically, one of the enthusiastic architects of this approach was Carl Gershman who, as executive director of Social Democrats, USA, had attended SI meetings as a voting member.

In 1981 Gershman had become a member of Jeane Kirkpatrick's staff at the United Nations. That was not surprising, since a good number of the "neo-conservatives" in the United States—Irving Kristol and Nathan Glazer among them—had come from socialist backgrounds. But when Gershman and others (including Norman Podhoretz, a lapsed liberal who had been part of the antiwar movement) became out-and-out Reaganites, that was something of a shock. By 1982 to 1983, Gershman had turned into such a trusted Cold Warrior that he was loaned to the State Department and sent to Europe to lobby his former comrades of the SI on Central American issues. Without, it should be added, much effect.

Were Gershman and the neo-conservatives simply hysterically wrong in their fears of what might happen in Nicaragua? I always felt that there were indeed "Marxist-Leninists" in that country, people who wanted to follow Fidel's example and shoot, jail, or exile the opposition. (I put "Marxist-Leninist" in quotes because that label is now routinely used in the Third World by any revolutionary who wants an excuse to establish a one-party state and has little ideological, much less intellectual, content.) I was aware in 1981 that there were important tendencies in the Sandinista revolution moving in that direction—and important tendencies opposed to it.

I thought then—and think to this day—that the United States acted as the recruiting sergeant for the "Marxist-Leninists," i.e., its policies provided proof that the simple-minded theories of American imperialism espoused by the "hards" were true. One is told that the Sandinistas' voting against the condemnation of the Soviet invasion of Afghanistan in the United Nations in 1980 is proof that they were Soviet agents from the very first. That is utterly simplistic.

The Soviet Union had not sponsored armed interventions in Nicaragua six times in forty years, nor had it supported the Somoza family until the very last minute of its despotic rule. Washington, of course, had. That a youthful leadership, fresh from an armed struggle against American-backed fascists—and a Latin American leadership from a region in which "Marxism-Leninism" is a cliché—would behave in such a fashion should not come as a surprise, and most certainly does not prove that a country has joined the Soviet bloc. There was indeed a deep and visceral anti-Americanism in the Sandinistas' Nicaragua. How in the name of heaven could it have been otherwise?

But the proper American policy was to have ignored all of the understandable hostility toward Washington and to seek to neutralize our own shameful history in this area by being friendly to those who didn't like us for very good reasons. I put the thought politically since I think that such an approach would have maximized the legitimate national security interests of the United States in the region. But I confess that there are theological echoes of my youth in my attitude: that sinners, like the United States of America, should prove their genuine repentance by making amends.

That 1981 trip of the Committee to Defend the Nicaraguan Revolution probably was the high-water mark of the SI's identification with the Sandinista Revolution. In the years that followed, however, the International remained resolutely opposed to American military action in the region, even if there was increasing criticism of repressive measures taken by Managua. At the Bureau meeting in Rio in the fall of 1984—itself a sign of the growing importance of socialists in Latin America and the Caribbean—the International came close to pulling off a political coup.

The governor of Rio province under the restored democratic system, Lionel Brizola, the leader of the Brazilian Labor Party, was our host. We found ourselves in one of the most breathtaking cities in the world, convening in a luxury hotel on a Copacabana beach thronged with swimmers, prostitutes, and petty criminals. Yet we were no more than twenty minutes away from the intolerable poverty of an urban slum. When I arrived I heard that there was talk that Arturo Cruz, the anti-Sandinista leader who was considering running in the upcoming Nicaraguan elections, had been invited to attend by Carlos Andreas Perez. I prepared for a bitter fight over whether Cruz would be granted official status, on the model of the traditional battle over the representatives of the Palestine Liberation Organization.

The dispute never took place. Soon after we arrived, Cruz and Bayardo Arce, the Sandinista observer, began to meet with Carlos Andreas to discuss a possible compromise that would guarantee Cruz's participation in the elections. Hans-Jürgen Wischnewski, a powerful figure in the German SPD, had played a crucial role in setting up this discussion, and my friend Thorwald Stoltenberg (now the foreign minister of Norway) was an important observer at the meetings. When the negotiations finally broke down, Carlos Andreas read a statement to the Bureau that Arce had approved on behalf of the Sandinistas. It included postponing the election—a Cruz demand to allow more time for campaigning—and extremely generous guarantees for the rights of the anti-Sandinistas (radio and television time, the free circulation of literature, including literature imported from abroad, etc.).

At the last moment, Arce had indicated that he was ready to sign on the spot, but Cruz demanded three days so that he could clear the arrangements with his colleagues. And that broke up the discussions.

I felt that the last thing the Reagan administration wanted was a Cruz "ticket" in the Nicaraguan elections. Since almost everyone conceded that the Sandinistas would win in a fair count, their prestige and legitimacy would be greatly enhanced if they had prevailed over the strongest opposition. Indeed, had that happened, it would have made it extremely difficult for the United States to continue working to overthrow a government whose claim to electoral rectitude would be considerably greater than that of Duarte in Salvador. (Duarte won on a ballot that effectively excluded a significant percentage of the population that supports the guerrillas.)

I therefore assumed that however decent and sincere Cruz might be, the influential presence of the CIA among his colleagues meant he would not be allowed to agree to any formula for fair elections—because Washington did not want fair elections. In late 1987, Cruz, who had by then broken with the Contras, gave an interview to the *New York Times* in which he confirmed my guess and regretted his failure to make the deal offered in Rio, saying that he had been under heavy pressure from Washington to act as he did.

The New Jewel Movement of Grenada was another departure for the SI. It had become a part of the SI. I talked to Maurice Bishop and other New Jewel leaders and found them both charming and unmistakably representative of a sixties' Black Power point of view. That is hardly the typical ideology of the International, even in its most radical Third World parties. The French had been in charge of screening applications prior to the 1980 congress, and I was willing to vote for anything approved by Lionel Jospin, the French Socialist Party's first secretary, who was hardly soft on such issues.

It was not long after the New Jewel had become a part of the International that we began to learn of the political prisoners being held in Grenada. No one wanted to move to expel the Grenadians—that, in any case, is an extremely rare procedure in the International—so every effort was made to persuade them to move in a democratic and civil libertarian direction. At a meeting in Amsterdam in 1981 I was told by the representative of a rather moderate Caribbean Labor party that we could have more of an impact upon the internal situation in Grenada itself if they were members and we could pressure them privately.

In the fall of 1982, at a Bureau meeting in Basel, Michael Manley, who had been charged to talk to Bishop on a more or less official basis, reported that he had been assured that civil liberties would soon be introduced and that a constitution would be written. I had my last conversation with the New Jewel leaders at the SI congress in Portugal in 1983. I argued in favor of democratic rights, as I always did when I spoke with them, and we agreed, in a most friendly fashion, that I would try to visit Grenada as soon as possible. If they might have been bothered by my relentless insistence on civil liberties, they also knew that I was equally single-minded in my opposition to American intervention.

I later learned from the press that in the months prior to the American invasion of Grenada, Bishop had tried to come to an understanding with Washington. I have no way of knowing—perhaps history will never know—whether he was motivated in part by the SI pressure to move in a more democratic direction. But I did become convinced at that time that Reagan was appalled by the idea of civil liberties emerging in Grenada. The President had an absolute horror of truly democratic revolutions because they cannot be opposed on Cold War ideological grounds, or at least it is more difficult to do so.

My judgment is not in the least contradicted by the fact that Argentina, Brazil, Haiti, and the Philippines all moved toward democracy while Reagan was President. In each case, and particularly in Argentina and the Philippines, we appeased and applauded the dictators to the very last moment. Jeane Kirkpatrick had wanted Washington to support the Argentinian generals in the Falklands-Malvinas crisis, and our refusal to do so was not based on the abhorrence of fascism but on a *realpolitik* concern over Reagan's favorite ally, Margaret Thatcher. (In all fairness, it should be noted that the Soviets behaved about as shamelessly with the Argentinian torturers as did the United States.) When the CIA organized the Contras to fight for "democracy" in Nicaragua, it turned without embarrassment to Argentinian officers who had honed their military skills in "disappearing" innocent people.

In the case of the Philippines, Mr. Reagan judged the election results in the race between Marcos and Corazón Aquino with marvelous even-handedness—each side had engaged in irregularities, he said—until the people overthrew the government. Similarly, in Haiti the United States supported two generations of Duvaliers and discovered the merits of freedom only when the people in the streets were on the verge of victory. The fact was, as Jeane Kirkpatrick put it so well, American conservatives normally prefer stable dictatorships to unruly democracies because they are fearful that the latter will go Communist. Thus I am convinced that the President, or at least his sophisticated advisors, must have been deeply upset when they learned that Maurice Bishop was moving in a democratic direction.

One of the spoils of war in Grenada was the capture of some New Jewel documents indicating that a number of SI member parties from the region had met with the Sandinistas in Managua to plot concerted action in the Socialist International. The State Department saw to it that every major socialist party in Europe received a copy, and the whole question was an issue at a meeting of the International in Brussels in 1984. And Seaga in Jamaica, who had of course supported the American invasion, was delighted to use this information to try to discredit Michael Manley. No one doubted that something similar to the meeting described by the Grenadian might have taken place, but that it was the "Leninist" conspiracy the State Department tried to make it was not at all convincing.

I had liked Bishop as a person and I could understand why masses of people responded to him. When he was first arrested, over ten thousand people had mobilized on his behalf, even though his captors had disarmed the populace. And when he was killed, I felt that the blood was, at least in part, on Washington's hands: if Reagan had cooperated with Bishop's attempt to democratize his revolution, then his death would have never occurred. That was why, in Rio in 1984, I believed that my country was tragically working night and day to undermine the possibility of democracy in Nicaragua.

V

Two personal experiences might illuminate the ambiguities and contradictions faced by the International in its turn toward the Third World in general and Latin America and the Caribbean in particular.

Guillermo Ungo is the leader of the Democratic Revolutionary Front (FDR) of Salvador, the political organization linked to the guerrillas of the Farabundo Martí Liberation National movement (FMLN). Ungo, the son of a founder of the Christian Democratic party of Salvador and the leader of a small social democratic party, the Revolutionary National Movement, had been elected Vice President, as Duarte's running mate, in 1972, but the military would not allow either of them to take office. When the dictatorship was overthrown in 1979, Ungo was named a member of the new government. By 1980, appalled by the strength of the Right wing and its death squads in El Salvador, Ungo and others had gone into opposition and made a bloc with the five guerrilla movements that had previously taken up arms against the dictatorship.

Ungo's Revolutionary National Movement was a member party of the International. He himself is the most unlikely-looking revolutionary one can imagine. Relatively short and bespectacled, extremely mild-mannered, he looked more like a kindergarten teacher than the defender of an armed insurgency. In 1981 in New York I took him to Rocco's restaurant one night; the next night I went with my son Teddy to an American League playoff game between the Yankees and the Brewers. There on the top tier of Yankee Stadium I discovered Ungo and two comrades, containers of beer in hand, watching the game. I desperately wished that a photographer had been along to capture this image of these dangerous revolutionaries.

Isn't my point a condemnation of Guillermo? Isn't it true—as many in the State Department and elsewhere believe—that he is only allowed to play the role as spokesperson of the FDR because it suits the purposes of much tougher revolutionaries in the FMLN?

I put that question to him on that New York visit. I asked him if he were not afraid that he would be the very first casualty of the triumph of his own cause.

The thought had certainly occurred to him, he told me. And had the FMLN been able to win power through a decisive military victory, it would have been much more likely that such a negative scenario would play itself out. (Kindergarten teachers do not, I think, thus discuss their own assassinations in measured and analytic fashion.) But since the struggle had become much more protracted, since the best outcome would result from political negotiation, the movement in all of its wings would need his ties to the democratic Left of the world. And therefore he thought that he could realistically play a significant role in this very difficult process.

The other relevant personal experience occurred in November 1985. Democratic Socialists of America (DSA) was holding its national convention in Berkeley, and we had invited Miguel D'Escoto to speak at our major mass meeting. About a month before, the Sandinistas had adopted a series of repressive measures, many of them, it seemed to me and others opposed to American intervention, aimed at legitimate internal opposition, including the unions, rather than at the Contras.

Shortly before the convention, Barbara Ehrenreich, the cochair of DSA, phoned me. She was deeply disturbed about the developments in Managua, a fact all the more significant since she had been a leading New Leftist in the sixties and seventies, and that movement had often been relatively tolerant of violations of civil liberties in the Third World effected in the name of revolutionary justice. We agreed that we would raise the issue with D'Escoto in private *and* that Barbara would also refer to it publicly in her speech to the mass meeting. In a sense, we had already defined our attitude by inviting a Polish exile to speak on behalf of Solidarność and to share the stage with Miguel.

When I spent time with D'Escoto on the day of the rally, I told him and the Nicaraguan ambassador, Carlos Tunnermann, of our concerns. They defended the government's actions, of course, but it seemed to me they understood what I was saying and knew that it was not motivated by any reactionary attitude toward American intervention. There was a classic Berkeley fund-raiser before the big rally, and the mayor, Gus Newport, a Leftist who had worked with us on many causes, attacked all those who were critical of the new restrictions in Nicaragua. The American Left, he said, should simply defend the Nicaraguans against the immoral actions of our own government and avoid any criticisms.

There were about 2,500 people at the rally. It lasted too long, of course—there were trade union, minority, feminist, and anti-apartheid speakers (the last, Mpho Tutu, the Bishop's daughter, who was admirably brief), since all Left meetings in recent years have been carefully designed to fulfill the requirements of political affirmative action. Barbara spoke just before Miguel and, within a context of decisive and principled opposition to American intervention, she told of how upset we socialists were by what had happened in Managua. It was only a passage in her talk, but a distinct and unmistakable passage.

The point is, for DSA as for the Socialist International, the engagement with the Third World is fraught with moral and political ambiguities. On the one hand, one cannot, particularly when meeting in a comfortable hall or hotel, tell the wretched of the earth to behave as if the history of their own suffering did not exist, demanding that they emerge from an often violent struggle against centuries of oppression as if it were a moderating experience, as if people were still not starving. Desperation is not necessarily a good school for civil libertarians and parliamentary democrats. Or as Bertolt Brecht put it: "First stuff the face. Then comes morality."

Of course. But then neither can one adopt an attitude of revolutionary colonialism—and this is what many on the Left have done in our time—and assume that the people of the Third World must, because of their past, be treated for an entire historic epoch as if they were children, that the "adults"—the revolutionary, self-appointed "adults"—have to tutor them until they achieve that lordly level found in Europe or the Soviet Union (depending on your politics). That is, after all, nothing but a "Leninist" version of what the French colonialists used to call *la mission civilatrice*, the civilizing mission of those from superior cultures. Human rights are *human* rights, and as soon as you begin making exceptions, even for the noblest of reasons or out of respect for the most imperious of historical necessities, one is on the slippery slope that leads to the defense of "progressive" torture and repression.

All of us in the SI had made the dangerous moral decision to try to involve ourselves in this contradictory world. We failed regularly, of course. But, as these examples from our work in Latin America and the Caribbean show, perhaps we actually took some first tentative steps in the right direction.

Will the International Free the Human Race?

C'est la lutte finale
Groupons-nous et demain
L'Internationale
Sera le genre humain.

E ugene Pottier, a Communard who spent a period of exile in the United States, wrote the song "The Internationale" in 1871. Literally translated, the last two lines of the chorus, quoted above, read, "The International will be the human race."

For the Europeans, the International (*L'Internationale*) was the name of the International Workingmen's Association, the First International of 1864 (and of its successors in 1889, 1923, and 1951). For Pottier, and the idea had deep roots in the French syndicalist tradition, the workers' organization itself would eventually "be" the human race. The notion was not at all as authoritarian as it might now sound, since it referred to a movement primarily composed of nascent trade unions and implied that the "associated producers"—the workers in the factory banded together to make cooperative decisions—would provide the model for the integration of all humanity.

History, of course, dealt brutally with that hope. In the seventies and eighties of the twentieth century the unification of the human race looked infinitely more problematic than it had a hundred years before. One of the most trivial consequences of that change was the debate in the United States over Pottier's lyrics. You could tell a Leftist's politics from how he or she sang the chorus of "The Internationale." The Communists sang "The International Soviet shall be the human race." The anti-Communist–Leninists intoned, "The International party will be the human race."

The anarchists rejoiced that the International Union would represent humanity. In my anti-Stalinist, ex-Leninist, Marxist-youth organization, after much discussion we decided on a libertarian translation, both grammatically and in terms of content: "The international working class shall free the human race." The whole dispute might well seem preposterous but, as is so often the case, the debate over those words turned on conceptions of the very nature of socialism. In the name of democracy and pluralism, our rendition of the chorus rejected the identification of any one organization with the human race. But the ideal, we implied, was therefore even more rigorous than any of those that had gone before: a world that would be both one and diverse.

There were times in the seventies and the eighties when at meetings of the International I was in near despair that it or any conceivable organization could ever move toward any unification of humanity. It is a cliché that one of Karl Marx's most profound errors was his underestimation of nationalism. At Brussels in 1984, at a Bureau meeting of the SI, a little incident, both humorous and sad, illustrated this key fact.

The Australian Labour party had sent a young man to represent it, and he had clearly not been informed of the etiquette of an international consensus organization. When the issue of French nuclear testing in the Pacific came up, he firmly and straightforwardly said that the tests were wrong and colonialist to boot. He therefore proposed that we vote to condemn the actions of the French Socialist government. The French delegate was furious. Are we, he said, going to begin to sit in judgment of one another? Is it the International's business to assess the wisdom and socialist morality of the actions of its member parties? If that is indeed the case, the French Socialist continued with not a little passion, then the issue may begin with nuclear testing in the Pacific but it will not end there. I translate his thought freely and irreverently into English: there are skeletons in the closet of more than one party in the International, and if we begin to sit as some kind of a court, then the French are not the only ones who are going to be censured. He added, of course, a defense of his government's policy.

Practically no one in the International supported the French representative on the substantive issue. Someone even suggested that if nuclear testing were as safe as he claimed, then it could easily be moved to some island right off the French coast. But everyone knew, alas, that he was quite right on the question of how the International should act. For all of our profound agreement on socialist values, for all of our shared history, no national party would accept that foreigners, even foreign socialists, no matter how impeccable their credentials, should tell it what to do or not do.

The Socialist International of 1889 (the "Second" International) and its post–World War I successor, the Labor and Socialist International, had both insisted that their resolutions were binding, when in fact each nation went its own way. The original Communist International of 1919 was designed precisely to counter this petty bourgeois indiscipline and to create a centralized general staff of the world revolution. That led to a world movement that was forced to follow every twist and turn of Joseph Stalin's line, e.g., the German Communists obediently followed the dictates from Moscow, attacked the socialists (who, Stalin said, were fascists in Leftist disguise), and thereby objectively helped the Nazis to power. So when the Socialist International was reconstituted in 1951 at Frankfurt and then reborn at Geneva in 1976, it realistically became a consensus organization in which, in effect, all major parties had a veto over any decision.

That was wise. It meant of course that the official proceedings of the International were often contrived and dull, a matter of set speeches that carefully avoided the real disputes dividing the member parties. At the same time, the discussions in the restaurants and bars were often candid and even bitter. In Paris one night in 1981 a Swede who had had a glass of wine, or maybe ten, told a leading member of the Left wing of the French Socialist party that his government's foreign policy was dragging the ideals of socialism through the mud. And obviously, such private frankness did regularly have an impact on public policy, perhaps more so than a resolution. We had, after all, serious moral claims on one another, which was one more reason why a powerless American like me could have a certain impact.

The policy was wise—and sad. For if one believes, as I emphatically do, that powerful economic forces are even now carrying out the de facto unification of humanity, then unless there is a de jure integration, catastrophe awaits the world. But how is that integration to be carried out if democratic socialists, who despite all their differences have so much in common, cannot be open about their disputes within their own organization?

That issue is all the more ironic in the setting of the Socialist International since 1976, because the organization was dominated by two of the most principled internationalists of our times, Willy Brandt and Olof Palme. What follows, then, has to do with some of the contradictions and paradoxes of trying to free the human race.

I

Some of the most bitter fights within the International had to do with the Middle East.

In the immediate post–World War II years, there was almost a Left consensus in favor of the defense of Israel, the homeland and refuge of the victims of the Holocaust. Since I became a Socialist right after the anti-Fascist war and during the Jewish struggle for self-determination in Palestine, I was personally and emotionally very much a part of that consensus.

Ironically, it was Israel's tremendous victory in the Six-Day War in 1967 that played a major role in changing that attitude. At that point the Jewish state went from being David to being Goliath in the imagination of a good number of radicals. At the same time, the justified response to the unconscionable Vietnam War often led the New Left to an uncritical Third Worldism. If the Vietcong was the chosen instrument of national liberation in Vietnam, it was argued, the Palestine Liberation Organization (PLO) was the freedom movement of the Middle East. Israel, which supported the United States on so many foreign policy issues—including, alas, Vietnam—was, they concluded, the agency of American imperialism in the Middle East.

I was clearly hostile to this line of reasoning, even though I shared some of the specific objections to Israeli policy. The Palestinians, I thought, did have a right to national self-determination in the region; but so did the Jews. The solution was not a single "secular and democratic" state, which was the PLO code word for the destruction of the Jewish state of Israel, but a Jewish state *and* a Palestinian state. American imperialism, I insisted, did exist and was pro-Arab, which was why both the Pentagon and the State Department opposed Harry Truman's recognition of the new Jewish state. After all, what was the economic value of a tiny country without oil? The American imperialists would have to be plain stupid to see their main chance in allying themselves with it—and they had not been that stupid.

When the Democratic Socialist Organizing Committee was created in 1973, our principled defense of the right of Israel to exist marked us on the American Left as "right-wing." But times changed. Cuba had already turned into an orthodox Moscow ally when it supported the Soviet invasion of Czechoslovakia in 1968, an attack on a "EuroCommunist" regime. The horrors of Pol Pot and the dictatorship in Vietnam put an end to some of the romantic ideas about liberation movements. And a fair number of Jews within the New Left went through a personal transition and discovered their own ethnic and cultural identity. By 1982, when DSOC and the New American Movement united, there were still sensitivities and differences on the issue, but there was general agreement on a "two-state" approach.

When I finally went to Israel in 1983 as a guest of its two socialist parties (the Labour party and Mapam), I experienced a certain confirmation of our position. As the guest of the Labour party—and, as a leader of an affiliate of the SI, theoretically coequal to Shimon Peres—there was a dinner in my honor hosted by Peres in Jerusalem. The leadership of the party was present, and as the evening drew to a close Shimon asked Abba Eban to propose a toast to the guest of honor.

Eban proceeded to give a passionate, eloquent statement of the Zionist case for peace with the Palestinians. If, he said, we remain the rulers of predominantly Arab territories, if the majority of the people within Israel are Arabs, then what becomes of the Jewish state that is the Zionist ideal? It cannot exist under such circumstances. It is not in spite of my Zionism, Eban continued, but precisely because of it, of my commitment to a Jewish state, that I am for trading land for peace. For me the moment was deeply moving, a confirmation of my stubborn insistence that there were Israelis who shared my convictions.

But then, no one in the International—with the exception of Walid Jumblatt's Progressive Socialist party of Lebanon—was hostile to Israel either. After all, the Brandt generation was defined by the struggle against Nazi racism, and Brandt himself symbolized the fact that there had been Germans who had struggled against the horrors that had led to the Holocaust. The Israeli socialists had been members of the Labor and Socialist International after World War I, and they were founding members of the revived International at Frankfurt in 1951.

And yet, even before that shift in attitudes that occurred in a number of Western countries in the mid-sixties, the Israelis were in a special position in the International, for they were the only party from a country whose legitimacy, whose right to exist, was not accepted by part of the world. I remember being saddened in 1963 at the Amsterdam Congress (when I was totally unaware of the undercurrents within the International) at how the Israeli delegate, Moshe Sharett, spoke only on the Middle Eastern question. He was clearly a brilliant man and a thoughtful socialist, yet life in a nation under siege meant that in the midst of a discussion of the political implications of the Moscow Test Ban Treaty, there was only one issue for him: the survival of his homeland.

Ironically, it was the very progressive decision made by Brandt in 1976 to reach out to the Third World that made the Israeli issue much more controversial. If one was going to engage in dialogue with nationalist, as well as socialist, forces in Asia, Africa, and Latin America, how could one relate exclusively to a single, quite Western, enclave in the Middle East? To be sure, most of the "socialist" formations in that region had little or nothing to do with the ideas of democratic socialism (some of them could even be accused of reinventing a "national socialism"). But Brandt and his comrades had made the moral decision to talk to all of the dynamic nationalist forces in the Third World. That posed a vexing problem regarding the Middle East: what kind of a dialogue could the International have with groups that wanted to wipe out the homeland of one of its own member parties?

At the same time, there was genuine justice on the Palestinian side. That did not give it the right to drive the Israelis into the sea, which was clearly the real program of the PLO in the seventies. It was ironic that the Palestinians were widely regarded as the "Jews" of the Arab world—as better educated and more competent than others among their ethnic brothers and sisters—and that the living standards in the UN camps were sometimes higher than that of poor Arabs in various established nations. Still, there were compassionate instincts that made the Europeans respond to the claims of a Palestinian people who had been homeless for a generation. Both the Labour party and Mapam shared the critique of Menachem Begin's invasion of Lebanon made by many of the parties in the International. Even so, there were obvious differences on the issue within the organization.

Bruno Kreisky was at the center of this dispute. He talked to the PLO and urged the Israelis to negotiate with them. In 1979, Kreisky invited the participants at the International's Hamburg Bureau meeting to come to Vienna and discuss the Middle East. Our talks were held in one of those ornate and quite imperial

Hapsburg palaces that have become the meeting rooms of the democratic Austrian state.

In personal terms, the encounter deepened my own sense of the complexities of the issue. I spoke on behalf of a Palestinian "ministate" composed of the West Bank and Gaza. Shimon Peres completely persuaded me that this was a formula for future disaster because such a ministate would have but one aim in life: to become a maxistate. That, Peres argued, was not because the Palestinians would be dishonest or malevolent, but because such a small entity with a huge population was simply not economically viable. It would have to expand or die. Peres also bridled at the use of the word *self-determination* for the Palestinians. In part, this represented a sense of what kind of language he would be able to defend back home. But insofar as Peres, using a standard argument, went on to say that there already *was* a Palestinian state—Jordan—and that the world did not need another, I felt that he was taking a dangerous tack. From the outset, the Israelis underestimated the force of Palestinian nationalism, which was ironic since the existence of the Jewish state demonstrated that the nationalist passion could move mountains. The Palestinians, Golda Meir said, were not a nation, only "South Syrians" (a thesis that the present-day proponents of a Greater Syria in Damascus, which would include Israel, could accept).

The fact is, even if the Palestinians are an ethnic majority in Jordan and play a critical role in its administration, that does not satisfy the drive for a separate, specifically Palestinian state. Clearly, any such Palestinian state would have had to have some kind of a federated relation with Jordan; hopefully that might lead to an eventual unification. But telling the Palestinians that they should accept Jordan as their already existing country is an incitement, not a solution.

I discussed these things abstractly in Vienna in 1978. Five years later, in 1983, Shimon Peres's Labour party gave me a chance to form more concrete opinions firsthand. (That the Israelis would encourage this kind of criticism is one more reason I respect them so.) I went to the West Bank and saw the visible signs of occu-

pation—the constant Israeli army patrols, the Arabs being carefully watched in their own land. I met with some Israeli Rightists—
Americans, of course, since most of the extremists in *Eretz Israel*
seem to come from Brooklyn—and asked them how they could
accept a Jewish state with an Arab majority. One young, articulate
woman from Gush Emunim, who received me in her West Bank
living room, carefully explained that there would be a nineteen-
twenties type Depression in the United States, anti-Semitism would
rise, and millions of American Jews would flee to Israel, thus saving
the Zionists from their demographic contradictions.

All of this, preposterous as it seemed to me, was said in a calm
and rational way. But suddenly the woman's eyes flashed as she
said, "But when the Messiah comes, then all this is irrelevant."

I did not know whether to laugh or cry. But when I met Ibrahim
Tarwhil, one of the West Bank Palestinian leaders, the talk was
more serious. He identified with the PLO *and* was ready to talk
to the Israelis when Labour came to power and negotiations were
on the agenda. What will you do, I asked him, if Arafat refuses
to come to the bargaining table? He will come, I was told. But
what if he doesn't? He will. And if he doesn't? Then we, on the
West Bank, will have to negotiate.

A failure to recognize that last possibility was one of the worst
mistakes of Menachem Begin's rule. The Palestinians of the West
Bank have, potentially at least, much more specific and concrete
reasons to negotiate a solution to the immediate problems of their
daily lives than the Palestinians of the diaspora. All things being
equal, then, it is in Israel's interest to have a maximum of Palestinian self-representation on the West Bank and in the Gaza Strip.
But it was precisely such a possibility that Begin worked to eliminate. One way was to increase the Jewish percentage on the West
Bank—and thereby create a future opposition to any tradeoff of
land for peace—by building subsidized housing and attracting very
nonideological Israelis to settle there.

In 1988 all of my concerns were tragically confirmed as the
Palestinians on the West Bank and in the Gaza Strip revolted
against the Israeli occupation. The *realpolitik* of twenty years of

repression turned out to be, in C. Wright Mills's memorable phrase, crackpot realism. That policy, it turned out, was not simply immoral but, just as so many of my friends in Israel understood before the event, had actually undercut the genuine security of the Jewish state.

There was, however, one moment on that trip to Israel that was almost humorous. Mapam, which had been somewhat more dovish than the Labour party, had attracted a number of Arabs who were Israeli citizens. I was taken to a dusty village and met with some of its most important people—all men, of course—and there was much sipping of both Coke and sweet Arab coffee. The twenty or so Arabs explained to me why they thought that Israel had to negotiate with Arafat. But then they began to ask questions. What was American socialism? Was I going to become President of the United States? I suspect that they were much too polite to tell me that they could not make head or tail out of my eminently dialectical answers.

On the subject of Kreisky, however, my Israeli hosts were not very dialectical. For the most part, they were profoundly distrustful of him. I replied that Kreisky was honestly trying to act as an intermediary between the Israelis and the Palestinians. That he sometimes did so in ways all but calculated to infuriate the Israelis is unquestionable. In 1982, for instance, he and Brandt received Arafat in Vienna as if the Palestinian leader were a head of state. I wrote Brandt a private letter at that time, explaining that I was all in favor of his having a dialogue with Arafat, but not under conditions that gave a kind of diplomatic recognition to the PLO before it publicly accepted the right of Israel to exist. It was subsequently clear that Brandt had received other such communications from socialists much weightier than I and that they had made an impression upon him.

Even though I had disagreements with Kreisky, I felt that a characterization of him as a "self-hating Jew" was unfair. Indeed, when I first heard that phrase—usually solemnly enunciated like a medical judgment as "Jewish *selbst Hass*"—I thought it no more than a literary flourish. Later, when I was working on a book on politics and religion, I realized it described a very real phenomenon: the disdain of the educated, middle- and upper-class Jews when their uncouth brothers and sisters were liberated from the ghetto by the French Revolution and its aftermath.

Otto Bauer, one of the founding giants of Austrian socialism (and of "Austro-Marxism"), wrote a youthful masterpiece, *The Social Democrats and the Nationality Question*, which was one of the first attempts to theorize the emergence of a Jewish nationalist tendency within the socialist movement. Sometimes it was Zionist in character, sometimes, as in the case of the Jewish Socialist Bund, it sought only Jewish cultural autonomy within a national workers' movement. Bauer thought that this nationalism was a product of the economic and social backwardness of the Eastern European societies in which so many Jews were to be found. In the advanced capitalist societies, he argued, the Jewish radicals assimilated into their own class movement as workers first and as Jews—even if with a distinct culture and language—second. Many Jewish socialists agreed.

Clearly Bauer did not anticipate the creation of Israel—the absence of a physical homeland for the Jews was central to his argument—and one can make this or that criticism of his analysis on the basis of informed hindsight. But it is plain to me that this was the context in which Kreisky defined himself, this was why he said—infuriating many Jews in the process—that he was not Jewish but an atheist and a socialist. Why go back to the very real self-hate of some of the Jewish upper class when explaining a man whose attitudes are so clearly the product of the Austrian working-class movement, many of its Jews included?

I knew that Kreisky took those socialist traditions quite seriously. When I was in Vienna for an SI meeting in 1980, I lectured at the Socialist party's school for advanced party workers. The Socialist government had given the party a grant to carry on its internal education, so the party had bought and remodeled an old palace as a school. As I talked, the Chancellor sat in the first row nodding vigorously in agreement, shaking his head when he thought I was wrong. It was this Kreisky who had made his definition of his Jewishness, or lack of it; and his actual policies, whether one thinks them shrewd or not, were meant to find a solution to the Middle Eastern crisis, not to sell out the Israelis.

The very necessity of this digression about Kreisky shows how the Middle Eastern issue within the International was so charged that it sometimes seemed impossible even to have a rational discussion of it. The International's congress in Portugal in 1983 raised the issue to the level of tragedy.

In typical SI fashion, it had been decided that no official representatives of the PLO would be invited, but that Palestinian "journalists" would be welcome. When I arrived at the congress site in Albufeira, Issam Sartawi, a moderate Palestinian and associate of Arafat, had come and asked for the right to speak. I was opposed to that kind of formal recognition and yet torn by conflicting feelings on the question.

The night before the final session of the congress there was a ceremonial dinner at a luxury hotel (Albufeira is located in the Algarve, a resort area of Portugal). We dined al fresco in a courtyard, and I told my comrades from DSA to note the security guards on the roofs around us. I also thought of going over and chatting with Sartawi, which I had wanted to do in any case, but decided to put it off until the next day.

The next morning we were in the final session at the congress hotel when there was a sudden commotion and white-faced people raced through the hall to speak to Brandt at the rostrum. There was no explanation, but we were told not to move. Then we heard the horrible news: Sartawi had been murdered in the lobby not far from where we were. When we were permitted to leave the room, his body, covered and partially concealed by some ornate wooden screens, was lying where he fell.

When we reassembled, Brandt and Peres spoke in memory of Sartawi, and the speech he had wanted to deliver—which I had opposed his presenting in person—was read. His death had purchased him the access that earlier we had denied him. It was not simply the shock of the moment that changed my mind on the issue. It had been dramatically demonstrated to me that there were at least some members of the PLO who were honestly committed to serious negotiations. That Arafat cynically did nothing to deal with the killers of his comrade—because that would have violated the consensus he tried to maintain between moderates and terrorist rejectionists—could not change that fact.

The day of Sartawi's murder, I learned from Brandt that the Palestinian had turned down special security. He had told the Portuguese that he knew sooner or later he would be assassinated because of his views, and that he had decided not to spend his entire life searching for the face of his appointed killer. Later I also discovered that Shimon Peres had been scheduled to have a private conversation with Sartawi the day after Sartawi was murdered.

Two years later in Vienna I was presiding over a discussion of the Middle East at the Bureau meeting of the International—Brandt had picked me, I think, because I was trusted by the opposing sides. Peres, now the Prime Minister, but with little room to maneuver, defended the Israeli air strikes against the PLO headquarters in Tunisia on the grounds that one had to respond in this way to terrorism. Egon Bahr, who had done much of the negotiating of the *Ostpolitik* with the Soviets, told of the anguish he and the other German Socialists had felt when they watched people being killed as they tried to get over the Berlin Wall. There was, he said, an obligation even more important than that to those who were thus murdered.

One incident while Shimon Peres was speaking gave a certain tone to the proceedings. Some official of the conference center came up to Brandt, who was sitting between me and Peres, and told him in English that the battery in Shimon's microphone had to be changed by a workman. "Make sure that he is a workman and that what he has is a battery," Brandt whispered back. He was indeed an electrician and the battery was changed without incident, yet I was powerfully reminded of how utterly unacademic this debate was.

Under these circumstances, it was not strange that Vienna in 1985 made me think of the Hegelian definition of tragedy: not the conflict between right and wrong, but between two rights, between Antigone's sacred duty to bury her brother and Creon's responsibility to enforce the law that he not be buried. Were the Palestinians and the Israelis on such a collision course? Here of course we are dealing not with abstract policies but with life and death. I am committed to resolving it short of tragedy. But the complexity of the issue, the passions it evokes among decent people sharing profound socialist values, makes me wonder if the human race, so infinitely more complex than our International, can ever find a moral and political unity.

I I

The complexities of the Middle East disturb any simplistic internationalism. So do those of the United States, as I learned in bitter and unfortunate detail while working on a very successful conference on EuroSocialism and America.

That this country is exceptional among the advanced industrial democracies is hardly a discovery. But I learned firsthand about two additional factors in this historic puzzle: the first was a bitter demonstration of how, even when events seemed to be favorable to American socialism, our past devours our possible future; the second had to do with the impact of mass communications on American politics in general and American socialism in particular.

The idea of the EuroSocialism conference came out of discussions in the DSOC office near Union Square. In the late seventies there was much journalistic attention paid to EuroCommunism, i.e., to the anti-Moscow, and even democratic socialist, trends in the Communist movements of France, Italy, Spain, and some other countries. Through our relations with the Socialist International we knew that something at least as dynamic as EuroCommunism was happening in that organization under Brandt. The Swedes were talking about "wage earner funds" and decentralized social ownership, the French about a workers' control socialism, and the SI itself was reaching out to the Third World.

We decided therefore that there should be a conference on EuroSocialism and America. It would do two things simultaneously: educate this country on the changes taking place in European socialism and reflect some of that European glory upon our own American movement, which was becoming a bit more visible and serious. We approached the German Marshall Fund—set up when Willy Brandt was Chancellor as a token of German gratitude for the Marshall Plan but with an American board. Its director, Jerry Livingston, was amenable to the idea. In fairly short order, and with little opposition on the board, our proposal was approved. For the first time in our experience we had the money in hand to do something about a brainstorm.

At this point we hired a DSOC leader, Nancy Lieber, to take on the project as a full-time job. A Ph.D. in political science, Nancy had been active in our group at the University of California at Davis. When she and her husband, also an academic, went to Paris from 1978 to 1979, she put her fluent French to work and developed ties with many of the French socialist leaders, François Mitterrand among them. As our official representative in Europe during that year, she attended various party congresses and extended her contacts. She was clearly ideal for the job.

Long before the actual conference, Nancy, who was working out of Washington, began to get rumors of determined opposition from the office of Lane Kirkland in the AFL-CIO. At first, I assured her, with all of my sophistication from years in the movement, that this was almost certainly no more than the jealous grousing of our critics from the SDs who had become an "old-boy"—and even occasionally an old-girl—network in the Kirkland wing of the movement. Little did I realize, until it had already gathered considerable momentum, that there was a full-fledged campaign to sabotage the conference.

One of the first things we had done after we had received the news of the Marshall Fund grant was to write, in March of 1980, some nine months in advance of the conference, to Kirkland, to the AFL-CIO secretary-treasurer, Tom Donohue, and to the president of every international union in the United States, telling them of our project and asking that they appoint a liaison to work with us on it. As we got more information on the attack against us, we found out that Kirkland's agents were telling people that we were attempting to hold an international trade union meeting and had never informed or consulted the AFL-CIO president in any way.

By August, the AFL-CIO campaign had become so serious— among other things, Kirkland's office tried to get the German Marshall Plan to cancel our grant—that I sent a long, conciliatory letter to Kirkland, reiterating our desire to work with him and the federation and asking for cooperation. In mid-September I received a frosty reply telling me that my arguments were not at all persuasive. By this time things had become so nasty that Nancy Lieber, on a trip to Sweden to participate in a conference, went by way of Paris and Bonn to make sure that our European friends were still behind us. Horst Ehmke, a German Socialist leader very actively involved, felt that my letter to Kirkland in August was a clear proof of our good intentions.

The faction fighting continued through the congress of the International in Madrid in November. Nancy and I spent at least as much time talking to the Germans and persuading them that we had acted responsibly as we did in dealing with the issues before the meeting. The Germans and Brandt remained behind us, but the constant need to defend our actions made it a tense and unhappy time.

I do not know to this day what personal role Kirkland played in all of this. He is a man of substantial intellect, wry humor, and great talent whom I had known briefly in the mid-sixties when he was George Meany's number two. I had, of course, disagreed with him as well as his boss on the issue of Vietnam and of anti-Communism—or, I should say, what I thought of as obsessive and self-defeating anti-Communism—throughout the late sixties and early seventies when Southeast Asia was the central issue of American domestic politics.

When Kirkland took over the Federation, I knew perfectly well that he was honestly, sincerely, and quite competently somewhat more of a hawk than George Meany. But when I discovered that his people were ranging the globe—in the midst of an economic and political crisis of the Western Left—to undercut the terrible danger of a conference organized by Michael Harrington, I did not know how much that represented Kirkland's own view and how much his name was being invoked by my enemies on his staff. In December, when most of the infighting was over, we came into possession of a March 28th memo from Tom Kahn, a Kirkland aide and Cold War social democrat who had once been a protégé and close friend of mine, advising Kirkland not to respond to that original letter informing him of our conference. It was proof that our communication had both been received and pointedly ignored, thus refuting one of the main charges against us. But it arrived rather late in the game and was not much use in our campaign of self-defense. (Kahn has since become the head of the International department of the Federation.)

The attack on the conference, a high official of the International Confederation of Trade Unions told me, had become so passionate that the ICFTU was told that whether the AFL-CIO would reaffiliate would be affected by any decision to participate in our project. This official assured me that he didn't believe the charges against us, that he was quite sympathetic to what we were doing, and that he would, of course, have to absent himself from Washington.

III

If all of this is seen as simply a personal vendetta against me and my friends, it is a bizarre anecdote and not much else. But something more serious is involved: how the failure of the old American Left—the Debsians before and immediately after World War I, the Communists in the days of the Popular Front—made it more difficult for the unions in this country to respond to the emergence of a new political force both here and throughout the Western world.

During the post–World War II period, the relative decline in the number of blue-collar workers and the growth of higher education and a salariat with college degrees, changed the class structure and politics of every Western country. There came to be two Lefts: one based on the classic proletariat, the other the product of the "new class" of the postindustrial economy. That the non-proletarians often spoke in the name of the "real" working class and against the attitudes of the actual workers should surprise no one. But on issues like the war in Vietnam, feminism, and the environment, the new strata were the proponents—even if sometimes dilettantish and irritating proponents—of critically important new values.

The conflict between these two Lefts occurred in every working-class movement in the West. In Holland, the result was the opposite of the United States: the New Left in effect joined the social democracy and both sides of the alliance were transformed. When I spoke at the congress of the Dutch Labor party in the spring of 1983, I witnessed the most spontaneous and natural feminist meeting I have ever seen. That is, without any affirmative-action provisions, women played a role in the proceedings in every way equal to that of men.

These trends surfaced in every party of the mass European Left. For instance, when Gro Harlem Brundtland became Prime Minister of Norway in 1986, she followed the procedures already in effect in her own party and appointed a cabinet in which 40 percent of the members were women. In Germany, particularly in the eighties and obviously in response to the political pressure of the Greens, the venerable Social Democratic party began to talk of "eco-socialism" and to provide for mandatory representation of women in leadership bodies. Moreover, the party's official spokespersons on both economic and foreign policies were former leaders of the radical youth. At the International's 1986 congress I worked with Heide Marie Wisczourek-Zeul, a prominent member of her party's delegation and a member of the European parliament. When we first met, during the seventies, she was known as "Red Heidi" because of her hair and her politics.

In the United States there are important activists from the New

Left who now play a significant role in the unions. And the counterposition of the two Lefts was never simply that, even in the days of their greatest hostility. For instance, major trade union leaders had opposed the Vietnam War. But the AFL-CIO itself was fundamentally hostile to the antiwar movement, dismissing it as a pseudoradical cover for privileged kids with student exemptions from the draft.

Meany, and then Kirkland, did respond on the issue of feminism, supporting the Equal Rights Amendment by moving an AFL-CIO convention from Miami to Washington because Florida had not ratified the ERA and supporting Joyce Miller, the first woman elected a member of the Federation's executive. And yet, there was a visceral, class-based hostility to the "new class" and its political activists, who resembled, more than a little, that of the neoconservatives (since some of the neo-cons came from the same tiny group as my former comrades around Kirkland, that similarity was not, as Marxists say, an accident).

But why had the difference between the United States on the one hand, and Europe and Canada on the other, persisted in the most left-wing of decades since the thirties?

The American past simply weighed too heavily on the socialist opportunities of the sixties. To put the point biblically, in the words of Saint Matthew, "For unto every one that hath shall be given and they shall have abundance; but for him that hath not shall be taken away even that which he hath." Europe had a mass socialist movement which, after many of the same screaming rows which took place in the United States between the old and new Lefts, was reinvigorated. The United States did not have a mass socialist movement, and events that might plausibly have begun to call one into life were aborted.

It was not just that a good part of the European New Left eventually decided to be realistic about transforming their society. As the youthful German Marxists of the seventies put it, marrying Mao and Social Democracy, they were embarking on "the long march through the institutions." That changed the mass social democratic parties and the New Left. Let there be no mistake about it, the Social Democratic old-timers were at least as hostile to these Leftist upstarts as Meany or Kirkland. But there was a framework in which that relationship could be worked out.

At the EuroSocialism conference itself, Joop Den Uyl, the leader of the Dutch Labor party and former Prime Minister of Holland, was quite specific on that European experience. "During the sixties," he told a plenary, "socialism began to lose its appeal for the younger generation in many countries. The revolt of the sixties was a movement that was antiestablishment, antiinstitutions, and antihistory. In Europe, it was first and foremost a movement directed against a form of democracy perceived as outdated and against a welfare state suffering from ossification . . . [and in] opposition to . . . regulating the affairs of the community and attending to its needs *without any real participation whatsoever on the part of the people for whom the arrangements were being made*" (his emphasis).

All the European Socialist parties, Den Uyl went on, "have assimilated the experience in different ways." But the point is, they did respond to, and even *assimilate*, the lessons of the New Left even if none did so as forthrightly as Den Uyl's own party. Listening to Joop at the EuroSocialism conference, I suddenly remembered that the irrelevant and nostalgic congress of the International at Eastbourne in 1969 had actually focused on the central theme of how to respond to the new political youth movement. That is, even beyond Willy Brandt's contribution on foreign policy, that event was not quite as meaningless as I had at first thought. In saying these things, I do not want to glorify the European socialists in order to denigrate the American trade unionists. On the contrary. My point is that on this count, the decisive (if not all-controlling) difference between Europe-Canada and the United States is to be found in history and social structure, not in the personal superiority of Den Uyl over Kirkland. The ongoing *institutional* effect of the New Left was less in this country than in Europe and the reason is an American catch-22 I have just described. Because this country is so exceptional in its non- and anti-socialism, it becomes even more exceptional even where there is, as in the sixties and early seventies, an extraordinary burst of left-wing energy.

Today, while working on this sorry history of Kirkland and the Federation, I was on the phone with people from the Steelworkers about organizing citizen support for their strike. For, paradoxical as it may seem, I *still* think that the American trade union movement, for all of its enormous problems, must be a decisive element in any progressive coalition. My loftiest ideals cannot even begin to be accomplished without the self-organization of the workers at the base, the minorities and women in the low-paid service jobs above all. And if I will continue to fight Lane Kirkland with all of my might on those foreign policy issues where we disagree, I am deeply committed to working with him and his movement on the multitude of issues where we do agree, the experience of the EuroSocialism conference notwithstanding.

I V

At first glance, the hidden history of the EuroSocialism conference might seem more fascinating than the event itself. But that was not true. The meeting was extraordinary in its own right, even though it was almost totally ignored by the American media.

Consider what the press found unworthy of coverage. At the small, invitational discussion prior to the big public plenaries, Rudolf Meidner, the economist of the Swedish trade union federation, talked about the wage earner funds he had originated. They became law a little more than two years later. Edith Cresson, who would be one of the most important ministers in the French Socialist government of 1981 through 1986, analyzed industrial dislocation, and Jacques Atalie, Mitterrand's chief economist, spoke of the policy framework of his movement. Ulrich Steger, then one of the leading Socialist parliamentarians and now even more of a major figure in his party, dealt with the technological revolution, and Norbert Wieczorek, a top German finance expert (and former vice president of the trade union bank in his country) analyzed problems of capital formation. Clive Jenkins, the president of the most important white-collar union in Britain, discussed the idea of workers' control of industry.

At a dinner for the small conference, Dennis McDermott, the head of the Canadian Labor Congress, spoke about his organization's political action program, which centered on "one-on-one" contact on the shop floor between union activists and the members so that they can discuss candidates and electoral issues. Bill Winpisinger, the president of the machinists, was so impressed that the next Monday he began to explore a similar strategy for his own union. In 1984, in those areas where the AFL-CIO was able to put such a program into effect, they had much greater success than anywhere else in the campaign.

American experts, such as Irving Bluestone of the Auto Workers, Carol O'Cleiracain of the New York Municipal Workers, and Brian Turner of the Industrial Union Department of the AFL-CIO (who came despite considerable pressure to cancel), made major contributions. The discussion was quite frank: Rudolf Meidner was openly critical of Olof Palme's version of the wage earner funds on the grounds that Palme expected too much of them. That turned out to be an ironic point since, when Palme's government actually put Meidner's idea into practice, the latter thought the legislation much too weak. Michael Roccard, who had just withdrawn from contesting Mitterrand for the Socialist presidential nomination, took an active part in the discussions and in private told several of us quite frankly that he too thought the Socialists would lose the presidency.

The major plenary speakers included Brandt, Palme, Den Uyl, Tony Benn of the British Labour party, Congressman Ron Dellums (I introduced him as the "Socialist caucus of the United States Congress"), Gloria Steinem, and Mitterrand. Felipe Gonzalez came to convene a meeting of the Committee to Defend the Nicaraguan Revolution, and though he did not participate in the formal proceedings—we had decided that we could only have one plenary speech, Mitterrand's, translated before we knew that Felipe was coming—he was introduced to the audience and was very much in evidence throughout the weekend. There was a small, private dinner on Saturday with the plenary speakers, Felipe, trade unionists such as Jerry Wurf of the municipal employees and Bill Winpisinger of the machinists, Steve Solarz of the House Foreign Relations Committee, and Ted Kennedy.

The *New York Times* did not cover any of these events. The *Washington Post* carried two modest stories, one of them on the style page about what socialists wear to such gatherings. The three networks did not mention us. One veteran reporter told us that we had assembled a bunch of has-beens. And all this on a fairly slow news weekend during the transition from Carter to Reagan.

Within two years of the conference, two of those in attendance had become Prime Ministers (Palme, Gonzalez) and one a President (Mitterrand). Where the French are concerned, I should be fair. I privately asked Mitterrand if he was going to win the presidential election in May, and he assured me that he would not, saying that he wanted to run this last time to make the case for his principles.

I cannot, then, blame reporters who did not realize that Mitterrand was going to become President, and that his aides would make an impression on France, since Mitterrand did not know it either. I can, however, fault them for totally ignoring the leader of the French opposition when he was in Washington on the eve of a presidential election.

After the conference, there was a comedy of errors—a very revealing comedy of errors—with the *New York Times*. A number of people had written outraged letters to the *Times*, protesting the absence of coverage in a daily that pretends to be the nation's newspaper of record. We received a range of self-contradictory excuses: the reporter assigned to cover the conference suddenly became sick; there had been a bureaucratic snafu; and so on. Two somewhat more interesting reasons were advanced by *Times* people, one of whom must remain anonymous for obvious reasons.

Some time after the EuroSocialism event, I chatted at a small party with Harrison Salisbury, by then retired but a venerable Pulitzer Prize–winning veteran of the *Times*. I told him the sad story of our noncoverage. He said to me, Abe Rosenthal, editor of the *Times*, is not at all sympathetic to you people. It's not that he told the Washington bureau to lay off the story. That would be too obvious. It is just that the people in Washington know that they get negative points when they write on such matters and that their stock goes up if they are known to have ignored such events. That fits in with David Halberstam's analysis of the American media.

In the early seventies, Halberstam recounts, the *Times*'s management called in its senior staffers and told them that the paper was getting too much of a reputation as a left-wing journal. This was a period when the corporate leadership was worried that it would lose the readers migrating in droves to the suburbs. Part of the response was to create weekly sections in the paper on food, homes, sports, entertainment, etc., to reach out to the baby boom market that was leaving the cities (or beginning to gentrify them). But, if one were going to thus identify with the aspirations, tastes, and fads of a privileged stratum now engaged in tending its own garden and appreciating fine wines, it was necessary to jettison the Leftist attitudes that had come into the paper during the mini-cultural revolution of the sixties when that same stratum was in a much more activist mood.

Halberstam's history coincides very much with my own experience. In 1972, my resignation as co-chair of the Socialist party because of my opposition to the Vietnam War was given significant news coverage in the *Times*. There was also another story on our plans to start the Democratic Socialist Organizing Committee (DSOC) and there were no less than three reports on our founding convention. Our second convention, in 1975, got a paragraph and after that we were ignored. Clearly, there had been some kind of a turnabout in attitude at the *Times*, and that would bear out Salisbury's comments as well as Halberstam's analysis.

There is another version of this story, somewhat less subtle than Salisbury's theory of self-censorship. It came to us from a responsible staffer on the *Times*, someone who is both trustworthy and in a position to know the events of which he speaks. The *Times*, our source said, had assigned a reporter to cover the conference, but that decision was countermanded from on high, i.e., from New York.

I have no way of knowing which version was true—or if a combination of all of them was at work. I do know that Rosenthal was upset by all the complaints he had received. When he first came back from foreign assignment to begin his trek up the ladder in New York, I had spent an evening with him showing him Greenwich Village (he was systematically touring the city's neighborhoods). We had quite a pleasant time, and it made him aware that I was an anti-Stalinist radical, not the least because I had praised his excellent dispatches from Poland during the anti-Stalinist rising of 1956. So he knew that I was not the "Leftist dupe" he might have imagined, and I think he felt he owed me an explanation.

When Rosenthal phoned, he simply conceded that it had been a mistake not to cover the conference and said that he had told Robert Semple, then the foreign editor of the paper, to see to it that the event was somehow covered. When I talked to Semple, he was understandably worried about how he would be able to plausibly cover a conference that had taken place some months earlier. How could he make that news? I had a suggestion. I was going to a Bureau meeting of the International in Amsterdam in April of 1981. Most of the leaders who had been in Washington would be there. It would be quite easy to include some paragraphs referring to the fact that these people had all been together in Washington in December.

Semple thought that a fine idea, and the *New York Times* reporter, Frank Prial, dutifully showed up in Amsterdam. He interviewed me, covered the Bureau deliberations, and I waited anxiously for the report that would partly right the wrong of the previous December. The article appeared and was totally and completely scrambled. By accident or design all of the transitions were omitted and the story read as if the December meeting in Washington had taken place in Amsterdam in April. For instance, Senator Kennedy was said to have been in Amsterdam at the Socialist International, which obviously he had not. After that, I simply lost heart in pursuing our protest.

This incident also has a larger meaning. In the early days of this century, when Gene Debs was the inspired tribune of American Socialism, he used to charge admission to his campaign meetings, speak for two hours, and pack in the crowds. That was America before radio and television, and an antiestablishment candidate could have an enormous impact simply by barnstorming. By the eighties, political meetings had turned into "pseudoevents," that is, they were designed for television coverage, and what actually took place was much less important than what appeared on the evening news.

In 1980, the environmentalist Barry Commoner ran for President on the Citizens party ticket. I told Commoner that I thought it was a mistake to run a third-party campaign when all it could do in practical terms was to take votes away from Jimmy Carter and, in effect, help elect Ronald Reagan. At the same time I thought that Commoner talked more sense than any politician in the country that year. Yet he was not mentioned once on network television. The only time he got any coverage at all was when a radio ad of his used the word *bullshit* and was able to do so because of special exemptions from the normal censorship rules for campaign speeches. It was an instant, one-day, story—the *New York Times* said that Commoner's people had used a "barnyard epithet"—and it had, of course, nothing to do with any political idea.

The United States, which had been so exceptional in not having a mass socialist movement ever develop, was now evolving in such a way as to make that exception institutional and permanent. For all of the emphasis on campaign reform in the wake of Watergate, perhaps one third of the Senate is now made up of millionaires, not the least because they can make unlimited contributions toward their own election. The *Times* is, of course, an elite paper. But one's credibility with the political class in this country—and one's ability to raise funds from that political class—depends on coverage in that paper. We had 2,500 people in Washington, and the *Times* knew that the event had been fascinating and exciting. The tens of thousands of activists and the small core of funders, however, did not even know that the leadership of the European democratic Left had come to this country to discuss our common problems.

With television, the issue is even more serious, for this medium controls access to the great mass of the American people, and not just to the elite. One can be a presidential candidate approved by the Federal Election Commission, but if there is not simultaneous recognition from the informal electoral commission formed by ABC, CBS, and NBC, the campaign does not even exist. It is not just that our conference, which cost about $100,000 to stage and involved most of the energies of a five-thousand person organization over a year or so, was turned into a nonevent. Even more significant, this means that Eugene Victor Debs and Norman Thomas could never happen again.

That is obviously bad for the American Left. But it is also intolerable for the rest of the world. If this country, the greatest economic, political, and military power of its times, is to remain the Great Exception, then what hope is there for any kind of serious internationalism?

The Internationalists

A t the EuroSocialism conference, Willy Brandt spoke on a subject that had occupied him—and Olof Palme—since they had assumed leadership of the International in 1976: how to bring North and South together on the basis of a common economic interest to solve a common economic crisis, a vision he carefully linked to big-power disarmament. That, I believe, is the key to any possibility of a serious and new international order. It is clearly Brandt's own sense of his legacy to the world, the cause to which he intends to devote the rest of his life. It was central for Palme, too, and it was clear he had intended to focus on it in the coming years.

I have written of that program in books and articles. But what of the men behind it? What of Willy Brandt and Olof Palme? They, perhaps more than any others, have stood for a genuine internationalism in our time.

The contrast between them extends to practically every aspect of their lives except one: their enduring collaboration until Palme's death in 1986, an event that shook Brandt to the very core of his being. Their backgrounds were very different. Brandt was born out of wedlock to a salesperson in a cooperative store and joined the party when he was still in high school. Palme's father was from a distinguished bourgeois family in Stockholm; his mother was descended from the German-Baltic nobility, and his wife belongs to one of the most aristocratic families in Sweden. His socialism, he once told me, was partly shaped by his experiences as a young man in the United States when he attended Kenyon College, a traditional, even elite, institution.

Yet Brandt, the son of the people, is courtly, even aristocratic, in his manner, an overwhelming physical presence, a man with an almost sculpted dignity. I have known him mainly in his persona as a statesman, yet there have been glimpses of boyishness and warmth, such as the time he rushed down from the dais at the Lima congress to tell Lionel Jospin that France had won a World Cup Soccer game, or his making an elaborate ritual out of cadging a cigarette he really shouldn't have. Still, he is clearly one of nature's noblemen and looks the part.

Palme, the scion of respectability and rank, was informal, perpetually rumpled, open and democratic. But there was also something reserved and deeply private about the man. On the surface, the two leaders of the Socialist International were virtual opposites.

Once, in a rustic setting at a Socialist youth camp outside Stockholm, I watched Brandt and Palme at dinner, and it seemed that there was not much small talk between them. Later I asked a Swedish Socialist friend who knew both of them well if I was right. Palme, he said, had never been totally comfortable as the leader of a workers' movement. He saw Brandt as the authentic representative of the cause he himself believed in so deeply yet came to as an outsider. Palme was in awe of him. When Palme was assassinated, Brandt, speaking at a meeting of the foreign socialists who attended Palme's funeral, almost broke down. At the Lima congress of 1986 when he referred to Palme in his opening address as *"nuestro hermano, Olof"*—our brother, Olof—his voice shook.

I
——————————

One night in April 1986, a small group of us attending the SI meeting in Gabarone, Botswana, ate together at a Chinese restaurant in that most modest of capital cities. We got to talking about Brandt and we all confessed to the same fact: that he was a personal hero for each of us. We were hardly politics-struck groupies; all of us had been privy to the inner workings of the International for at least a decade. That, in a way, is precisely the point.

For a valet, Hegel liked to say, those whom he serves are not heroes. That does not mean, he added, that these people are not heroes, but only that the valet deals with them in their very unheroic persona of eating and drinking and dressing. To which I would add that, for much the same reason, people who chair the committees on which you sit for long, often boring and sometimes contentious, hours are not heroes either. Except for Brandt.

As a young man, I had looked up to him, for he was an anti-Nazi who had fought the crimes of his own homeland and then become the leader of the resistance to Stalinism in a Berlin surrounded by Soviet and East German troops. In June 1953, when the workers of East Berlin, and then of East Germany as a whole, had gone out on strike in the aftermath of Stalin's death, he was the man on the tightrope who supported their cause yet worked against any actions in West Berlin that could be taken as a provocation.

I had first seen him from afar at a mass meeting in the Berlin Sportspalast in 1959 when I was there for the meeting of the executive committee of the International Union of Socialist Youth. I was not disappointed. It was obvious to me that his speech was vibrant and powerful, even though my reading knowledge of German, based on the vocabulary of Marx and Hegel but not of ordinary life, did not enable me to grasp any nuances.

I had followed his brilliant rise to the Chancellorship with enthusiasm and then been stunned by his resignation from that office because of a spy scandal. When I first met him face-to-face in 1976 in a New York hotel room, I was still shy and awkward in the presence of a genuine hero. He talked that day of the importance of drafting a new statement of basic principles for the International. Developments like those in the Italian Communist party, he said, required that we think through the old dogmas. The idea that a serious, practicing politician might be concerned with ideology, and even philosophy, struck me as gloriously un-American.

As I got to know him, I realized that he was dead earnest about his socialist principles. That sounds like a strange, even patronizing way to begin, so I should explain.

The European movement, I knew in painful scholarly detail, had made compromise after compromise. Irving Howe once said to me that he wondered if, after that most fundamental betrayal when most of the socialists violated their solemn pledge and supported World War I, socialism could ever again be innocent. It was not at all strange, therefore, for me to speculate that socialism, for the European leaders, might be merely a rhetoric; that what divided them from their liberal counterparts in the United States was simply a tradition, a history without substantial present meaning. Brandt and Palme and several of the other European leaders convinced me that this was only a partial truth. They really were, and are, socialists.

This is not to say that Brandt was stuck on some youthful vision of the perfect society. It is to argue that even after all of the necessary compromises, he is possessed by the ideal of a genuine community of the human race, of a radical transformation of the human condition. What was it that took this man of seventy-three on a long and arduous journey to South Africa, to be booed at the airport by some of the German colony in Johannesburg and then to preside over a little meeting in which he and Gro Harlem Brundtland were the only major European leaders present? It was not the instinct of compromise. It was an enduring passion.

I suspect one of the reasons I have always been so sympathetic to him is that he incarnates the "long-distance runner" I imagine myself to be. He became the Chancellor of the Federal Republic against extraordinary odds: how many politicians who fought against their own country's war have later been elected to the highest office in that country? He lost that post in a way that would have crushed a lesser man. Within months of his downfall, however, he was creating a new life for both himself and the world socialist movement within the International. There are some superficial similarities to Richard Nixon's return to political respectability in the United States. But Nixon was undone because he lied to the people and Brandt, once his serious error in judgment was revealed, forthrightly resigned. More to the present point, Nixon waited patiently for history to heal his wounds and went through a deep depression in the aftermath of his disgrace. But Brandt, with that enormous inner drive—that socialist vision—continued the struggle he had been engaged in throughout his life.

Much less dramatically, but no less important, he is a man of utter patience who actually listens to speakers. At the Lima congress of the International in 1986, there was one endless session in which various Latin politicians indulged themselves in a rhetorical overkill that seemed designed to confirm every stereotype of their culture's verbosity. I usually sit through such experiences, if only out of loyalty to Brandt and to help disguise the fact that nothing is happening. But this time I couldn't take it and went to get coffee and quiet. As I left, Brandt was not only presiding, but, it seemed to me, actually listening. For I knew from experience that if an occasional point of substance were made in the midst of all that rhetoric, he would catch it. (The American educator Robert Hutchins was the only other person I ever met with this quality.)

When there are angry disagreements in the International, Brandt's genius for locating a mollifying consensus is legendary. After bitter exchanges, Brandt will begin, "Could we say that . . ." and sketch out some middle way. Then, when everyone is trying to grasp the exact implications of his intricate formula, he will look around the table and say, "Agreed?" If no one objects immediately, he will proceed to the next point without skipping a beat. Yet, strange as it may seem, most of his formulations hold up. Small wonder, I used to think when he negotiated one of these problematic moments, that he got a Nobel Prize for peacemaking.

Inevitably there were a few times when that magic did not work. On three or four occasions, he simply accepted the impasse and decided to let time do its work. But there were two times, one of them relatively minor, when I saw a streak of stubbornness not easy to reconcile with the consensus personality. It was as if that infinite patience suddenly snapped and gave way to an implacable intransigence.

The serious occasion when he became unyielding was the only time I really felt at all in conflict about Brandt. Bernt Carlsson had been elected general secretary of the International in 1976 when Brandt became president. He was, I thought, an incredibly hard-working, imaginative, and effective executive for the organization—and a personal friend. My friend and comrade Jim Chapin, a Socialist historian who regularly worked as staff for the International at its big meetings, shrewdly observes that the European Left is critical of America and likes Americans (we have the most socialist and egalitarian style in the world, even though we lack a mass socialist movement); the European Right admires our system but often doesn't get along with its individuals. Carlsson is certainly a case in point, an activist in a party that has been severely critical of U.S. policy and a man who enjoys our country and its citizens. He liked to laugh at my very American irreverence; I deeply admired his very Swedish sense of solidarity and morality and his not-so-stereotypical sense of humor.

Shortly before the 1983 congress of the International I learned that Brandt was opposed to Carlsson's re-election. I was against that on both personal and political grounds. In the period leading up to the congress, and at that meeting itself, I lobbied as best I could for Carlsson. But at a small, private meeting of leaders of the SI, Brandt made it emphatically clear that he would not stand again for president if Carlsson were to be the secretary. To this day, I do not know why he was so obdurate on this count—or even why he decided to get rid of Carlsson in the first place. Yet I knew from past experience that when Brandt dug in his heels, there was no force in the world capable of moving him.

Those events were upsetting, but they did not change my basic attitude.

In Lima in 1986 I saw the much more typical, heroic Brandt at one of his best moments. On an issue of principle—whether we should protest the effective execution of prisoners by the army of the government that was hosting our meeting—he was steadfast. Yet at the same time he managed to convey a sense of sympathy and solidarity to the beleaguered Peruvian socialists whom he had to pressure. The event made me proud both of our principles and our humanity, and it was Brandt who managed to integrate them in the most extraordinary way.

About his small talk I know little. We met at working meetings and, in any case, I am a shy person in general, more so when in the presence of those I greatly admire. Once we sat together and chatted on a bus taking us from a dinner at the President's house in Helsinki back to the hotel. He was, I think, a bit surprised that I knew some of the history of the Socialist Workers Party of Germany—the SAP—a Left socialist formation that united the more radical wing of the SPD and some of the dissident, expelled Communists in the period just before Hitler's rise to power. Brandt had been a member and talked nostalgically about those times, delighted to discover that a friend of mine, a veteran American Trotskyist, had attended an anti-Fascist conference with him in the thirties that had been broken up by the police.

Brandt broke into an infectious grin when I told him of my hilarious arrest in New York as part of the protest against apartheid in South Africa. The demonstration was quite serious, of course. But it took DSA about two weeks to negotiate my right to be arrested, and when the news came that I had been accepted, I was told to report on the appointed day to a high-ranking police officer. I did, and he made sure that I was on the list and instructed me on the procedures of the arrest. At the actual moment of the extremely civil disobedience that day, a veteran civil rights activist went limp and we had to explain to him that this was an arrest in cooperation with the New York police department. For Brandt all this was wonderfully American.

Clearly, I make no claim of knowing him intimately. I found him likeable and relaxed, yet it is hard to discuss the weather with someone who, morally and historically, is twenty feet tall. What I did see, though, was the passion, the decency, and the intelligence of the man coming through in the close quarters of a political meeting. And since I so completely share his vision of a disarmed world in which the North and South would both advance their particular interests by doing the common work of global justice, I am more than satisfied to do whatever I can to help our cause. So, too, with Olof Palme.

Brandt thought of Palme as almost a son and probably as an heir.

I first met Palme at the Eastbourne congress in 1969 when he was the brash young Prime Minister who had succeeded the venerable Tage Erlander. He struck me from the very start as being "un-Swedish" in many ways. Most of the Swedes I have known, including those who are drinking companions, are quite reserved, at least until *vino* produces *veritas*. Jim Chapin and I used to discuss endlessly the national personality differences we observed around the table: the beer-drinking, cheerful, and outgoing Danes; the Norwegians, who struck us as the Scandinavian equivalent of Americans; and the Swedes, with their cards held close to their vests. Chapin, with the advantage of being a professional historian, would document with scholarly references our insights as political tourists. The Swedes, he demonstrated, had never really recovered from being the imperial power of the region. So they still felt responsible for the world.

Palme clearly felt such a responsibility, but he didn't look "Swedish" when he acted on it. With his clothes in casual disarray and his glasses perched on the edge of his nose, he sometimes had the air of an absent-minded professor. And yet, when he argued, there was a sharpness, a polemical precision, that sometimes puzzled his own comrades. Legend has it that in one campaign television debate, he so completely demolished his opponent that he won the man sympathy votes. Actually, I think these seemingly contradictory aspects of his personality were a function of his disdain for the decorous and proper style in both dress and debate.

When he came to the United States in 1970 he was Prime Minister, but was in this country on a private visit to Kenyon College. I helped organize a small reception for him the day before he returned to Stockholm. On this visit to a land he knew well and admired, he was furious. Because of his opposition to American policy in Vietnam—and his participation in a famous demonstration that included the North Vietnamese ambassador—the Nixon administration was being so childishly sullen that it would not even admit that a foreign head of state was present within our own borders. Washington also ignored, of course, the fact that Palme had participated in a huge demonstration to protest the Soviet invasion of Czechoslovakia in 1968 because that reality interfered with their picture of him as a Communist dupe.

There was a bizarre prelude to the reception. I had decided not to invite the American press, to allow Palme to have more time to meet the trade unionists, civil rights activists, and intellectuals we had assembled. I had invited Pete Hamill in his persona as a political activist, not as a journalist. I did not know it when I asked Hamill, but he was then seeing Barbra Streisand and brought her along. For the Swedish press following Palme her presence, not any discussion with Leftists, was, of course, *the* story. But once the photo session was over, Palme was openly bitter. "Finally," he said, "I am officially welcomed to the United States. The chairman of the Socialist party of America greets the chairman of the Socialist party of Sweden."

Many years later he was in New York shortly after a visit to Moscow as the guest of the Central Committee of the party. What was the mood in the Soviet Union with regard to their invasion of Afghanistan? I asked. About the same as that of the sophisticated people in your government late in the Vietnam War, he answered with a smile. They would like to get out, but they don't know how. And, he added with a boyish grin, the Central Committee chauffeur likes rock and roll.

In 1976, at the Geneva congress of the International, Helmut Schmidt, then Brandt's successor as Chancellor of the Federal Republic, gave a remarkably conservative speech about the evils of excessive government spending. Palme was being interviewed when Schmidt was at the rostrum and asked me what he had said. When I summarized the talk, Palme commented wryly, "I didn't know that Schmidt talked German with such an American accent." The last time I saw him, at the SI disarmament conference in Vienna in the fall of 1985, he was almost impish when he whispered to me about Boris Ponomarev, the leader of the Soviet delegation. "He is a real Stalinist. When I went to see him in Moscow, he had Dimitrov's old office from the Communist International days."

For me, the quintessential Palme moment occurred in 1970 on my first trip to Sweden. He was Prime Minister then, yet when my wife went to the party office to attend a meeting I was having with him, Palme and his predecessor, Tage Erlander, walked in off the street like two ordinary mortals and waited for the elevator with her. But the quality of "Prime Minister's Night" at the University at Lund was even more remarkable. Pierre Schori, then the International Secretary of the party—and now the number two in the foreign ministry—was my host on the whole trip and translated for me.

"Prime Minister's Night" had been initiated by Erlander. Palme walked alone into a packed gymnasium while a band played "The Stars and Stripes Forever" and "The Internationale." He sat at a little table, and the students who questioned—or, more accurately, harangued—him, did so from the podium at the front of the hall. The interrogators had been elected by their fellow students, and the Maoists had run a successful campaign, winning nine out of the ten spots. So student after student attacked Palme for being a right-wing traitor to the working class and socialism, a lily-livered phony radical who was unwilling to resort to that violence which was the only language the bourgeoisie would ever understand.

Palme's replies were intense, angry, and extremely effective. Violence, he said, may be necessary in this or that situation; he was not a pacifist. But socialism could not possibly be built with violence, for it was based on voluntary cooperation. What happened in the Third World when a national liberation movement did come violently to power? They almost always dispatched a mission to Sweden to find out how to deal practically with issues such as health and education. Yes, Sweden still had a long way to go, but so long as it was possible to proceed democratically, nonviolently, that was the only way, for ultimately that was the path to socialism. Such events made me want to bring the ideas and spirit of the Swedish socialists back to the United States. But I soon learned another complexity of internationalism: that political solutions are, more often than not, national, and do not travel well.

Sweden, I realized after my first trip there in 1970, cannot be a model for the other countries in the West, above all the United States. It is a small nation, with its own uniquely Scandinavian history—there were peasants in the parliament by the last quarter of the nineteenth century!—and a relatively homogeneous (white, culturally Lutheran) population. It has traditions of cooperation and self-help that long predate the emergence of the socialist movement and give it some of its exceptional characteristics. This is not to say, however, that the "Swedish way" is to be explained by some theory about the genetic or cultural tendency of this nation to search for compromise.

My friend John Stephens, a socialist who has written a remarkable book on Sweden and the transition to socialism itself, has documented the bitterness of the class struggle in Sweden. The debates over creating a funded pension system in the fifties or over the wage earner funds in the eighties were intense, even nasty. When Palme tried to implement the wage earner–fund concept of decentralized social ownership, he was attacked—unfortunately with some effect—as proposing to create the *gulag* in Sweden. That was patent nonsense, but it was one of the reasons the government adopted such a modest version of Meidner's idea.

The stupid ferocity of the rich in that debate may well have something to do with Palme himself. For upper-class Swedes, Palme was a "traitor to his class," not unlike how some Americans viewed Franklin Roosevelt. But preposterous as the *gulag* description of a program of economic democracy was, Palme's critics did intuit something important. Palme was not satisfied with the best of capitalist welfare states; he did want the great mass of the people to make decisions that had long been the preserve of the elite. Palme was the living proof that the Swedish Socialists did not compromise for the sake of compromise. He went as far as he dared; he pulled back when he was forced to.

At the same time, there is a historic tradition that has made the resolution of those class struggles different from the outcome in any other country. The word that sums it up is an important one for the Swedish social-democracy: solidarity.

The unions in Sweden have long had a "solidaristic" wage policy, i.e., in negotiations, they always fight to give the largest increases to the lowest paid, and the least to the highest paid, thereby decreasing the differentials within the working class. This policy has had an extraordinary feminist impact, since women, in Sweden as everywhere, are concentrated on the lowest-paid rungs of the occupational ladder. The reduction of differentials within the working class has also meant a sharp diminution in gender discrimination.

Solidarity is also key to Swedish foreign policy. I once told Palme that when I was in Dar es Salaam in 1976, I concluded that the typical Tanzanian must be blond and blue-eyed because there seemed to be as many Swedes as Africans in that city. Palme's passionate dedication to the internationalist vision, which he and Brandt shared, translated into linking big-power disarmament and the development of the Third World by using part of the money not spent on arms to fund a vast transfer of money and technology from North to South. When the SI met in Botswana shortly after Palme's murder, I was struck by the genuine grief that the Africans felt over his death.

The memory that sums up the man as I knew him came from a meeting of the International at Boomersvik, the lovely socialist youth camp not far from Stockholm. The big formal dinner that is a standard feature of these conferences was held this time in a rustic camp dining hall instead of an international hotel. Palme, like the rest of us, was in casual clothes and therefore appropriately rumpled. Butz Aquino, the brother of the slain Filipino leader, was at his side, Brandt and Michael Manley sat across from him, and I was between Aquino and Anker Jorgensen, the leader of the Danish party.

Palme talked exuberantly about his days in the youth movement and his first visits to Boomersvik, joking with the young socialists who were serving the dinner. But mixed in with those reminiscences were passionate comments about and analyses of the Third World and disarmament. He was a man of solidarity even in his relaxed moments; that informal and unassuming individual was possessed by a vision that turned him into a dynamic orator and often dominated his table talk. His death did not put an end to his ideal of a disarmed globe with justice for all, but it was a heavy blow for those of us who must struggle for that ideal without the help of one of its most decent and exemplary proponents.

I I

Brandt and Palme and the International made some progress with their proposals for a new world order. Ironically, sophisticated conservatives understood that they had a point—which the Right, of course, proposed to exploit for its own purposes.

Thus it was that in the fall of 1985 James Baker, the United States secretary of the treasury, proposed to an IMF meeting in South Korea that government aid to the poorer countries was essential to help them deal with their debt. It had begun to dawn on Baker and others that the world economic crisis was indeed a "common crisis"; developing nations required to run a large balance-of-trade surplus to pay off their debts would not be any kind of a market for the advanced economies. Or, as the *New York Times* put it in a pragmatic 1986 editorial: "The Rich Must Lend or Wither."

Under those circumstances, the congress of the International in June 1986 should have been a triumph. One of its main political themes was now being acknowledged or even espoused by the Right. The host was Peru's President Alan García, the young, charismatic Socialist who had made global headlines when he announced that his country would not spend more than 10 percent of its export income on servicing its international debt; therefore there would be a marvelously appropriate celebration of the tenth anniversary of the historic Geneva congress at which Brandt declared the new turn toward the Third World.

The congress was a disaster. The reason it was illustrates how difficult it is for the International to even begin to free the human race. It also provides an insight into how these internationalists interact with a most unhappy history.

Peru is not simply a poor country with a turbulent political history. That hardly distinguishes it from most members of the United Nations. But its politics are unique. García, its President, is a democratic socialist and his party, the APRA (the acronym for the Spanish of the name Revolutionary Popular Alliance of the Americas), belongs to the International. The main opposition in the 1985 campaign was, however, to García's Left, the Marxist United Left. And on the far, far Left—with disconcerting similarities to Pol Pot's Khmer Rouge—was the guerrilla group Sendero Luminoso, the Shining Path, an organization that fled from the university and found a base in the Indian population, that is, the marginalized majority of the Peruvian population.

That extraordinary diversity of Leftist politics was related to a cultural inheritance. Two of the major theorists of Latin American socialism, Victor Haya de la Torre and José Carlos Mariategui, were Peruvian. De la Torre founded García's party, the APRA, and gave it a distinctly anti-imperialist emphasis even though at certain points he cooperated with conservative forces in the country. Mariategui wrote extremely sophisticated Marxist analyses of Latin history, and it was his stress on the Indians that had inspired the militant, terrorist simplifications of Sendero Luminoso (which cannot, of course, be blamed on Mariategui).

Sendero Luminoso obviously regarded a conference of traitorous social democrats as a great opportunity for making points, so the Peruvian authorities anticipated trouble. I arrived the Sunday five days before the congress opened, because I was the secretary to both the resolutions committee and the committee on a new declaration of principles. The hotel was surrounded by troops, and on Monday morning the first thing I had to do was to get a badge, with a photo, in order to cross police and army lines.

To be guarded by armed men and women tends to make you feel important. I had known that ever since I had visited Sargent Shriver during the 1972 campaign when he was a vice presidential candidate and protected by the secret service. As we talked, agents patrolled the spacious grounds of Shriver's suburban home, a most visible sign that there were powerful, important people within. At some SI meetings—particularly those in Vienna—there was fairly tight security, but one did not feel the threat of real danger. The fact that there were detectives in the hotel corridor, or that going by bus to some function we were accompanied by people with automatic weapons, gave me a sense of being in the presence of real power, something I rarely felt in the United States.

This was different. The possibility of being assassinated, particularly by some indiscriminate act, makes one fearful, not self-important. From the outset we were told to take care in moving around the city and to remove our SI identification badges as soon as we got beyond the security perimeter. Bombs had exploded at a García rally a week or two before, and Thorwald Stoltenberg, the Norwegian socialist who was the chair of the resolutions committee, got security reports because he was checking out whether his Prime Minister and party leader, Gro Harlem Brundtland, should come to Lima. Thorwald told me that García had recently fired a large number of police on grounds of excessive violence and that they had kept their uniforms and guns. The fact that someone was dressed in the livery of the law did not exclude their being disruptors or even assassins. It was enough to make one paranoid.

When Thorwald, Jim Chapin, and I went out to a restaurant on Monday night, we worried about whether the friendly cab driver was actually a potential kidnapper. One night when I was washing my hands in the men's room, the Peruvian next to me casually placed a large pistol by the washbasin before he began his ablutions. Under such circumstances one's imagination becomes both fearful and fanciful.

On Friday morning, Brandt summoned the leaders of delegations to a special meeting that delayed the opening of the congress. We knew from rumors and fragmentary reports in the press that there had been political rebellions in three prisons. We had also heard that in suppressing them the government had in effect executed some of those involved by shooting them after they had surrendered. Brandt began by stating both our solidarity with the government and our concern about human rights. Armando Villanueva, the APRA Secretary General, gave a report that, it later turned out, was much too optimistic. (From everything that happened afterward, including an attack on his own home, the evidence is that he was speaking truthfully but in ignorance of what had actually taken place.)

There were a number of socialists present who seized on one critically important contradiction in the official version: that ten of the government force had been killed, but more than one hundred and fifty of the rebels had lost their lives. Joop Den Uyl, the thoughtful leader of the Dutch Labor party, was one of the most outspoken. "I have been a Prime Minister," he said to Villanueva. "I was not opposed to the use of necessary violence then and I am not against it now. But the death toll among the prisoners strongly suggests that excessive violence was employed." Lionel Jospin, the leader of the French delegation, made the same point with his usual Cartesian clarity: not to defend democracy with necessary violence is to lose democracy, but to defend democracy and excessive violence is also to lose it.

Ed Broadbent, the leader of the New Democratic Party (NDP) of Canada, was another leader who strove mightily to see to it that the SI met the requirements of morality as well as of politics. He was living proof that even in North America an intellectual can be a serious and effective politician—he regularly tops the Canadian polls as one of the most admired figures in his country. Indeed, when I spoke in Canada I often said, thinking of Ed and his comrades, that I came from the politically underdeveloped country to the south. In this case, Broadbent also demonstrated that ethical sensitivity and passion had a crucial play in our movement.

A small committee headed by Den Uyl was appointed to talk to García. We did not know that even as we were meeting over the prisoners' rights, a woman who was trying to shell the convention center with a bazooka blew herself up. That news reached us as we prepared to go to the formal opening of the congress. It was hardly an auspicious beginning. Yet that first meeting was in its own way impressive. García, who is extremely tall in a nation where most people are not, marched down the center aisle, and he and Brandt embraced, Latin-style, at the podium. A choir intoned the Peruvian national anthem, "The Internationale," and then the Aprista hymn, which is sung to the tune of "La Marseillaise." The president delivered a fascinating speech on the history of the Latin American Left in general and the concept of the multi-class radical party in particular. Brandt, speaking in Spanish and English, reiterated his, and the International's, perspective on disarmament and development. The only thing out of the ordinary was that our delegation held a brief conversation on how we would hit the floor in the case of a terrorist attack.

But the continual bombings around Lima, and the revelations indicating that the Peruvian army had in fact carried out executions in its attacks on the prisons, cast a pall over the proceedings. I had been working for three years on no less than five drafts of a new declaration of principles and there would have been problems under the best of circumstances (it is extremely hard to write a consensus document for more than seventy parties and say something substantial at the same time).

When my draft came up for discussion, the debate lasted a mere twelve minutes, and most of that time went to one of my critics. Indeed, resolutions were passed with such speed that the business of the meeting was completed at the end of Sunday evening, a good half day ahead of schedule. I went to the hotel desk, prepared to take any plane going north the next morning, but was able to get a flight to New York. For the last three days the official advice had been not to leave the hotel: we socialists from the West and from the Third World had been prisoners in a Lima hotel at our own congress.

Garcia, it turned out, was as good as his word. During the weeks following the congress he ordered the arrest of the officers responsible for the massacre even though that act could have led to a coup d'état.

In all of this, it seems to me, the International had acted decently in an impossible situation. During that long discussion with Villanueva on the morning the congress opened, Joop Den Uyl had said: "If we do not protest an injustice here, where we are the guests of a friendly socialist government, who will ever believe us when we attack some similar action in Chile or South Korea?" That is, our internationalism does not make exceptions even for those we know are fighting the good fight; and if it recognizes historic necessity, its task is not simply to respect it but to develop whatever possibilities for freedom exist within it.

I do not want to idealize the events in Lima. On the whole, the Latin Americans, who have lived under the turbulent constraints of the Third World, were more understanding of what had taken place than the Europeans. "Such things happen in this region," was the fatalistic explanation of one leader to a journalist. Indeed, the English and Spanish texts of the congress resolution on the issue differed slightly—and not by accident. And yet, Carlos Andreas Perez, the most prominent of the Latins present, was very much a part of the delegation that talked with García about the necessity of publicly investigating the killings.

The Europeans were not monolithic, either, for the situation was one in which utterly sincere internationalists could disagree. Michel Roccard, Mitterrand's longtime "social democratic" antagonist (in a party that has now become quite social democratic, but with Mitterrand still at its head), gave a characteristically brilliant speech in which he uttered some telling words about the violent events outside the meeting hall.

"This congress is astonishing in so many ways," he began. "It is our first congress in the Third World . . . and also our first congress guarded by troops. That should remind us that misery leads to despair and despair to violence. . . . None of us has the right to say that he or she is surprised. In coming to Lima, we all knew that we would find a violent situation. Let us not be naïve about that: democracy is not the right to be weak. The Commission of Inquiry [which García had announced] will tell us, and this is essential, if the democratic requirements of consultation and of a search for a negotiated solution were fulfilled. But I am far from thinking that the Peruvian government actually had the possibility of choosing solutions which we would have found more tolerable."

That was clear enough: an insistence that justice be done within the context of the limits faced by García and his comrades. Others, like Joop Den Uyl, put much more stress on a universality of human rights no matter what the mitigating circumstances. Joop obviously understood the historic necessities that caused the Peruvian Socialists to be caught in a crossfire between fanatic guerrillas and the sullen forces of order. Roccard just as clearly insisted that the commission of inquiry do its work even if that meant risking a coup d'état.

After the event, I suddenly realized that my anxious days in Lima reminded me of an incident at the Catholic Worker. Roccard had said that we had no right to be surprised at what took place. That may well be intellectually true—and I did anticipate the possibility of being killed in Lima to the point of writing a little note to my sons explaining why I had gone there even with that knowledge—and yet I *was* surprised.

The experience at the Catholic Worker that echoed in my mind, when I reflected on my own fear and surprise at Lima, took place in a little bar on Second Avenue in the early fifties. Those of us who lived at the Worker were voluntarily poor, but the supporters of the movement who came to our Friday-night lectures often took us out for beer afterward. A group of us were sitting in a little working-class bar engaged in intense conversation about our commitment to an existential Catholicism. None of your desiccated abstractions are for us, we told one another. We approach Life as pulsing, irrational, contradictory. (I think it was Jürgen Habermas who said that when people start talking about Life they are usually deep in the realm of abstraction.) As we were celebrating our realism, a husband came into the bar, discovered his wife with another man, and in accents of sheer, homicidal rage threatened to kill the interloper. The scene became deathly quiet; there was the scent of animal ferocity in the air, of life, not Life. The husband stormed out with his wife and we, to our credit, quietly departed in a common recognition of our profound superficiality.

I felt like that again in Lima. I had traveled fairly extensively in the Third World and even seen the police trash a deaf and dumb man—they did not know his condition—in an incident in Old Delhi. I had been moved by the miseries of Calcutta and Mexico City, by the sight of women stooped under the weight of firewood in Kenya. I had carefully explained in books and articles that this was an intolerable and daily violence, a Golgotha that struck me as more terrible than the one Christ suffered. And I had walked by Issam Sartawi's body in the lobby of the hotel in Albufeira. Yet I had never before Lima been in a situation where violence could at any moment have taken my life; I had never been on the fringes of a massacre. I knew the possibility of such things, much as I knew about Life before I entered that Second Avenue bar.

Brandt must have felt these things far more than I. As I knew from that experience in Vienna when he questioned whether a workman might be a terrorist, he—and I assume all leaders of his rank in these times—looked upon assassination as a possibility. At the opening session of the Lima congress when I occasionally scanned the galleries to see if anyone might be lurking there, it occurred to me that Brandt and García, rather than the unknown members of the American delegation, would be the prime targets of any attack. The bomb slated to go off at that opening session, we later found out, had been timed for the ceremonies when both Brandt and García would be together.

And yet it seemed to me that Brandt, as was so often the case, held the contraries in a remarkable synthesis. From the first moment that we discussed the killings in the prisons to the end of the congress, he insisted on the principle of protesting any violations of human rights *and* of sympathetically understanding the incredible pressures under which the Peruvian Socialists had to act.

There was a very small reception to commemorate his tenth

anniversary as our leader. It took the place of a much grander event at the Presidential Palace, which had been canceled for obvious reasons. Our celebration was held in a small room at the hotel guarded by the police and army. Kalevi Sorsa, the Prime Minister of Finland, presented Brandt with an ornamental gavel and then, typically, the latter simply made a gracious, even humorous speech in response, joking about the problems of internationalism in the face of the World Soccer Championships. (Brandt said, in keeping with the European usage, World *Football* Cup and then, in his usual, courtly way, paused, looked at me, and said: "We call it football; you call it soccer.") Brandt went on to talk about the problems of the International. There were now so many vice presidents, he remarked wryly, that perhaps we ought to make every leader a vice president and let it go at that. I was impressed, I suppose, because the attention to that relatively trivial detail in a room under armed guard conformed profoundly to my notion of the long-distance runner. It is easy enough to participate in the apocalypse, since what has to be done is obvious. But in between those decisive turning points in history—that is to say, during most of one's life—there is the more difficult task of being patient with your impatience, of maintaining the visceral and immediate and overwhelming sense of outrage against injustice and thirst for justice, *and* worrying about the details of the organization.

I end this account of my work in the Socialist International on this somewhat unheroic note for a good reason. The world is becoming one in fact and—within the framework of that famous "long run" which Keynes said is a fit subject only for undergraduates—will become one in political fact. That unification could be totalitarian or authoritarian—or it could be democratic. Internationalism is, then, an inevitability, not a utopian dream, and all that is in doubt is the essential: whether it will be the means of a liberation or an enslavement, whether the people can actually take control of this destiny, which until now has been the creation of gigantic national bureaucracies and multinational corporations. Paradoxically, even though only the most romantic of politicals can now believe that the International will free the human race, that ideal—understood in a chastened, patient way—has become more relevant than it was in its simple, visionary days.

The utopian dream is long since dead, yet the struggle to which it summons people goes on. Only now, as Brandt and Palme and all the rest of these Internationalists knew so well, it proceeds by way of increments of change, of defeats, and disappointments like the Lima congress. And sometimes it must be begun again in the shadow of a massacre, in a little hotel room guarded by the police, where the internationalists decide to plan not so much for the final conflict in which the International will become the human race, but for the decades of difficult tomorrows that lie ahead.

Life and Death

T his chapter is about the ordinary and the profound: about some of the mundane and even egotistical experiences of being a writer. And about facing death.

I

In many ways, the praise lavished on *The Other America* spoiled me forever when it came to being reviewed. But it also meant that I have lived for thirteen more books—this is the fourteenth—in its shadow. It is an astounding experience to have your first book turn into a kind of a classic, even a legend. It is also dispiriting to read on the cover of every succeeding work, "By the author of *The Other America*." If all writers are understandably sensitive about their reviews, I was even more so, not because I kept waiting for the lightning to strike again in the same place, but simply because I wanted people to realize that there was more to me than "the author of *The Other America*."

In what follows I will act, in part, on a fantasy that I suspect obsesses every writer: to review the reviewers. By doing this it should be clear that I am entering a domain that is at least as irrational as the libido, and probably more so. Back in the fifties,

I sat next to Murray Kempton at a Civil Liberties Union lunch where we were both speaking. Murray chatted about Irving Howe's review of his book *Part of Our Time*. "I know," he said to me, "that what Irving said was fair and accurate and that he, among all people, would never let personal attitudes interfere with his judgment. Only I wake up in the middle of the night screaming, 'I'll kill the bastard!'"

The reader is warned.

The week *The Other America* was published in March 1962 there were portents that I did not recognize. *Newsweek* magazine ran a news story on the book, taking it quite seriously. I also received a daily review in the *New York Times*—a distinction conferred on only seven or eight books a week—on publication date. The latter, by Herbert Mitgang, was positive and respectful but, it later turned out, perhaps the least enthusiastic assessment I was to receive. Abe Raskin's Sunday *New York Times* review was much more upbeat, comparing me to the prophet Jeremiah. I liked that.

Indeed, there was no negative review, with the possible exception of a brief comment from the Kirkus service, which does critical summaries of hundreds of books. I had written in *The Other America* that the American poor needed a Dickens to render the sight and smell and touch of their misery and then noted that I was not up to such a task. The anonymous critic at *Kirkus* thought my sad admission was one of the most persuasive parts of the book. On the whole, however, no one even laid a glove on me.

As I have described on a number of occasions, it was a review that actually made the book. Dwight Macdonald had called to say that he was writing something about *The Other America* for the *New Yorker*, and we spent one rather alcoholic evening—which lasted until lunch the next day at a summer place—talking about it and everything else. But my hangover passed and so did the memory of the discussion, and I left for the traditional writer's pilgrimage to Paris on January 4, 1963. It was in Paris that I received tear sheets of Dwight's review in the *New Yorker*—it ran to around forty pages—and I did not realize that he had engineered a second publication date much more important than the first. Thus it was that when I returned to the United States, just before Christmas of 1963, I suddenly discovered that I had turned into a minor celebrity, a Writer.

During that year in Paris, I had been working on a book, *The Accidental Century*, that was to appear in 1965. My life was to be involved in it more deeply than I could have imagined.

I had started writing about what I called "the magnificent decadence" in the mid-fifties. Originally I had in mind an entire book on the subject of how the giants of literary modernism—especially the trinity of Proust, Joyce, and Mann—were both the products and evidence of a breakdown in Western society *and* inspired geniuses precisely because of that breakdown. In a dialectical mood that has been with me ever since I can remember, I argued that the decadence that made their extraordinary accomplishments possible was also the stuff of a social catastrophe, that a political or even ethical evaluation of the outrages that gave rise to their insights would be different from, even opposed to, an appreciation of the insights themselves. Shelley's reading of Milton—that the Devil is much more interesting than God in *Paradise Lost*—had always impressed me, and I concluded that these writers were great, and positive, precisely because the times forced them to be such nay sayers. They belonged, I said, in citing Shelley, to the "Devil's party."

That exclusively literary book never came to be. But I worked intermittently on an article for *Partisan Review* on this theme for years and never succeeded in satisfying myself or the editors at *PR*. In a way, I viewed the writing of *The Other America* as an interruption in my serious work, an exercise in popularization rather than probing analysis. I had made the decision not to talk about socialism in *The Other America* because that would deflect attention from the poor. But I had said to myself that as soon as I finished the book on poverty, I would return to the theme of the magnificent decadence in a specifically socialist mode.

Now, many books later, I can look back and realize that there was, and is, a remarkable continuity in my writing; that it is—if one can abstract from the pretentiousness of the term—an *oeuvre* and not just fourteen separate volumes. The failed essay of the mid-fifties turned into *The Accidental Century* in 1965 and reappeared again as *The Politics at God's Funeral* in 1984; the concerns of *Toward a Democratic Left*, a programmatic book for the progressive coalition in the United States, which came out in 1968, were taken up again by *Decade of Decision* in 1980 and *The Next Left* in 1987. Indeed, I had completely forgotten that my autobiographical *Fragments of the Century* (1973) and a book I did with the photographer Bob Adelman, *The Next America* (1981), both contain brief statements of what was to become a complex, even scholarly, book, *The Politics at God's Funeral*.

Socialism (1972), which received more praise than any other of my books after *The Other America*, was clearly treated to my very scholarly reconstruction and application of democratic Marxism in *Twilight of Capitalism* (1976). And I read a scathing denunciation of that latter volume by Sidney Hook in the *New Republic* one jet-lagged morning when I arrived back from Africa where I was working on the study of Third World poverty that was to become *The Vast Majority* (1977).

These books, I assume it is clear, fall into three distinct, but related, categories—immediate politics, theoretical politics, cultural criticism—and this often confused the reviewers. *The Accidental Century* was the first to suffer from this situation. Let me try to explain.

In the last volume of *Remembrance of Things Past* Proust is struck by the continuities of his life in Time—a spoon striking a plate, an uneven paving stone in the courtyard of the Guermantes house, the memory of the famous tea and madeleine, evoke a lifetime and seal the decision to write his book. And yet he is more impressed by change than by continuity, by the way an aging and sick Baron de Charlus ceremoniously greets a woman he would have snubbed in the old days. Everyone, it turns out, is not one person, but many successive persons in time, or even simultaneously many persons, depending on the face they wear in a particular relationship.

I think that is an important truth, yet my own experience is better explained by Hegel than by Proust. For Hegel, as I noted in the first chapter of this book, individuals and societies must, after exhausting effort, become what they already were in the first place. Looking back, I have the illusion of the inevitability of my life, the sense in which it forms a whole, the way in which themes that fascinated me as a young man keep returning in a dozen different guises—and in more than a dozen different books. What the reviewers could not understand—through no fault of their own—was that my various personae were simply versions of the same person. That is why so many of them were bewildered by *The Accidental Century*.

Most of the book review editors gave that volume to their social problems specialists, which made sense given that it immediately followed *The Other America*. But then experts on the economy and poverty were confronted by a work that contained only one chapter that concerned itself with the economy. As much space in the book was devoted to the novels of Thomas Mann. But since that one chapter did talk about technological revolution, even if in the context of Aristotle's treatment of the myth of the statues of Daedalus, the critics could then take me to task for not writing a book that I had not tried to write. They imagined what the sequel to *The Other America* should be and then discovered, quite accurately, that I had not produced it. Had those critics been aware of the conscious principle that unified my seemingly disparate selves— that I was a democratic Marxist and viewed a society as a complex and interacting whole in which the slums of *The Other America* and the mountain sanatorium of *The Magic Mountain* were utterly different and yet the parts of a common process—they would have understood that my second book was very much connected to the first.

My hurt over being attacked for not writing a book I had not intended to write was compounded by my having much more of my ego invested in *The Accidental Century* than in *The Other America*. I had first written on poverty because Anatole Shub at *Commentary* suggested the idea to me, and when that article generated three inquiries from book publishers, I ignored them until Emile Capouya at Macmillan and a few of my socialist friends convinced me that no one else would translate the available data into readable English. When *The Other America* turned into a success, I was astounded. Like the Zen archer who hits the target because he does not aim at it, I had given birth to a kind of classic without thinking too much about it.

The Accidental Century was for me a much more serious effort. I had been reading in and around the theme for more than ten years, and it was going to prove that I had integrated my youthful literary studies with my later Marxism and thereby prove myself worthy to be taken seriously by the New York intellectuals who were my peers. I desperately wanted someone to compare it to Camus's *The Rebel*, which I had first read (in French) in 1951 or 1952 and which I greatly admired precisely as a marriage of commitment, literature, and philosophy. I was, in short, being true to my radical contempt for mere bourgeois success and also being more than a bit of a snob. I wanted to show, in terms of a classic French distinction, that I was not simply a *journaliste* but also an *écrivain*, a man of letters and not simply a popularizer. But no one mentioned Camus, and I was mainly attacked for having written the wrong book.

My unhappiness was compounded by *The Accidental Century* appearing during the worst moments of my nervous breakdown (which I described in *Fragments of the Century*). I remember getting a copy of *Life* magazine, with the usual puzzled review, when I was hiding out in Santa Barbara trying to recover my shattered control. The day, of course, then went to pieces. Back in New York, I ran into my friend Norman Mailer at a party and complained to him about the injustice of it all. Norman, who had also gone through the experience of an enormously successful first book, was Hemingwayesque in his response. We are, he told me, professionals, and we expect to be mauled around, and we shouldn't complain. It was excellent advice and I have tried to live by it ever since.

As it turned out, my next two books were praised in front-page reviews in the *New York Times Book Review*, the make-or-break vehicle for any new work. I would, I have long said, gladly trade a rave in *TBR* for complete condemnation in every other paper and magazine. But then, if the *Times* did hail a book, it would not get bad reviews in most other papers. That is precisely the point why the *TBR* is so critical. I discovered this in a negative way in 1973, when *Fragments of the Century* appeared.

The *TBR* assessment was by Martin Duberman, a man I knew slightly and liked. He went after me on two main counts. I had decided that *Fragments* would be a "social," not a private, autobiography, in the same sense that I described at the outset the present work. In his study of Black Mountain College, Duberman had publicly revealed his own homosexuality in courageous fashion. He was, like so many of the activists of the sixties, convinced that the "personal is political." And he found my own book too impersonal. At the outset of *Fragments* I had written, "My remembrance of things past is selective: I will not tell you whether I had trouble going to sleep." Duberman, who somehow missed the clear reference to the opening sentence of Proust's novel, seized on this as evidence of a cowardly refusal on my part to come out of an insomniac closet. There was also a charge that I had slighted my wife, Stephanie. In writing about my nervous breakdown I had commented, in passing, that she had been a lifesaver to me. But then, Duberman said, why does Harrington only mention her six times in the course of the book? Since this was 1973, a time of militant feminist sensibility, it seemed that I was guilty of yet another sin against the personal that is political, this time of sexism. In fact, when I began to write *Fragments*, Stephanie, a woman with a high sense of her own privacy, had told me that she did not want to be reduced to a character in my life and insisted that I not even mention her. That proved to be impossible, but each time I did refer to her—it was more than six times—I had to negotiate the passage with her. Indeed, it was precisely a feminist consciousness that led her to this attitude.

Later, when I read the reviews from around the country, I discovered that, by some strange coincidence, Duberman's point about

Stephanie had independently occurred to critics in Florida and Iowa and points in between. Indeed, they all chastised me for making a mere six references to my wife—the *TBR* figure—when in fact there were about twice that. This was not an era when one wanted to be attacked for sexism in front of the American reading public. But the point is that it was a stunning demonstration of the power of the *Times*.

In other cases I suffered simply because the reviewer was not capable of dealing with the book. In his daily *New York Times* review of *Decade of Decision*, Christopher Lehmann-Haupt, who had liked some of my earlier work, tore into me for faulty economics. But then in the middle of the notice he commented that some of my facts were indeed quite disconcerting to him and that perhaps he had not understood the book. I wanted to write him and tell him that this was the most profound sentence in his entire analysis but, true to the Mailer code, I resigned myself to the occupational hazards of my trade.

I was not so stoic, though, when editors gave my books to political enemies. When, for instance, the Sunday *Times* gave *The Politics at God's Funeral* to Peter Berger, that was an invitation to an attack, which was indeed forthcoming. Perhaps that is why I have sometimes bent over backwards when dealing with the work of conservatives. For instance, two of my reviews on volumes by the black conservative Thomas Sowell were somewhat positive even in their disagreement. That was, to be sure, my genuine reaction, but I think I took a certain malicious pleasure in being so ostentatiously fair to a political enemy. On one occasion, though, I simply bowed out of this process. I picked up a copy of *Commentary*, saw that a book of mine was being discussed by a foe, and decided that the day is sufficient to the evil thereof and there was simply no point in making myself feel bad. So I didn't read it.

The frustrating, and superficial, character of this whole process was driven home to me by one of the best reviews I ever received. It was a discussion of *Twilight of Capitalism* by Kenneth

Arrow, the Nobel Laureate in economics, and appeared in *Partisan Review*. Arrow was not at all uncritical, and in a memorable line that made a lasting impression on me, noted that I used the word *brilliant* more often than any book not on diamond cutting. And yet he really understood what I was trying to do in recovering Marx from those who claimed to be his friends as well as those who were his sworn enemies. Moreover, he pointed out clearly that I had developed no coherent alternative to the mainstream economics I criticized, yet found my insights worth remembering.

The irony was, this review appeared about two years after the book itself. That is, it probably did not sell a single copy of *Twilight*. But it, and Dwight Macdonald's essay on *The Other America*, showed what real criticism, as distinct from journalistic reviews, could be. On the whole, however, the experience of being a writer in America exposes one to the most chancy, arbitrary judgments, and they, in turn, have an immediate impact upon sales and the advance for the next book. I know whereof I speak, since I was once a spectacular case in point of the evil that I now denounce.

There was a period in the fifties when my friend Bill Clancy was the book review editor of *Commonweal*. We were quite close, charter members of the "meat counter intellectuals," the small group that used to meet at the end of the bar at the White Horse where they kept the assorted *Wurst*. I was in the full flush of my first encounter with Marx, an experience as exciting as a love affair, and was therefore an expert on everything. When I would drop by *Commonweal*, as I did regularly, Clancy would lead me into a room where the review copies were stacked, and allow me my choice. In a brief period, I magisterially commented on a book about ballet (about which I really did know something not found in *Das Kapital*), André Malraux on art, a study of the Chinese Revolution, and a novel by May Sarton.

To be sure, I did less damage than one might imagine, since I only picked books that I thought I would like. And I got over my polymathic pretenses fairly early on when a more serious reading of Marx convinced me that it was useful to know what you were writing about. But what was an amusing little incident of youthful intellectual bravado is, alas, the way so many reviews are written in the United States to this day.

I cannot really complain, however, since I am one of the lucky ones. Even though I have fled the success of *The Other America* for twenty-five years, it was an extraordinary stroke of luck that the book received the acclaim it did and then went on to have a minor but real historic impact. On balance, the comments on my work have been far more positive than negative. Moreover, I have been able to live for a quarter of a century from being a writer and, of course, from the spin-offs from writing—professor and lecturer—and thus belong to that rarest of companies in the contemporary world, the fraternity-sorority of those who spend their lives actually working at what they believe in.

The ultimate truth in this area is, of course, Proustian. It is time—Time?—that will tell. Perhaps all of my intellectual exertions will add up to nothing more significant than a footnote in a very scholarly book or a doctoral dissertation by an unimaginative candidate who found that all the good topics had already been taken. Perhaps the future will be kinder. But neither I nor my friends and enemies will ever know, for we will all be quite dead when the judgment is made.

I I

One day in November 1984 I was driving to Princeton University to participate in a symposium in honor of the hundredth birthday of Norman Thomas. At a traffic light my hand idly encountered a bump on the left of my neck.

As a modern man in the age of terror over cancer, I was immediately concerned by the discovery of what could be a growth. But I decided to hope that it was a swollen gland of no importance and drove on. When I came back to New York I made an appointment to see my doctor. He checked it out and told me that it was a swollen gland of no importance. Delighted to be told that nothing was wrong, I proceeded to spend the next five or six weeks in coping with the holidays and making two trips to California. I felt fine and even got in some tennis out on the Coast. The bump persisted, but I knew that it was not significant.

At the end of January I went to see the doctor for a routine physical. All went well until, at the very end of the examination, he was checking out my neck. "What is that doing there?" he asked. Had the bump been a swollen gland, it would have long since disappeared. I had had the same thought on other occasions, which had proved to be false alarms, but at that precise moment it occurred to me that perhaps my life had just turned a corner. It had.

Dr. Kislak immediately referred me to a surgeon, and a few days later I found myself in the office of an open, ebullient man by the name of Dr. Robert Eberle. He felt the bump, examined my throat most imperfectly while I gagged furiously, and then did a needle biopsy on my neck, extracting some fluid from the growth. After he examined it, he became quite jovial and said that it did not look cancerous. But, he continued, he would have to send the sample off to the lab just to be sure. On Saturday, he said, he would call, hopefully to give me good news.

On Saturday, the news was ambivalent. I would have a definitive judgment by Wednesday, Dr. Eberle said. I spent Monday night and Tuesday in Miami Beach talking to union leaders at the midwinter executive council meeting of the AFL-CIO about a new programmatic coalition meeting in the Democratic party (it turned into the Democratic Alternatives project described earlier). But the whole time, the back, and often the front, of my mind kept wondering about the tests. The labor meetings were in Bal Harbour, where I had spent happy summers with my family, freeloading at my mother-in-law's apartment just up the beach, so I also kept encountering the ghost of myself as I walked around the place.

On Wednesday morning the issue was resolved. Dr. Eberle called and said that, unfortunately, the tests showed that I had a metastatic carcinoma. That is, the bump on my neck was a derivative cancer; the primary cancer was somewhere else, most likely in the area of the head and neck. I went to Queens that afternoon and lectured on power in America, but throughout a voice kept screaming at me, You have cancer.

There was another, not quite so spontaneous, thought. In a debate with my one-time friend Max Shachtman over the class nature of the Soviet Union—whether it was a "degenerated" workers' state or a new form of class society—Leon Trotsky had, with his usual polemical brilliance, entitled an article "From a Scratch to the Danger of Gangrene." Now that phrase echoed in my mind as a way of describing an insane causality, from a bump on the neck to a metastatic carcinoma.

I have always prided myself on never having let go of my youthful self who tried to be a poet. I have long thought that the success of *The Other America* was partly a result of its being written by a man who was as literary as he was political, and much more of both than a social scientist. But now I discovered the dangers of being imaginative. For a period of about three weeks, I fantasized about the site of the primary cancer everywhere in my body: in the brain, the eyes, the vocal cords, and, when there was the least murmur from any part of me, everywhere else.

I tend to be a man of delayed reactions, and my response to grief in the past has been that I am initially benumbed, with little or no visible reaction, and then gradually face up to my feelings. I had noticed, for instance, when I was on Robert Kennedy's funeral train, my own repressed emotions could be suddenly released if I saw someone else in tears. Every time I looked out the window of the train and glimpsed the people lining the tracks, some of the men saluting, my face and my composure crumpled. So now with myself. I could not imagine my own death. As an adept of the German classical philosophy, I knew perfectly well that one cannot imagine *nothing* except by the negation of something—but I would suddenly conjure up a memorial meeting for me, and as an imagined member of the audience, I would weep over my fate.

It was at this juncture that I turned fifty-seven; it was one of the most depressing birthdays conceivable. This time, between the diagnosis and the first stay in the hospital, was the worst period, above all because it was so utterly uncertain. To the extent that I coped, it was because I kept on working. I taught my classes at Queens, led a Gauss seminar at Princeton, attended a meeting of the executive committee of DSA, and pursued a regular schedule of research and writing. The Princeton seminar, though, had an unexpected irony.

The largest individual contributor to DSA was a marvelous woman, Muriel Gardiner. The daughter of an extremely wealthy Chicago meat-packing family, she had become a socialist as a young girl, studied medicine in Vienna in the thirties (where she got to know Freud and his family), participated in the revolutionary socialist underground movement in that country during the time of clerical fascism, and become the lover and then the wife of the leader of the underground, Joseph Buttinger. (Parts of her life were apparently appropriated by Lillian Hellman in the story of "Julia" in *Pentimento*.) Joe and Muriel had long been staunch supporters, and when Joe had to go to a nursing home, I met with Muriel to chat—and to ask for money, which was always forthcoming. At one of our recent meetings, I had suggested—she was in her eighties—that she might put us in her will, and she had agreed. Then she phoned to say that she was dying from cancer, and we made an appointment to meet at her home, near Princeton, on the day of the first Gauss seminar.

But Muriel died a day before our appointment and I dedicated the seminar to her as a victim of cancer. By the second session, I, too, was a victim of the same disease, an irony that did not help my concentration.

Before I went into the hospital, I also had to arrange to let the movement know what was happening. I didn't want vague rumors to spread, but I also didn't want to broadcast my plight. So I decided that at least our leadership should be given honest information. I turned naturally to Jack Clark. He was a good and trusted friend as well as a comrade of long standing, a respected leader of the organization and someone to whom I could talk. He therefore was given the dubious distinction of being the first person, aside from Stephanie and the doctors, to know that I had cancer. And he had the difficult job of informing the rest of the committee.

Early in March I went into St. Vincent's Hospital. There was to be a surgical procedure of undetermined outcome: they would search for the primary cancer, and if they found it, they might well wait until some later date, after further treatment, to remove the lump; or, if they failed to find the primary, they would forthwith excise the lump, and part of my neck with it. This was the first time that I had ever been in a hospital as a patient and my reaction puzzled me. It still does.

I have lived my life in the sure knowledge that I am a physical coward. In part that was common sense, not a character flaw. I was not a tough or aggressive kid and early on I figured out that in almost any fair fight I would lose. So I had carefully arranged things as best I could to avoid violence. When my political convictions required that I risk myself, fears and all, I did so with my heart in my mouth. The week I spent touring Mississippi in 1964 as a civil rights activist was, for instance, a time of galloping paranoia and fright.

But on my two trips to the hospital, I was utterly calm. There is a section in a memoir by Bruno Bettelheim on his experience in a concentration camp where he tells about being beaten, for no reason at all, when he was first imprisoned. He felt, he said, like a disembodied presence hovering over the scene where the guards were beating someone else. So with me in the hospital. When there was a minor malfunction in the CAT scanner and I was immobilized inside of it for over an hour with only a few inches between my face and the tubing, I was quite uncomfortable but not, as I would have anticipated, panicked. I had to wait almost a whole day to go down to the operating room, and yet I bore the experience with a curious, unexpected equanimity.

I did not give much thought to my reaction until November, long after those hospital stays were finished. At the DSA convention in Berkeley, our executive director, Guy Molyneux, introduced me to give the keynote and, alluding to the events of the year, remarked on the fact that the staff had been impressed by my courage in adversity. Until that moment, it had never occurred to me that I had been courageous, and the idea was in profound conflict with my own self-image as a coward. Indeed, I still don't know how to describe my reaction. If it was indeed courageous, then that virtue is less valuable than I had thought because all it was for me was an eerie absence of fear in a frightening situation. For that matter, if it was courage, I think it takes a much greater moral effort to be a coward. But I digress.

When I did go to surgery, they discovered that the primary cancer was on the base of my tongue. Radiation was the indicated therapy, followed by an operation to remove the growth that they had not touched in the first procedure since it, too, would be affected by the treatment. So I went home and began one of the strangest periods of my life.

For one thing, as the news spread that I had cancer, people who had conquered one or another variant of that disease began to call. It was as if I had joined a club (one to which, as Groucho Marx put it, I really didn't want to belong since it was willing to accept me). One woman friend told me that she had gone through radiation therapy for breast cancer at a time when I saw her—blissfully unaware of her problem—quite regularly. My friend Bob Lekachman had waged a gallant war against cancer of the colon, and he called to encourage me. The sociologist Robert Merton, whom I knew slightly, telephoned to urge me not to trust blindly in doctors, to pursue second opinions, and so on. He was talking out of the experience of having fought, and mastered, cancer of the jaw in the early seventies. And my friend Dr. Sol Moroff became a sort of informal consultant as I reported each diagnosis and suggested therapy to him.

It was in this period that I also wondered why I had been singled out for the disease. After all, I had dutifully quit smoking on New Year's Day 1965, almost twenty years before that lump appeared on my neck. One friend, who had also had cancer of the tongue and who had survived it through radiation, told me that her doctors said that this variant of the disease was becoming more common and that they suspected environmental causes. Dr. Eberle and

Dr. Ghossein, the radiologist, would only say that the incidence of the problem seemed to have some relation to smoking and drinking.

I had, in short, blundered into an experience as quintessentially modern as any work at the Museum of Modern Art. It has created a strange fraternity-sorority of those of us who have been stalked by this deadly quiet killer, and particularly those who have survived the experience, for a while at least.

The radiation therapy was as strange as the disease itself. I liked the radiologist. Dr. Ghossein was Lebanese-born and French-trained, with a lively interest in the world outside of medicine. We often chatted in French, and when an eminent specialist from Paris visited, there was an almost festive conversation in which both assured me that I would beat the cancer. But my neck and chest were permanently tattooed with little guide marks, and then temporarily sketched with lines that marked off the zone of the day's treatment. One day I forgot to wash off the latter and found myself walking down the street in Larchmont looking like a fugitive from a Halloween party.

I would be left alone on the table in the treatment room while the radiation actually streamed into my body. It was strange: a destructive power was being carefully introduced into my system in order to save me, and yet there was no sensation at all. But that is doubtless appropriate when you deal with a disease which in its earliest stages, as mine was, does not hurt. All the while that my tongue and neck were hosts to my own premature death, I was going about my ordinarily hectic schedule, even playing tennis.

But that is the modern world. We are afflicted by illnesses that take years, even decades, to gestate and then strike without warning. My friend Paul Jacobs may well have died twenty years after the fact from witnessing a nuclear test in Nevada in the fifties. I on the other hand had no such noble political reason for my illness. It was simply an absurd, existentialist dimension of life.

But if the radiation did not hurt, it had unpleasant consequences. The machine was aimed at my neck and tongue and one of the side effects was that, gradually, I lost my sense of taste (it later came back, though not completely). Worse, most food became nauseating to me—but I had not lost my sense of smell, so that I could still desire it. Eventually I was reduced to "eating" a concoction that contained some essential nourishment and was designed for people in my situation. By the end of the experience, I had lost about 40 pounds and weighed in the neighborhood of 130. I did feel quite sorry for myself when in the evening I would go upstairs and consume my barely tolerable "meal" while watching television.

Strange to recount, the experience sounded a Proustian echo in my mind. I had long thought that the comment in *Remembrance of Things Past* that you must be careful what you wish for, since you will probably get it, but not under the circumstances you had imagined, was a profound insight into the ironic impact of time upon our lives. That knowledge now turned into an infinitely sad joke. I was encouraged to try to get down some actual milk shakes as another way to fight the weight loss. When I was a little boy at St. Rose's School in St. Louis, I had dreamed that becoming an adult meant that you wouldn't have to write in that beautiful penmanship the nuns taught and that you could drink all the milk shakes you wanted. Now I was practically under doctor's orders to drink milk shakes and I could not even tolerate the taste of them.

Work had been my salvation when I had had a nervous breakdown, and so it was now. When I first found out about my illness, I called Dick Seaver, my editor at Holt and my friend. I told him that I had cancer and that I wanted to propose a contract for a new book. Astoundingly—or so it seemed to me—he not only agreed to the project but arranged for a prompt advance. His faith was rewarded: that proposal became *The Next Left*, which was published in 1987.

After that exploratory procedure in early March, it became likely that, whatever else happened, I would not die in the near future, so I used to spend my time in Dr. Ghossein's waiting room taking notes on books I was reading for what would become *The Next Left*.

In June the seven weeks of daily radiation had come to an end. I could eat somewhat better, and I was waiting for surgery. So I went to a meeting of the Socialist International at Boomersvik, that socialist youth camp just outside of Stockholm. Michael Manley had only recently recovered from an illness, so Willy Brandt opened the session by welcoming back the "two Michaels," and that was a tonic to me. My work, my continuing involvement in the movement in the United States, and that trip to the International, all had a positive effect on my health.

Still, there was major surgery to be faced at the beginning of July. Shortly beforehand, my cousin Peggy Fitzgibbon, a Cenacle nun, was in New York, and I took her to lunch at Rocco's. Peggy and I were only six months apart in age, and as toddlers had been closer than many brothers and sisters. So I felt I could talk to her frankly and freely. I had, I told her, been forced to reconsider my atheism given the fact that I was going to undergo a serious operation. Having done so, I had concluded that the possibility of my own imminent death was no reason to turn my back on my atheistic convictions.

I did not go into the complex reasons for my attitude with Peggy, though I suspect she sensed them generally if not specifically. Ever since I had left the Catholic Church at the end of 1952, I had always respected, even loved, it. I was never one of those militant ex-Catholics who had to kill their one-time God over and over, since I found the Church, in its highest expressions, profound and beautiful. My only problem was that I did not believe in it. Even so, all kinds of religious phrases were spontaneously appearing in my mind. It did not bother me in the least that, as I noted earlier, when I was possessed of a sense of beauty or suddenly felt that I had grasped a particularly intricate idea, an inner voice would break out into the opening lines of the Magnificat, "My soul doth magnify the glory of the Lord" (and, yes, the voice often spoke in Latin: "*Magnificat anima mea . . .*).

In any case, I told Peggy that if I did die on the operating table and discovered, to my astonishment, that there was indeed a God and an afterlife, I was not afraid of meeting my maker. I don't think you should be, she responded to my arrogant, utterly un-Calvinist a-theology. I then added that in case I did encounter God face-to-face, I was going to accuse Him (Her?) of mumbling to humankind.

I woke up in the recovery room, not at the judgment seat, and I remember practically nothing of the week or so I stayed in the hospital. It was, I assume, moderately uncomfortable since I was plugged into an IV part of the time, but it passed like a slightly unpleasant dream. The pathologist said that there was no sign of cancer in the nodes they had removed from my neck. So I had survived. For a while at least.

At first I was too busy simply trying to cope to think much beyond the immediate future. My saliva glands had been impaired, and water had to be constantly at hand, particularly in the middle of the night when I would wake with a parched mouth; a part of my neck was missing and some muscles and nerves had been cut to give me a crooked smile and a left arm that could not do everything it should. My first public speech was at the American Sociological Association at the end of August and, even though I looked like a wraith, I delivered it with no great trouble. Then I began to gain weight and to return to my normally hectic existence of teaching, writing, and organizing.

What, then, have I learned, of society and myself, from this experience? Nothing but clichés—but therein lies a sad but important truth.

I first read about it in Pascal, who commented that the very same words in the mouth of a young person and in that of someone who has lived a full life have a profoundly different meaning. Astonishing to me, I later encountered the same insight in, of all places, Hegel's *Introduction to the Greater Logic*. Now, however, it is part of my life, not a matter of scholarship. That is, what I know from this brush with my own death is trite and almost everyone else already knows it, too, including people quite young. But the *way* in which I know it—that has changed and changed forever.

Were I the great poet I wanted to be when I was a young man, perhaps I could express this extraordinary knowledge of the ordinary, this epiphany of the commonplace. That, after all, is the subject of most art. But I am not that poet. Having cancer was for me something like losing my virginity: it transformed my inner life and I assumed that everyone on the street must read that transformed consciousness in my face. But, of course, they can't, and the best that even the readers of this book can do is to take my word for it that my words mean more than they seem to mean.

Yes, I know that Norman Mailer's preposterous notion—that cancer is a product of society and what society does to the individual—does not seem preposterous at all any more. Indeed, on a more prosaic level, perhaps I have been victimized by that environmental irresponsibility that I have denounced for years. More broadly and more bookishly, I have an unsought appreciation of that strange and even poetic section of Volume I of *Das Kapital* in which Marx describes how, under capitalism, the highest achievements of science and technology seem to be ghostly and inexplicable happenings, demons rather than the servants of the genius that created them. It is quite possible that it is one of those demons who invaded my tongue and my neck.

I also know why my mother, toward the cruel end of her life, called the doctor "Father." I grew to like both Dr. Eberle and Dr. Ghossein, yet both were also priests of a mystery and held my life and death in their human hands and I had no way of judging them. But then that gets to one of my profound disagreements with my mentor, Marx. He thought that if justice would combine with science so that no one had to die because they were poor, then there would be no need for God, no religious anxiety. But under those circumstances, everyone would still have to die, only they would perish now, not because of injustice, but because of their essential, finite, mortal humanity. And if I did not turn to God, I certainly felt that religious anxiety.

But it would, of course, be absurd to pretend that the whole experience mainly affected the way I know social truths. It also, or even primarily, transformed my knowledge of my most private self.

When a high-ranking official of the Ford Foundation wanted to give the Catholic Worker a large grant in the early fifties, Dorothy Day turned it down on the grounds that the followers of St. Francis of Assisi could not have a balance in a bank account. We were living, she said and I heartily agreed, precariously. Only, until the cancer came, I had never really been at that edge where the hungry and homeless and the dying dwell. And, for that matter, I have thus far only had a brief tour of that genuine precariousness. Since I come from a Catholic tradition, I have not been "born again" in one of those decisive moments of conversion that seem to happen to Protestants. There are periods in which I happily forget everything that happened since my hand grazed against the lump on my neck. But there are many times when I do not.

Strangely, it is the experience of my own teeth that has been most existential. They were never particularly good in the first place (certainly out of carelessness and perhaps out of a genetic Irish tendency). But when I immersed myself in the "destructive element" of radiation in order to live, there were consequences (there always are). One of them is that my battered saliva glands do an even poorer job of carrying away the detritus of my food. Another is that when I get into dental trouble, my mouth does not respond as well as it should. So I have spent hours upon hours in dental chairs and a twinge of pain in my mouth—or the shattering of a tooth, which happened on New Year's Eve 1986—is a kind of memento mori.

At a meeting of a Young Socialist League committee a thousand years ago in 1954, a very romantic comrade said, mouthing a famous revolutionary formula, "We are all dead men on leave." Almost all of us, thank God, snickered, for if we were beleaguered and persecuted in Joe McCarthy's America, no one was seriously proposing to put us to death. But, I now know, something is. And in my most somber moments I do wonder how much of my leave has been exhausted.

So I have read a bit more poetry than usual, returning to some of the literary haunts of my youth. My teeth make me think of a line from Auden about how "a crack in the teacup opens a lane to the land of the dead." And when I reread the *Duino Elegies*—or listen to the Goldberg Variations—I am at times overcome by the poignancy of a life in which it is indeed true that "Beauty's nothing / But beginning of terror we are still just able to bear, / And why we adore it so is because it serenely / disdains to destroy us."

Ultimately, I hope for a death like my father's. He came downstairs one morning, having seen me off to New York the day before, put some water on the stove to boil his eggs, went into the living room, and died. When my mother came down, the water had not even boiled away, but his life had ended. It was terrible on the survivors, marvelous for him. And I fear a death like my mother's. For three years her body, and then her mind, were savagely assaulted as if by a fascistic nature. Then, mercifully, she died in the middle of the night.

I have no idea what the future holds or how long it will be. I know now that the most bitterly profound line in our literature—when the chorus in *Oedipus Rex* tells us to call no man happy until he is dead since no one knows what will happen before then—is apt and true. And yet, even after this experience, if I may hazard a provisional judgment and dare the fates, I give thanks that I was born.

Postscript. In the fall of 1987, after I had completed this manuscript but before I went over it after copy editing, I noticed that I was having trouble swallowing. So I went to see Dr. Ghossein, who sent me to have a barium X-ray, which confirmed that I had cancer of the esophagus, a much more deadly form of the disease than the earlier cancer.

One thing led to another, and a surgical procedure in November revealed that the tumor was inoperable. I was then told that I had between six months and two years to live. As I make the final preparations for this book, I am about to enter the hospital for the fifth time in five months for a four-day period of continuous chemotherapy. There is some evidence that my previous visits had had good effect and perhaps that my chances for survival had been pushed to the positive side. But there is no sign—or possibility—

of a cure, and however long I live, it will be with a daily sense of how precarious my very existence is.

The moment I received my medical sentence, I began to work on a new book, which will summarize over thirty years of reflection on democratic socialism. At this point I have written six chapters in draft form, and when I go into the hospital again next week, I will be writing on legal pads until the chemotherapy makes me too miserable to go on working. But the book is a kind of salvation, for it gives me a reason to fight to live and it distracts me from the knowledge that I may not. If fate, which has not been overly kind in recent times, allows me to finish that project, I already have another in mind.

This new cancer makes the old one seem almost benign. Here I thought that I had earned my veteran's decoration in that previous encounter with death, but it turned out to be only a practice session. The situation is made all the more ironic by the signs that a new mood is beginning to form in America, that my ideas, which were so profoundly unpopular during the Reagan years, are about to have a rebirth of relevance. And here am I, at that very moment, pushed rudely aside, unable to take full advantage of the moment I have waited for for so long.

No matter. I see no reason to take back what I said just before this postscript—just before my own death became so palpable and real. I give thanks for the life of a long-distance runner, whenever it ends.

Epilogue

*I*n January 1987, I testified before the Senate Committee on Labor and Human Resources.

It might have seemed a kind of minor culmination of the political strategy I have described in this book. I was warmly greeted by the chair, Senator Kennedy, and by his economist, David Smith, a friend. I said hello to Tom Donohue, the secretary-treasurer of the AFL-CIO, and to Bishop Joseph Sullivan, who was representing the National Catholic Conference. There were various other trade unionists, academics, and feminists whom I knew. I was accompanied there by a reporter from the *Los Angeles Times*, who was working on a cover story about me for the paper's Sunday magazine. And that morning I had had breakfast with E. J. Dionne, now the national political reporter for the *New York Times*, a friend and a person who took my ideas seriously enough to occasionally take notes about them.

Hadn't I beautifully succeeded, then, in legitimatizing democratic socialism, in bringing it from the margins of society, where I found it in 1951, into serious discussions among men and women of power?

I was on a panel with Barry Bluestone, a brilliant economist whom I had known for years, and Karen Nussbaum, a feminist organizer and trade unionist. It was the end of a long session, and we each took only about five minutes to make an oral presentation of much more extensive written testimony. It seemed that the hearing would end with a few positive questions by Senator Kennedy, the only member of the committee who remained in the room. I noted a slight, somewhat unassuming man, who had taken one of the senatorial chairs, but since I didn't recognize his face I assumed he was a staffer acting somewhat informally.

He was, in fact, Senator Gordon Humphrey of New Hampshire, who, I later learned, was one of the flakier Republican conservatives in the upper Chamber. His questions were all directed at me. Didn't I have some kind of political identification? Wasn't I connected with some organization? And when I assured him that, yes, I was a socialist and the cochair of DSA, he got to the real point, which was to attack Kennedy for stacking the meeting with Leftists, myself above all, but also Tom Donohue and Bishop Sullivan speaking on behalf of a pastoral letter that was Left of Center. The Committee had invited a socialist, Humphrey said. Why was no one invited to defend capitalism?

Kennedy answered with growing irritation that the complaint should be addressed to the ranking member of the Republican minority, who had been given four weeks notice about the hearing and had not proposed any witnesses. Moreover, Kennedy said, the secretary of labor had been a witness on behalf of the Reagan administration, and that certainly gave voice to a conservative point of view.

But Humphrey came back at me with questions based on the ignorant assumption that socialists wanted the government to run everything. I surprised him by describing the decentralist and participatory themes critical to contemporary socialism, but he persisted in his questioning even after admitting surprise about some of the things I was saying. There was another exchange with Kennedy about packing the hearing, and after a while the latter gaveled the session to a close.

The incident is of no political importance whatsoever, and most of the press had left when it occurred. But it was, in terms of my political strategy, a striking illustration of how little I had accomplished. That is, socialism was still an alien and suspicious idea—indeed, for most, "un-American"—which could be exploited by an affable demagogue to launch a serious attack on the most important liberal politician in the United States. I was legitimate among liberals and intellectuals, but as far as the real politics of the country were considered, I was an outsider, of no real consequence.

But then, hasn't my long-distance run been an exercise in futility? Perhaps in the name of a noble, plucky, romantic futility, but futility nevertheless? And if that were the case, was I not simply another Quixote, the charming representative of an idea whose time had long since gone?

My friend Norman Thomas, who ran for the presidency on the Socialist ticket six times and was *the* socialist of his generation, had run into a similar problem. When I first met him in 1951 he had been turned into a kind of Leftist icon by established power. That is, it was convenient to have a socialist around who threatened no one and nothing—who was a palpably decent man of conscience and commitment—who could be revered on ceremonial occasions and cited to prove that the country was genuinely tolerant and democratic. It used to infuriate Thomas, who had been a courageous advocate for his cause and braved mobs on its behalf—in 1963, when he was in his late seventies, he was chased around the back roads of Mississippi by racists who were furious at his integrationist agitation—that he had been relegated to the position of a preacher, good for Sundays but not the practical working days of the week.

Had all of my long-distance running only resulted in creating a lesser Norman Thomas? Why, friends sometimes asked, did I insist on dragging in this vexed, European, un-American word, *socialism*? Why not settle for good left-wing liberalism and even go to Congress on its behalf? After all, the immediate demands I fight for are liberal, since the issue of capitalism versus socialism is not exactly on the American political agenda. Why insist on a romantic futurism?

Because the fundamental truth of these times is radical. It is not my use of the word *socialism* that creates problems for me. It is that the word asserts the need for a systemic and international transformation if humankind is to live in freedom in the twenty-first century. And that, I think, is true and even the only possible practicality. The utopians, in the negative sense of that term, are the pragmatists who mystically believe that society can survive political, economic, social, and military upheavals—can cope with what is a transition to a new civilization—by squatting in the middle of the road. The men and women of power who think that are wrong, and time will brutally destroy their illusions. All of which does not mean that I am right, that it is indeed possible for the vast majority of humanity to control, democratically and consciously, the massive forces that are changing the very conditions under which we live. That may not be. Human history could turn out to be a tragedy and the dream of freedom an interlude. But *if* the best values of humanity are to survive, then we will have to go down the road upon which I have been running.

In my lifetime there has been a revolutionary internationalization of the global economy. I will never forget standing in Nairobi and watching poor people making napkin rings and learning that some of them would be sold to fashionable people who shop at Gump's department store in San Francisco. It was a revelation, specific as the shabby square where I stood with boxes in which some people were living, of the oneness of the world. It is simply not serious to think that the new planet being created by our revolutionary economic ingenuity can be forever run on the basis of a nation-state system that dates from the eighteenth and nineteenth centuries.

There is a technological revolution under way that may change the very determinants of biological life as well as the material production process. There is, as I described in *The Politics at God's Funeral*, a crisis in values, a dissolution of the ethical and religious certainties that provided the ideological integration for human society. That this sometimes provokes a desperate fundamentalism, in the United States or the Third World, is simply one more demonstration of how radical and irrepressible the trends are.

How will freedom—and beauty and decency—survive in the world of biotechnology and photonics, of billions of human beings? That is a radical question, which requires a radical answer. That a rather simple-minded senator from New Hampshire can reduce such complexities to an innuendo, useful only to attack a decent liberal, is a matter of no consequence. That many of the best people in the society, the ones who must become aware of the need for fundamental change, think me odd, if persistent, because I am a long-distance runner, is much more disturbing.

My impossible vision, I am saying, is practical in terms of the era, even if it seems Quixotic in the context of Ronald Reagan's America. But that America will pass, and I most certainly hope that I will be around to speed its departure. I am, in my own way, as militant as I was when I first became an active radical in 1951 and infinitely more radical than when I encountered that slum house in St. Louis in 1949. I have been enriched beyond belief in the struggle, and I would not trade the life of a long-distance runner for any other, particularly now when death has become such a personal possibility.

A few months before his assassination, Leon Trotsky wrote what I feel. He said: "Natasha has just come up to the window from the courtyard and opened it wider so that the air may enter more freely into my room. I can see the bright green strip of grass beneath the wall, and the clear blue sky above the wall, and sunlight every-where. Life is beautiful. Let the future generations cleanse it of all evil, oppression, and violence and enjoy it to the full."

Amen.

Index